Entrepreneurial Management

Entrepreneurial Management

Edited by
Shivganesh Bhargava

Response
Business books from SAGE
Los Angeles ■ London ■ New Delhi ■ Singapore
www.sagepublications.com

First published in 2008 by

Response Books
Business books from SAGE
B1/I-1 Mohan Cooperative Industrial Area
Mathura Road, New Delhi 110 044, India

SAGE Publications Inc
2455 Teller Road
Thousand Oaks, California 91320, USA

SAGE Publications Ltd
1 Oliver's Yard, 55 City Road
London EC1Y 1SP, United Kingdom

SAGE Publications Asia-Pacific Pte Ltd
33 Pekin Street
#02-01 Far East Square
Singapore 048763

Published by Vivek Mehra for Response Books, typeset in 10.5/12.5pt AGaramond by Star Compugraphics Private Limited, Delhi and printed at Chaman Enterprises, New Delhi.

Library of Congress Cataloging-in-Publication Data

Entrepreneurial management/edited by Shivganesh Bhargava.
    p. cm.
Includes bibliographical references and index.
    1. Entrepreneurship.   2. Management.   I. Bhargava, Shivganesh, 1959–
HB615.E59746   658.4'21—dc22   2008   2008002615

ISBN: 978-0-7619-3615-2 (HB)   978-81-7829-779-8 (India-HB)

The SAGE Team: Sugata Ghosh, Vaijayantee Bhattacharya and Trinankur Banerjee

In loving memory of
my late mother Sreemati Dhurpati Devi Bhargava
and my late father Shri Raghav Ram Bhargava

Contents

List of Tables

List of Figures

List of Abbreviations

AFT	Asia Fair Trade
AGFI	Adjusted Goodness-of-Fit index
ANM	Auxiliary Nurse and Midwife
ANOVA	Analysis of Variance
APR	Asia Pacific Region
BI	Business Incubator
CFI	Comparative Fit Index
CO	Customer Orientation
CPO	Competitor Orientation
DFID	Department for International Development
EF	Economic Factor
EIF	Electric Induction Furnace
EP	Entrepreneurial Propensity
EIGSEP	Entrepreneurship-linked Income Generation for Self-employment Programme
FDI	Foreign Direct Investment
GFI	Goodness-of-Fit Index
GLM	General Linear Model
HRF	Human Resource Factor
IB	International Business
IFAT	International Federation for Alternative Trade
IFI	Incremental Fit Index
INVs	International New Ventures
ISRO	Indian Space Research Organization
MT	Market Turbulence
nAch	High Need for Achievement
NBIA	National Business Incubation Association
NEED	Network of Entrepreneurship and Economic Development Self Help Group
OBF	Organizational and Behavioural Factor
OLL	Ownership Locational License
PACS	Poorest Areas Civil Society
RBV	Resource-based View
RMR	Root Mean Square Residuals

ROI   Rate of Interest
SD   Sustainable Development
SEM   Structural Equation Modelling
SME   Small and Medium-sized Enterprises
SSI   Small Scale Industries
TC   Transaction Cost
TF   Technical Factor
THADCO Tamil Nadu Adi-Dravidar Housing and Development Corporation
TLI   Tucker-Lewis Index

Foreword

Technological advancement, developing economy, competitive market, knowledge explosion, focus on research and development, concern towards environment and improving quality of life of people—make this century appear much brighter than the past.

Many imaginations and dreams are finally seeing the light of day. I personally feel that this century has endless opportunities for entrepreneurial initiatives and we must utilize them constructively. Here, lies the importance of entrepreneurial management.

I realize that the probability of making an organization an entrepreneurial one has a better chance with the leaders, who are able to balance their drives for motivating, influencing and developing their people better than their competitors. There is a need for the leaders to go extra miles in order to create and develop the spirit of creativity and commitment among people.

Leading and managing (knowledge-based) faculty resources are essentially quite different in terms of channelizing the creativity and innovation of the faculty. Moreover, financial and infrastructure support to the newly recruited faculty allow them to develop a base for generating more funds, better laboratories and produce creative outcomes. The formation of the Society for Innovation and Entrepreneurship (SINE) to encourage technology incubation and to become business partner has attracted faculty members to apply their knowledge to productive business.

The entrepreneurial march requires not only knowledge but also the wisdom that one can get beyond the knowledge of core discipline such as arts, aesthetics, politics, history, environment and literature.

I am happy that my faculty colleague, Professor Shivganesh Bhargava, has compiled papers in the form of an edited book *Entrepreneurial Management*, published by SAGE Publications India Private Limited.

I wish and hope that this book comprising papers with diverse approaches and methodologies (survey-based, field-studies, case-studies, experience-based and theoretical) will help entrepreneurs survive and thrive in their business ventures. This book also reflects global access to the available entrepreneurial opportunities and throws light on how to start up as well as expand a business. Students of entrepreneurial management, corporate strategy, entrepreneurship, financial management, marketing management, organizational behaviour and human resource management may find it to be a useful reference book.

Ashok Misra
Director, Indian Institute of Technology
Bombay

Preface

The importance of entrepreneurial marketing, international entrepreneurial finance, technology incubation, and start-up business have occupied a respectable place across the disciplines in recent years, where creativity and innovation are the key determinants. Infusing creativity into products and turning innovation into measurable outcomes have become the main contemporary challenges of the globe. Students of entrepreneurship can contribute significantly in facing such challenges and making entrepreneurial management an emerging field of study. Managing entrepreneurs and entrepreneurial organizations are important aspects of the entrepreneurship development process. Some are being able to do well and are also benefiting from this while many are struggling and lagging behind.

Entrepreneurs are directly involved in the dynamic but complex inter-relationship between financial management and business strategy. The development of any society depends on the transition of its technology and economy. To introduce dynamism in the growth process of a society, entrepreneurial management is essential. It is also essential for improving the productivity of any process. It is the practice of taking entrepreneurial knowledge and utilizing it for increasing the effectiveness of new business ventures and small and medium-sized businesses.

Entrepreneurship has established its own niche in business, market, corporate world and national development. Entrepreneurial environment facilitates the process of entrepreneurship development and this makes the economy of a nation strong. It is a myth today that individuals from only a few nations/communities/castes can become entrepreneurs. Rather, the proposed thesis for validation is that every person can develop entrepreneurial competency and has the potentiality to excel; but it is also a fact that only some people are able to do while the rest are not. Here, an enterprising attitude, influenced by family, society, social institutions, governance and leadership can play a significant role.

An organization has to always understand the nerves of its customers and strategize policies towards achieving its goals of maintaining the position of its innovative product in the market. Those who are able to properly align and adapt themselves with the dynamic changes of the market will excel and those who fail in doing so will eventually disappear. This also shows the difference and intense interrelationship between entrepreneurship and entrepreneurial management.

In today's economy, technical and business skills are not enough to operate a business. Entrepreneurial skills are also required to anticipate changes, identify opportunities and create a high-performance working environment according to the realities demanded by the global competition. The development of entrepreneurship amongst engineers and general graduates is going to be an effective mechanism for technological innovations, helpful in the removal of regional imbalances and sustainable growth of small industries.

To be successful, particularly in business, everyone must have some basic skills: technical skills (proficiency in specialized information, methods, processes, procedures and techniques involved in product/service), behavioural skills (knowledge of understanding people), business skills (ability to operate in the market/environment), evaluative skills (ability to appraise the value of a process) and execution skills (ability to get work done within the constraints of time, money and people). These skills are particularly essential for today's entrepreneurs. Personal qualities (mindset, entrepreneurial vision, intrinsic motivation, hard work and professional values), technical knowledge, business skills, communication and management skills, capacity to utilize the available material and human resources, knowledge of how to get/take advantage of the available business/market opportunities and culture-fit have also been perceived as the core entrepreneurial characteristics. However, fast technological advancement has forced professionals to move at an equal pace with the fast changing skill requirements of this century.

Developing and preserving an entrepreneurial spirit should be a concern of all who want to convert their conventional business as a professionally managed corporation. There is no single capsule that could be prescribed to achieve this as all organizations are striving hard to reach this goal through various ways. All these organizations have the potentiality to excel but only some are able to do so and many are unable. Our analyses of the interviews of many entrepreneurs show some common challenges: competition, resource scarcity, shortage of power, capital, technology upgradation and the cost of production, talent, customers' loyalty, professionalism and inadequate infrastructure of the established entrepreneurs.

Often managers are asked to function as entrepreneurs and additionally, to surpass the competitors, entrepreneurs are also advised to act as managers. This means that actually both managers and entrepreneurs have overlapping responsibilities to perform. A manager has to learn how to develop the drive for utilizing/exploiting opportunities from an entrepreneur while an entrepreneur could learn from a manager how to optimally utilize resources for achieving target/goals. For a successful chief executive office (CEO), both are essential and required.

Data reveal that many companies do not achieve the targeted financial value and it has become a universal phenomenon. According to the recent Harvard Business Review Entrepreneurship alert report, nine out of 10 new products launched normally fail. Literature reveals that strategic failure, leadership ineffectiveness, motivation of people, product quality, marketing and business environment play an important role in the success and sustainability of a product in the market. Strategic, marketing and technology management gurus have a lot more to say on how to face such challenges.

By creating and developing an entrepreneurial mindset of the people involved in the product (outcome) development, an organization can face such challenges of making a product stay long in the competitive market. Additionally, to steer business and motivate (involve) employees to pursue breakthrough growth, capable leaders are required to navigate both external and internal conflicts. Thus, the role and importance of entrepreneurial leadership and management become important for students as well as professionals.

Therefore, in order to understand, explain and predict the behaviour of entrepreneurs, entrepreneurial teams and entrepreneurial organizations examine the interrelationship among different environmental (market/business), sociocultural and organizational factors as the predictors of entrepreneurship development and validate the existing framework/models of entrepreneurship development. Entrepreneurial management has the potential to emerge as a new field of study in management which can face the contemporary challenges of the globe.

This volume on *Entrepreneurial Management* comprises a set of 14 papers by management gurus addressing the above issues. The contributors of these papers are the faculty and research scholars of management and behavioural sciences, managers, consultants and administrators, who contributed their research-findings, thoughts and experiences.

The first paper is *Entrepreneurial Management: Emergence of a New Field* by Shivganesh Bhargava. In the paper, the author tries to present a case that entrepreneurship is an emerging interdisciplinary field of study and entrepreneurial management is very important for economy and development. He reports a shift in the mindset of the people, the organizations and government policies as a positive sign in the entrepreneurial context. This has enhanced the involvement of private corporations, increased the participation of new entrants in the market and created a culture of entrepreneurial transformation in a nation like India. The paper discusses some key challenges and puts forward a few directions to follow. The author emphasizes on treating social capital as the foundation of development and also on developing leadership that is truly professional and beyond transformation.

The next paper is a case study: *Network of Entrepreneurship and Economic Development (NEED): A Facilitating Organization of Microenterprise and Self Help Groups* by Shailendra Singh. The author identifies and describes the contribution of NEED in promoting microenterprises and self help groups (SHGs). This training model consists of six modules—namely, motivation training, project guidance module, training in management issues, operations and production issues, escort phase consisting of practical issues in an enterprise formation and the follow-up stage. The study throws some 21 outcome indicators of women empowerment and records the familiar voices of SHG members who enumerate the changes/developments that have come about after they joined SHGs. The author concludes that India, with more than 110 crore population, cannot provide employment to its eligible people in the organization sector, thus providing opportunities for self-employment as it is the most plausible route. Evaluation of Entrepreneurship-linked Income Generation for Self-Employment Programme (EIGSEP) revealed success of the intervention in terms of improved quality of life measured through social and political empowerment, income generation, poverty reduction and enterprise sustainability.

Deeksha A. Singh's paper, *A Resource-based Perspective to International Entrepreneurship* presents the new firms that emerge from the economies of the Asia Pacific Region (APR) and are making their presence felt in the global market place. The author looks at the issue of international entrepreneurship from the perspective of the firms arising from emerging economies and provides an alternative framework based on the resource-based view to explain the rising phenomenon of international entrepreneurship from emerging economies. Further, the paper argues that even though the emerging economy firms may not have the traditional proprietary advantages enjoyed by big multi-national enterprises (MNEs), yet they have different kinds of resources, which satisfy the criteria of being rare, valuable, inimitable and non-substitutable. It is these resources that provide a competitive advantage to these firms over the domestic firms in foreign markets. In the paper, the author examines a few assumptions and highlights the role of some key factors in explaining the rise of international entrepreneurship from emerging economies.

The next paper is *Developing Entrepreneurial Workforce for Sustainable Growth of the Small Scale Sector* by V.P. Wani. The paper presents the theory that the small scale industries (SSI) sector has acquired a prominent role in the socioeconomic development of the country and has contributed to the overall growth of the gross domestic product as well as in terms of employment generation, removal of regional imbalance and export. Due to some business challenges, many units of this sector are facing numerous problems resulting in their sickness. To minimize these, an entrepreneur has to adopt innovative product processes, productivity improvement techniques and effective technology management for the sustainability of the units. The paper examines the factors responsible for the growth or sickness of small scale industrial unit and proposes the model with strategic approach for developing entrepreneurial capabilities among engineers.

In the next paper, titled, *Does Human Resource Factor Matter in Achieving Energy Efficiency in Small Industry Clusters? An Empirical Study*, the author, N. Nagesha, argues that the level of energy efficiency in a small scale industry depends not only on the production technology adopted but also on other non-technology factors and therefore, analyzes the factors including entrepreneurial and human resources, in the context of two energy intensive SSI clusters. The analysis of empirical data from 42 iron foundries and 41 textile dyeing units located in two South Indian states establish the significance of non-technology factors and identify the key variables in achieving energy efficiency. The findings show the importance of human factors in energy efficiency levels in the selected SSI clusters. The paper underlines the need to involve non-technology factors in the prevailing technology-centred energy-efficiency improvement initiatives in the small industry sector for discernible improvements in the long run.

Another paper, *Effect of Market Turbulence and Market Focus on the Firm's Performance in Small and Medium Scale Manufacturing Firms* by Sanjay S. Gaur and Hari Vasudevan ascertains the effect of market turbulence and market focus on the performance of small and medium scale manufacturing firms in India. The study found that firms perform better during the time of market turbulence and components of market focus like customer orientation and that competitor orientation of the firm were not directly related to the firm performance. However, the study found that during the time of high market turbulence, firms with better market focus, that is, which are more customer-oriented and competitor-oriented, perform better. The paper shows that the scales used (for market turbulence and market focus) in developed countries like the USA are reliable and valid in the context of small and medium scale manufacturing firms in India also.

The next paper, *Student Expectations of Entrepreneurs: A Survey* by Francis Jose, is based on a survey of postgraduate students in Chennai, wherein the author presents the expectations of the students from entrepreneurs in terms of the personality qualities. He also examines the interrelationships that these characteristics have with their demographic profiles. Tests of difference on the 18 qualities among students in their varied backgrounds reflect the sociological trends and mind patterns, which primarily reflect the hidden needs and ambitions that the young educated Indian have about entrepreneurship. The analysis also suggests that entrepreneurial qualities like confidence, enthusiasm, intelligence, honesty and creativity can be built up and furthered in society, which will help governments and social institutions identify and develop specific strategies to enhance the global and societal consciousness of our entrepreneurs.

The next paper by Kailash B.L. Srivastava is on *Examining the Relationship of Sociocultural Factors and Entrepreneurial Propensity among Professional Students.* Here, an attempt has been made to explore the reasons why young students choose the entrepreneurial career and the role of socio-cultural factors in selecting such a career. Analyses of the results show that management students reported greater levels of entrepreneurial propensity on each dimension of the study. The effect of sociocultural factors on entrepreneurial propensity is also found. The author has also outlined some directions for the future.

A paper by R. Raghunathan on *Motivational Factors Influencing Industrial Entrepreneurship in Rajasthan* argues that stability serves as an engine for economic growth. Identifying the factors that influence an individual's choice to pursue an entrepreneurial career that has an impact on economic growth and development, he further argues that although a large number of leading industrialists of India belong to Rajasthan, yet the state is still economically backward. In his survey among industrial entrepreneurs, the role of non-economic factors on starting a business was clearly visible.

The next paper is *Psychosocial Perceptional Differences: An Empirical Exploratory Study on Indian Food Processing Women Entrepreneurs* by R. Ganesan, R.P. Pradhan and R.C. Maheshwari. The authors argue that change in the perception of women in India has yet not occurred in totality. It could be that women still need more support from their mentors, the successful enterprising women, who will impact their perception and thus bring change in terms of the social system and socio-background deviations. The analyses of women entrepreneurs/actors, who were running food processing enterprises/start-ups, show a significant effect of socio-background variables on psychosocial variable and the authors discuss these accordingly.

Following this is *A Study of Life-situation Antecedence, Personality and Motivational Patterns of Small Scale Women Entrepreneurs* by T.J. Kamalanabhan and V. Vijaya. The paper focusses on the psychological aspects of the entrepreneurial intention of small scale women entrepreneurs in the manufacturing, trading and service sectors. The variables incorporated for study were life situation antecedence, personality, entrepreneurial motivation and business-related variables. The tools used for the study were life situation antecedence scale, personality questionnaire and entrepreneurial motivation scale. The results reveal the significant effect of life situation antecedence, personality and business related variables on entrepreneurial intention in small scale women entrepreneurs, who were found to have lower psychological support, poorer work condition and lesser competence compared to women non-entrepreneurs in life situation antecedence. The authors have made an attempt to explain the differences in the entrepreneurial intention of women entrepreneurs in the manufacturing, trading and service sectors.

The next paper is a case study also on *Women Entrepreneurship: A Case of Microenterprises* by N. Manimekalai and A. Mohammed Abdullah. The authors argue that most of the researches in the field of entrepreneurship have been centred on male entrepreneurs and business communities. To inculcate the spirit of entrepreneurship among new communities, institutional efforts are the need of the time. There is also an urgent need to encourage women entrepreneurs, who contribute significantly but have hardly been accounted in the national income to become owners of enterprises. The paper presents the case that their contribution cannot be ignored now.

In the paper on *Strategic Role of Engineering Institutions for Entrepreneurship Developments in India,* Dinesh Khanduja and Rajeev Khanduja attempt to re-establish the important role played by engineering education on entrepreneurship development. They opine that the engineering institutions of India have mostly played a passive role in discharging their responsibilities and that resulted in establishing many myths and fears regarding entrepreneurship among students. They found the abundance of entrepreneurial aptitude among students but ironically, they could also find a lack of entrepreneurial capability among them in the absence of proper inputs on entrepreneurship. The paper also gives an account of the growing trend among engineers to choose wage employment/self-employment as a career option and analyzes the prevalent myths and fears on entrepreneurship. The authors propose a remedial measure of strategic counselling by engineering institutions in order to significantly improve the involvement of engineering faculty for the sustainable growth.

The last paper titled *Building Entrepreneurial Society in India through Business Incubation* is by M.K. Sridhar and M.V. Ravikumar. In this paper, the authors outline the historical roots of entrepreneurship and emphasize on the fact that the source of livelihood is wealth. They further argue that wealth enables the creation of more wealth. An entrepreneur is an economic leader, who possesses the ability to recognize opportunities for successful introduction of new products, techniques and new sources of supply and that all political ideologies of a nation treat entrepreneurship as the essential for economic development. The paper reflects on the government's efforts on overall entrepreneurship activity including survival and opportunity-based entrepreneurship. The authors presented these efforts as the growth and contribution of the small scale sector, which has the maximum employment generation ability with comparatively low investment and potentiality to minimize the regional imbalance in industrial development. For establishing an entrepreneurial society, a nation has to have a stable and efficient handholding mechanism available at low cost, to start-ups as well as family-based entrepreneurs for diversifying their efforts into new sectors. This paper proposes that establishing *business incubators* suiting regional conditions and local resources based on appropriate and effective framework on a public, private, in-company or co-operative basis could be the ideal method to build an *entrepreneurial society.*

The authors conclude that the *business incubator* has the potentiality to demonstrate its transformational role in developing the economy if a proactive policy support, knowledgeable governing council and effective incubator management are in place for an entrepreneurial society. The paper also cautions that designing such an overarching strategy is not going to be easy as it also depends on the cooperation and resources of a number of stakeholders in society, such as administrators, educators, financiers, social organizations, technologists, social scientists and entrepreneurs themselves. The authors put forward a positive note that it is possible to design an *entrepreneurial society* for the all-round development of the nation.

The society has to create entrepreneurial leaders, who aspire to be not only at the top in the environment but also feel the need to nurture people on whom the nation's economy stands. It is possible only through a comprehensive understanding of the sociocultural as well as economic aspects related to starting and expanding business ventures. Entrepreneurs must balance internal resources and they also need to focus on continuous improvement of their people by creating a hassle-free, free environment, achieving both growth and innovation.

In this techno-competitive era, physical boundaries are reduced. Communication has become easy, and information about everything is easily and timely available. The consumer, too, has a variety of similar as well as competing products to choose from. Getting money from the banks has become smoother; converting ideas into action is no longer just a dream and the market is dependent on the customers' interest and the brand name. The time has now come when the need of creating and developing an entrepreneurial organization where business starts with ideas of people incubated to define products/services matching the market realities through an effective implementation must be realized by all. All these are possible through an enterprising attitude of people, where family, society, social institutions, governance and leadership all play their role, thus enabling individuals as well as the small/medium enterprises, which are a very vital segment of the economy, to gear up their business operations professionally for rebuilding nations.

All organizations will find it hard to maintain their position in the global market for long. Hence, it is possible only by being an entrepreneurial system, where one has to move from effective leadership to effective entrepreneurship. The positive expectations of entrepreneurial leaders from their colleagues' performance will exert a powerful impact on an individual colleague's performance. This will allow organizations to face challenges related to the loss of knowledge and experience of talented people for an edge on competitiveness and profitability. Hope this volume will provide a direction in this field.

Shivganesh Bhargava

Entrepreneurial Management
Emergence of a New Field

SHIVGANESH BHARGAVA

We are in the era of entrepreneurship. Historically, entrepreneurship could be traced back from the development of human civilization and therefore, one can say that it is as old as history itself. As a field of scientific enquiry, it drew attention and momentum only in the last few decades. Today, a phenomenal growth in the research interest and outcomes are clearly visible across disciplines in this field and it is considered as the backbone of the economy of any nation.

Many issues are important and need to be understood in the context of developing an economy but two main aspects need to be addressed while understanding entrepreneurship. One is the factors that facilitate the process of entrepreneurship development and the other is identifying the processes through which an organization/enterprise has to pass through to become an entrepreneurial one.

Entrepreneurship is the creation of a variety of novel businesses. Many definitions are available in the literature of entrepreneurship (Morris, 1998) and all have their own merits. It suffers from the problem of definition, nature of its relationship with uncertainty and its identity crisis (liability of newness or on novelty). Keeping a cognitive structure of the people of a society, the economic structure of a nation and its socio-political system and an overall scope for business, one may attempt to understand entrepreneurship effectively and then define it.

In this process, probably, the economists should be remembered first. They differentiated an entrepreneur from an ordinary performing employee (worker) or a change-agent/catalyst/leader from a sincere manager.

Later on, other scientists too joined this field looking at the role and importance of non-economic factors contributing to the process of entrepreneurship. Today, it is an interdisciplinary field of study.

Some define entreneurship as the creation of a new (not duplicate) or novel business. Others treat it as a new entry in business. For some, it is the creation of a new enterprise and the process of utilizing available opportunities for productive and cost-effective development. For a psychologist, it combines both behaviour and outcomes. For a management scientist's demand of the product in the environment (society and market) is an additional component with behaviour and outcome. All these lead towards economic development, technological advancement and making the economy sound.

We see different perspectives of defining entrepreneurship. The only thing common in all is its interdisciplinary nature. This enables a scholar to respect the operation of the other scholar. It means it could be studied applying the framework of all concerned disciplines, such as psychology, sociology, economics and other sciences.

Entrepreneurship: Strategic Aspect of Business Development

Entrepreneurship has to be treated as a long-term competitive strategy, though for some organizations it could be only a part of the short-term strategy. In fact, the role of entrepreneurship has also changed drastically in the last decade, particularly after liberalization and globalization have become the acceptable framework of national development across the world. As a result, one can see a dramatic shift in the mindset of people, organizations and government policies. Fast growing organizations even go for audits of non-quantifiable functions as they are ready to invest in anything, where there is positive outcome but not on something that appears non-productive. This reflects a sense of involvement, concern on cost effectiveness and preparation of the mindset of all kinds of organizations for entering innovatively in the new/novel fields.

These enhanced involvements of private corporations and increased participation of new entrants in the market have created a culture of entrepreneurial transformation in a nation like India. For example, privatization in the field of telecommunication in the last decade has shown an increasing involvement of private corporations and impact of governance and management control on creating opportunities for entrepreneurs and influencing the economy (see Table 1.1).

Table 1.1   Ranking of Fortune Top 10 Companies of the World

Fortune 2006 Ranking of World's Companies*
General Electric (Electronic)
Toyota
Procter & Gamble
Fed Ex
Johnson & Johnson
Microsoft
Dell
Berkshire Hathway
Apple Computers
Wal-Mart Stores

Source: Philadelphia: USA (http://www.haygroup.com/ww/Media/Press_Release. asp?PageID=911)

Notes: 1. *March 15, 2006. Ranking of the world's most admired companies.
  2. The following criteria were applied to rank the above companies: ability to attract and retain talented people; quality of management; social responsibility to the community and environment; innovativeness; quality of products/services; wise use of corporate assets; financial soundness; long-term investment value, effectiveness in conducting business globally.

Table 1.1 shows the recent ranking of the top 10 companies of the world. While ranking companies, one is free to apply their own criteria to meet the timely requirements and they could be sound criteria as well but it will be hard to treat same criteria for understanding and predicting entrepreneurial management of an organization. From the success of the above-ranked companies, one is able to make out that the entrepreneurship-oriented strategy of the companies put them ahead of the others. A careful analysis of 10 years' *Economic Times* ranking of the companies (Agrawal, 2006) has shown that the companies which treated entrepreneurship as an integral part of their business strategy succeeded in maintaining top ranks for years. Others disappeared soon.

Entrepreneur: The One Whom Every Society Follows

An entrepreneur is that individual who is involved in an entrepreneurial service and one who has novelty in terms of ideas, processes and outcomes. He could be judged on the basis of the impact on the economic system, business environment, market and stakeholders that form the entire society. For some scholar (Kilby, 1971), an entrepreneur is like the 'Heffalump', a large animal, who has been hunted by many, who have used all possible devices but without success. It is interesting to note that all those who see him describe him as enormous but disagree on particulars. Same holds true with the definition of entrepreneurs and entrepreneurship that originated among the French first.

We have seen the process and behaviour of entrepreneurship and entrepreneurs. It requires examining the venture process, the venture capital, resource assessment, talent availability and business environment. All entrepreneurs could be categorized broadly as entrepreneurs (general/all), women, technical and social. Here exists scope for small business management, performance of entrepreneurial organization by examining issues related to survival as well as growth and inbreeding professionalism to convert all organizations into corporate entrepreneurship.

Entrepreneurship also refers to the mindset of the entrepreneurs, to the degree of proactivity they possess for being ahead of the competitors as well as the risk-taking ability and innovation in the outcomes of the organizations. Here, economy, market, technological advancement and the sociopolitical environment play important roles. The time has now come to encourage entrepreneurs develop themselves and initiate entrepreneurial strategies to benefit.

For most, the market is an allocative process. For some, it is a discovery process and for others, it is seen as a creative process. Such frameworks form the background to explain the variations of entrepreneurs on perception of risk uncertainty and the gain involved with the opportunity. Product market conditions and organizational contexts help in creating new business, where the developmental level of society and industrial environment play an important role. Societies and nations have to keep these in mind and must put visionary efforts to involve large numbers of entrepreneurs available everywhere.

Systems Framework of Entrepreneurial Organization

Evidences show that dispersed corporate entrepreneurship failed in most cases when the organizational conditions were unfavourable for entrepreneurial initiatives. One has no option but to take into account all micro and macro level factors that contribute in making the conditions favourable. An analysis was made on why some organizations manage favourably while others, under the same conditions, do not. This could be explained well within the systems framework. In an entrepreneurial system, a single unit, such as business development, is not the only key organ of entrepreneurship. Rather, all units require attention. Similarly, every employee has to be treated as an important stakeholder in this process.

Paying more attention to core business units and ignoring the peripheral units will lead to disequilibrium (ineffectiveness) in the long run. Similarly, focusing more on the high performers/achievers and ignoring the low performers/achievers will also lead to disequilibrium and eventually, in the long run, to ineffectiveness of the organization. Therefore, organizations aspiring to be entrepreneurial ones must be open to the external environment and apply social systems framework (Katz and Kahn, 1978) to function effectively. Although it can be sensed that small and flexible systems have an advantage over their bigger counterparts, yet to me it is not so. All social systems have to keep all their sub-systems checked in order to increase the span of their healthy business life.

Entrepreneurial Management and 21st Century Organizations

In the past, opportunities that we find today did exist and were available across the globe but these were neither thought of or imagined, nor were they visualized then. This simply means that organizations have to have people, who are capable of applying their innovation and identifying what needs to be done where. Some are already able to progress in this direction while others are looking at opportunities in the times to come from the environment around them. Organizations have seen the era and the outcomes of bureaucracy, participative management and quality management. Only innovative and entrepreneurial organizations will survive in this competitive environment. Hence, the future belongs to innovation that leads to entrepreneurship.

Literature examines the merits of entrepreneurial organizations and strategies that facilitate developing entrepreneurial management. Many issues obtained space in literature but I have restricted myself to the scope of people management contributing towards the entrepreneurship development of a system. It requires different approach in terms of looking at the environment (market) for identifying initiatives to be undertaken, people to be deputed for the projects, projects to be undertaken, teams to be selected, strategy to be applied, cooperation and co-ordination of competitors to be understood, assessing the strength of the organization and its health, and finally, preparing organizations to be entrepreneurial.

The thesis is that any organization, irrespective of its nature, size and sector, has the potentiality to be an entrepreneurial one if it is able to face the challenges arising out of the following common issues raised. The successful ones face them innovatively and those that are unable to do it fail, which is not uncommon. The desire of learning from failures could change the status again.

Learning How to Explore and Utilize Business Opportunities

In this era of entrepreneurship, competitions within, as well as among organizations have become important aspects of business. This creates an unprecedented market for the consumer as well as industrial products, where customers are offered choices and the entrepreneurs/organizations are able to maximize their business. However, everybody does not benefit equally from this process and some are ahead of the others. The latest ranking of the top 500 Indian companies (*Economic Times Survey*, 2006) clearly shows that only around 18 per cent of the companies existed in the ranking even after 10 years but it is difficult to present here the reason for what happened to the other 80 per cent companies. What emerges from this is that to be successful in the field of entrepreneurship, one has to know and learn how to explore and utilize business opportunities. Entrepreneurship is the alertness to new opportunities and also the actions following its discovery, which involves all kinds of learning processes.

Retaining Innovative Talent

Although entrepreneurship and uncertainty have an unpredictable relationship, yet when these two elements work together, their relationship could bring about many positive outcomes. Within an organization, entrepreneurship depends on its ability to utilize talents and the available resources effectively. It is not knowledge alone but also integration of different pieces of knowledge that facilitate the process of entrepreneurial activities. Retaining any kind of talent has become a major challenge to business leaders across the sectors but retaining innovative talent and knowledge workers is relatively more serious. All reward and people management strategies are being experimented but their significant impact has not been reported so far. Efforts like culture building and development, psychological contract and intrinsic motivation strategies got more respect than the financial rewards but again, nothing specific in the form of a model or framework is available. It is only suggestive and directional.

Today, technological advancement has diverted the attention of the globe towards itself. Silicon Valley is an example of entrepreneurship and innovation—inseparable aspects of the economic development. Innovation does not entail just the development of novel and creative products but also involves building loyal customers, adapting and applying cost-effective technology, strategic decision-making, as well as identifying, selecting, developing, managing and retaining competent people. People do make a difference. Organizations have to identify talents who could explore opportunities for product development. Therefore, retaining talent is one of the major challenges of the chief executive officers (CEOs), particularly in R&D, learning and entrepreneurial organizations. By retaining innovative talents, many entrepreneurial organizations and places like Silicon Valley could be created, developed and managed.

Role of the Senior Management

Another major challenge of corporate entrepreneurs today is to explore, identify and recognize the opportunities available for developing new business enterprises. Large enterprises face such challenges more seriously than their counterparts, as the utilization of opportunities is crucial in the outcomes of entrepreneurship. Also, such organizations do have the problem of middle management crisis and conflict between the young talent and the old experts. The middle management, particularly in large enterprises, is passing through a stage of transition. It does not see any space for contribution in decision-making or self development. Dissatisfaction of all kinds is clearly visible, leading to ineffective utilization of available talent for organizational effectiveness. Senior management can play an important role here in creating an environment supporting entrepreneurial initiatives and asserting their value for the organization.

Fostering Entrepreneurial Competency

There are also evidences to highlight the role that the government policies, and regional and cross-cultural factors play to facilitate entrepreneurial activities. Utilization of available opportunities and creation of market could be positively related to as entrepreneurial success. It is an outcome of making use of the opportunity to come out with a product that will be used in the market by the customers looking for a particular product.

Every individual has some talent or the other while in some this talent can be identified, in others, it remains hidden. Entrepreneurship is not restricted to a specific person or group. It is an ability to explore, create and utilize the available explored and unexplored opportunities for novel or unexpected innovations and solutions. Therefore, to facilitate and create business, some competencies could be identified and fostered as per the requirements of the entrepreneurship. It will help to realize where the scope for starting and pursuing entrepreneurial venture exists (sensing market). An entrepreneurial personality ignores the role of individual differences. Rather, it lays emphasis on the role of cognitive factors, and therefore we see substance in terms of entrepreneurial intentions and entrepreneurial thinking, which occupy significant space in understanding the process of entrepreneurship. Encouraging all individuals towards developing competency that leads to the road of entrepreneurship in any field is the demand of the time and organizations must foster it.

Entrepreneurial Culture

One can see clear regional differences in the same society or nation for the desire to establish entrepreneurship and further advance ahead. This however, does not mean that people of some places are made (gifted) for entrepreneurship and others are not. I am of the opinion that any place in this universe is a fit case for an entrepreneurial activity. Some are able to sense (get insights) while others do not. Even getting insight alone will not be adequate enough for entrepreneurship unless the skills to exploit the market and utilize the resources as well as opportunities are not adequately developed.

An entrepreneur always has to have space for unexpected happenings in the process of any entrepreneurial venture. Market turbulence and unpredictable environment, organizational factors like strategy, structure and leadership, managing people and resources including technology, political stability, and sociocultural factors play a very crucial role in developing entrepreneurial culture in society. Organizations will find it difficult to involve a majority of the people if they are unable to create a culture where most are oriented towards innovative activity, leading further towards entrepreneurial outcomes.

Leadership beyond Transformation

Today, many organizations disappear from the list of successful business organizations on the popular ranking of some professional bodies (Agrawal, 2006). One of the factors generally reported as its root cause is the failure to manage innovation within the system. A critical psychological analysis of the attitude (statements as reflected on interviews to the media or the address of the Annual General Meeting) and behaviour of the respected business leaders and CEOs (as actually perceived by the group within or insiders, who really know the person well) reveals a wide discrepancy. It cannot be objectively established but inferences could be drawn that probably Indian business leaders and successful entrepreneurs possess a common style of managing people. At some stage in every level it is the personal relationship that matters in the final decision-making. This is based on the perceptual response analysis of those who aspire to get a chance to lead the organization.

In case my thesis gets empirical support and validity, then the absence of entrepreneurial leadership in India requires further empirical examination. Thus, this leads only to routine success and normal achievement, which could be relatively better in that business environment. Any global business/entrepreneurial leader of this century has to go beyond personalized relationships and feelings of insecurity (loss/absence of power) in order to compete and keep going. Therefore, societies, where leaders say something and do just the opposite, will have difficulties in fostering and developing an entrepreneurial existence. The role of the top management in an organization is crucial in making an entrepreneurial initiative, a reality and the process effective. Here, a CEO has to go miles away from the transformational leadership if he/she is willing to take the organization ahead.

Synergetic Approach

One can find a significant difference between the outcomes of different subsystems and managers of the same organization working at different levels and such differences consequently have their impact on making an organization an entrepreneurial one. Thus, individual, group, social, organizational and environmental factors have to be carefully examined for making an effort to convert any organization in an entrepreneurial one.

Changing, Building and Developing Positive Mindsets

Changing the mindset is one of the major challenges, on which today's organizations must concentrate for carving their niche in the market. It could be asked that what was so distinct about the top ranking companies presented in Table 1.1 than the other companies and a single answer would not be acceptable to all. The degree of disagreement will be lesser if one puts forward an argument in favour of entrepreneurial management as a strategy that puts them ahead of others.

Conclusion

The paper discussed entrepreneurship as a process, where an entrepreneur and an entrepreneurial organization are alerted to uncertainty, unexpected dangers, new ventures and outcomes. Organizational routine leads to only accomplishing something routine but not an innovation. An organization can be converted into an entrepreneurial one by focussing on people in the centre of the entrepreneurial process and realizing the importance of social, cultural and political systems for creating something innovative. Based on literature and consulting expertise, Bhargava (2005) proposed the following 20 points as directions that can be followed in order to convert an organization into an entrepreneurial one, subject to their empirical validation as several external and organizational factors are not taken into consideration:

1. Begin with entrepreneurial initiatives
2. Respond to economic uncertainty
3. Explore corporate venturing
4. Select corporate venture funds
5. Identify suitable technology
6. Sensing and knowing market
7. Encourage and promote innovation
8. Look for competitive strategy
9. Mix strategy with exploration and utilization
10. Translate strategy into action
11. Turn strategies into reality
12. Assess business needs and competencies/capabilities
13. Identify, develop, manage and retain world class talent
14. Develop world class (global) leaders
15. Mobilize people to achieve business goals
16. Create competitive reward strategy
17. Create performance culture

18. Manage performance
19. Develop distinct culture
20. Create an entrepreneurial mindset

I can see that the future belongs to entrepreneurship. I can clearly see the unexpected available opportunities as well as the unlimited unexplored opportunities for creating new ventures in any field. Today, no nation can afford to back out from the process of liberalization or has the option to interfere in the open market economy that has opened new avenues to the new generation living in a technologically advanced world.

Call centres are the outcome of the last decades but an increase in the number of small and medium-sized enterprises (SMEs), particularly in de-veloping nations, reflects the attitude of the people towards entrepreneurship that was not as intense in the past. In fact, for business activity, one does not require to be only at the developed places (cities)—one can engage in an economic generation activity leading to business anywhere. This gives hope to those nations that possess a rural base.

There is a need to differentiate between the objective measures of support and the support that is being perceived by the prospective entrepreneurs. The entrepreneurship process could be well explained within the social psychological framework and sociology by applying the relationship between the social interaction and entrepreneurial behaviour. In fact, entrepreneurship has implications on the economic growth and consequently on social policy. Therefore, for an effective entrepreneurial management, the policy makers and business leaders have to see beyond the economic framework grounded around technology only. If nations aspire and desire to have an entrepreneurial society, they must lay more emphasis on social capital as an investment process in the future, wherein knowledge has an edge over others. It is now up to the business leaders to pay attention to make social capital as the foundation of development.

The implications of the model of achieving society (McClelland, 1961) are visible across the globe, where innovation and entrepreneurship play key roles in the process of developing economy. To maintain their place in the globe, all nations are mostly putting these characteristics at the top of their main economic-political agenda. Some are able to see the results while others are positively expecting for good results. My thesis is that an achieving society is possible not only by having achievement-oriented employees but also competent as well as talented people. It demands a leadership that is truly professional and beyond transformation.

References

Agrawal, A. 2006. 'Beyond Transformational Leadership', Term paper for the Progress Seminar, Shailesh J. Mehta School of Management, Indian Institute of Technology (IIT), Bombay.

Bhargava, S. 2005. 'Entrepreneurship in the Developing Societies', Unpublished report, Shailesh J. Mehta School of Management, Indian Institute of Technology (IIT), Bombay.

Economic Times. 2005. *Economic Times 500 Companies Performance Ranking.* Mumbai: M/s Bennett, Coleman & Co Ltd.

Katz, D. and R. L. Kahn. 1978. *The Social Psychology of Organization.* New York: John Wiley & Sons.

Kilby, P. 1971. *Entrepreneurship and Economic Development.* New York: Free Press.

McClelland, D. C. 1961. *The Achieving Society.* Princeton, NJ: Van Nostrand.

Morris, M. H. 1998. *Entrepreneurial Intensity: Sustainable Advantages for Individuals, Organizations, and Societies.* Westport, Conn: Quorum.

Network of Entrepreneurship and Economic Development (NEED)
A Facilitating Organization of Microenterprise and Self Help Groups

2

SHAILENDRA SINGH

This case study identifies and describes the contribution of the Network of Entrepreneurship and Economic Development (NEED) in promoting microenterprises and self help groups (SHGs). With fire in his belly, its facilitator, Mr Anil Singh, has founded NEED with the mission to help the deprived citizens acquire their rights. The founder strongly believed that maximization of human resource potential of a nation is possible through enabling women and children, which in turn will change all spheres (socioeconomic, political, environmental and cultural) of their lives. While pursuing its mission, NEED's major concerns include: establishing women's self help groups and mainstreaming gender issues, microcredit with multiplier effects, microenterprise, fair trade campaign from village to global levels with entrepreneurial skills, a child-centred development approach, health, education, agricultural diversification, income generation activities, capacity building and networking towards grassroots action. NEED developed a model of women's empowerment through SHGs that includes awareness training, skill development, exposure visits, and sound financial management for sustainability.

For microenterprise development, NEED conceptualized a comprehensive gender-sensitive model called Entrepreneurship linked Income Generation for Self-Employment Programme (EIGSEP). This training model consisted of six modules, namely, motivation training, project guidance module, training in management issues, operations and production issues, escort phase consisting of practical issues in an enterprise formation and the follow-up stage. The case study also records an evaluation of the EIGSEP model. The study has thrown some 21 outcome indicators of women empowerment. The case study has also compiled the feedback of volunteers who observed NEED's functioning while promoting the SHGs. Based on his vast experience, Mr Anil Singh has identified certain features of successful microenterprises and has suggested ways and means to replicate the successful experiences of microenterprise development in other areas. The case study has also described small case experiences of three SHGs and the struggles and achievements of their members. These are stories of crises and fighting hostile circumstances and coming out victorious. Women described in these case studies are truly empowered. They have learned various craft and developed skills in the groups promoted by NEED and have utilized these skills to start up their own businesses. Finally, the case records the familiar voices of SHG members stating the changes and happenings that took place after they joined SHGs.

NEED, as an organization, is Voluntary Development Organization established in mid-1995, to become a network of people-driven development models. NEED works for empowering women and children for their dignity and rights. Apart from working directly at the grassroots in about 600 villages spread in seven districts of Uttar Pradesh and facilitating 1250 self help groups, NEED has also networked with many voluntary and development organizations spread all over the country and is managed by an international advisory council which appraises the organization's performance with the objective of enhancing the efficacy of its interventions. The members of this council are management experts, professional trainers, behavioural scientists, grassroot level workers, and women development specialists with at least five years experience in their fields. There is a governing board consisting of seven members, including several women members from the grassroots who were earlier NEED's trainees and have now successfully started microfinance groups. The governing board is headed by the founder and the chief executive Mr Anil K. Singh. Its members are engaged in entrepreneurial activities and have evolved as outspoken leaders in their own communities.

The Facilitator

Mr Anil K. Singh has a postgraduate degree in social service with a specialization in rural management from the Xavier Institute of Social Service. In 1980, he came in contact with the Indian Institute of Management, Ahmedabad as Senior Research Fellow to undertake research projects in remote tribal villages where he worked closely with faculty members including late Ravi Mathai—a person with an exceptional human touch. Since Mr Singh himself comes from a rural background, he realized the difficulties, agony and social problems faced by the underprivileged people. He always aspired to develop an institution from where he could work to promote self-reliance of the underprivileged through socioeconomic and political empowerment. He worked for many years in the formal sector. Ultimately in 1995, he resigned from his job as the head of a government training institute to set up his own organization. Thus, NEED was born on 22 May 1995. His 25 years' long experience of rural economic management is very helpful in the successful running of the activities at NEED. Mr Anil Singh has also been recognized, both nationally and internationally, as a trainer in the field of rural socioeconomic management. He has given his experiential talks in the Princeton University, Colombia, US and also with many international agencies in the USA. Along with this, he has travelled to many European and South Asian countries as a resource speaker. In recognition of his contribution to social entrepreneurship, Anil has been conferred with the Ashoka Fellowship.

Mission

Mission of NEED, as an organization, is to create an impact upon the rights of deprived citizens of society by enabling women and children. It is possible through enabling women and children, to change their all spheres of lives. The mission focusses on the following:

• Maximization of their human resource potential
• Creation of positive change in socioeconomic, political, environmental and cultural spheres of life
• Upliftment of deprived citizens of society, especially women and children

Vision

NEED works to bring social action and change, which should be environment-friendly and sustainable, keeping in perspective the human resource and socioeconomic status of community as its nucleus point. Therefore, the broad vision of NEED is women-centred development—women being the most deprived section of our society—which leads to the process of empowerment.

Objectives

NEED's principal objective is the socioeconomic empowerment of deprived communities—targeting the women and children of these communities—by facilitating the development of grassroots organizations, creating economic and social opportunities and by enhancing existing human resource capacities in an environmentally sustainable manner.

While pursuing its mission, vision and objectives, NEED feels that the major areas of concern are:

- Women self help groups and mainstreaming of gender issues
- Microcredit with its multiplier effect
- Microenterprise, conservation-linked livelihoods, fair trade campaign from village to global level with entrepreneurial skills
- Child-centred development approach, family, and community
- Health, hygiene and sanitation education, agricultural diversification, income generation activities, and so forth
- Women rural asset management including natural resources
- Capacity building and networking towards grassroots actions

Steps and Processes in Group Formation

NEED conceptualizes the entire group process in six phases, namely, pre-formation stage including deep understanding of local context, formation process, stable group phase I, stable group phase II, growth phase, and finally, expansion phase. NEED believes that groups do not come up instantaneously. Rather they require meaningful and sustained efforts to come into existence.

Pre-formation Stage

In the pre-formation stage, facilitators are required to develop an understanding of the area and its problems, people, and the context. NEED's approach to group formation process is summarized here:

- Understanding the area profile: understanding the people, caste, locally available resources, Panchayat, village profile, possible opportunities-based interest of people in producing traditional skills and artisans
- Identification and selection of target: landless labourers, small and marginal farmers, artisans, small businessmen/women, and so forth
- Means of entrée: showing sensitivity to the social, economic and political problems faced by rural poor and by initially pioneering discussions on these issues and encouraging the people to generate alternative solutions of such problems through SHGs
- Providing awareness regarding various poverty alleviation programmes and making constant efforts to network with government and other offices concerned with development
- Interacting with the *sarpanch/pradhan* or social workers without any condition or pressure

Group Formation Stage

Once the workers understand the issues of the community, they can initiate the group formation process. Groups should be of 10–20 members and can be exclusive male or exclusive female or mixed ones. The steps involved are:

- Initial contact for developing an understanding of the community, fixing the date and time of meeting with the help of the community members and inviting local social workers, the *pradhan*, and other interested people for this meeting.
- Organizing the meeting effectively. Presenting benefits as well the requirements of the groups that would be fulfilled. Presenting

themselves as helpful, understanding, motivating, and approachable so that the community members can ask questions to clarify their doubts. Organize cultural programmes highlighting the positive points of the groups.

- Threadbare discussion of local problems among group members and their sources of income and expenditure.
- Identify the underlying human capital present in the group and presenting the structure of SHGs.
- Encourage open discussions on issues in the meeting and identify people who are motivated to be a part of the proposed groups.
- Request group members to evolve group rules regulation through in-depth discussions so that a vibrant group can be established.
- Develop synergy in various kinds of programmes implemented within and through the groups.

Stable Group (First Phase)

In this phase, meetings are commenced on a regular basis. Additionally, saving funds is initiated in consultation with and cooperation of the group so that enough funds can be saved for inter-loaning. Group members themselves decide the course of action to be used for saving, inter-loaning, and repayment. This also clarifies whether the individual members are worthy of receiving a loan or the members have the capability of utilizing the funds effectively or not. Attendance in the meetings is more than 80 per cent and timely repayment of loan is 90 per cent or more. A proper maintenance of records is also necessary. There are discussions on domestic and public issues of importance. This phase gives an emergence to the executive leadership of the group.

Stable Group (Second Phase)

This phase establishes the identity and values of the group through a continuous effort to network with the government department and social workers related with the developmental work. The group also tries to start income generation activities based on local resources while maintaining prestige and self help principles. The group encourages the entrepreneurial system that creates a culture in which members require mutual help and realize the value of interdependence.

Growth Phase

The group provides a stable forum to individuals for dialogue with the government, panchayats and other participatory and development institutions. If the group is working well, they get the opportunity to participate in these forums on their own, depending on their level of confidence and development managerial capability.

Expansion Phase

This is the phase where groups develop as full-fledged participatory and empowering institutions. The group's strength, however, depends on commitment to its objectives, feeling of mutual trust and cooperation among its members, and transparency in its dealings. Many matured groups, after developing the understanding of participatory philosophy, should form federations at panchayat, and then at the block level to undertake more challenging projects. Experience suggests that earlier federations were formed under two conditions: 1. When the groups had to take projects at community levels, for example, the work of sanitation or of drinking water. In such projects more than one group joined hands. 2. When the groups realized that they can save money when they purchase agricultural inputs and implements in bulk. It suggests that when the goals of many groups are common, then the interdependent conditions for the formation of the federation are ripe.

Women's Empowerment through Self Help Groups

Self help group (SHG) has now become synonymous to the developmental process. It is recognized as an important way of achieving economic and social force. SHG not only ensures people's participation but also establishes their collective force, which is very important. The case of Tahrulnisha from Sitapur district, discussed later in the article, clearly suggests that she could get freedom from the clutches of the moneylender only due to the collective force of the SHG and the fear of direct action by the group. NEED is working very sincerely to make SHGs a tool for empowering the deprived people, socially. They believe in giving freedom to SHGs and not spoon-feed them so that vibrant leadership can emerge. The people should become more responsible towards society. SHGs should be developed as a platform to find solutions of the issues, needs and concerns of the community. This regular process has enabled group members to free themselves from the clutches of moneylenders. The group members recognize their capabilities and translate these into income generation activities.

Skill Development

NEED is working to develop the skills of group members by providing them training in learning *chikan* embroidery work and *zardozi* on cloth, jute products manufacturing, ready-made garments, candle, *agarbatti* and *dhoopbatti* manufacturing and so forth. Many women have been trained in making ropes, undergarments and blouses that can be sold at the village level. These efforts have started giving returns.

Non-formal Education Centre

NEED has started several Non-formal Education Centers (NFEC) in the villages where the work is going on. In these centres 25–30 children are educated. These children are mostly girls who were deprived of access to formal education because of inadequate resources. The school regularly meets for four to five hours. The children are taught by members of the self help groups of the village.

Exposure Visits

The children enrolled in these NFECs are taken for exposure visits to local village leaders, and many other places including historical sights in Lucknow. This certainly helps in increasing their awareness. Many exposure visits are arranged for SHG members to give immediate practical experience for the functioning of other groups. The experiences gained through exposure visits are passed over to other members of the community. They can interact with others and discuss various problems and solutions. They also visit microenterprises, which give them knowledge, as well as inspire them to do something. These visits also give them an opportunity to widen their vision.

Sustainability of the Group

Sustainability of the group depends a lot on the economic stability of the group. The groups should have sufficient finances through their regular savings and minimized unrecoverable debts. It is also of great importance that the group is linked properly with the bank. For this, the group should have an effective financial management and must keep a watch on how the amount of loan is being used. The loans should be given to members keeping in view the nature and habits of the borrower, purpose of the loan, intensity of need, and the amount being asked for.

Microenterprise Development

The majority of government-sponsored programmes are one-sided and provide only basic training skills and a start-up kit. Mr Singh emphasized that it is the quality that ensures sustainability such as management skills, knowledge about backward and forward linkages, familiarity with government regulations and other follow-ups, which have not been cultivated. Despite these impediments, the poor, disadvantaged, isolated and long-exploited communities are expected to circumvent economic and cultural handicaps and produce successful entrepreneurs.

To bridge the identified drawbacks, NEED has developed a comprehensive gender-sensitive action training model called, Entrepreneurship Linked Income Generation for Self-employment Programme (EIGSEP). There are six modules in this program designed to meet the challenges of a specific dimension of entrepreneurship development. The six stages of the programme are summarized in following lines:

1. Entrepreneurship Motivation Training: It familiarizes trainees with the concept of human capital. This is the entry point for NEED where rapport is quickly built with the trainee groups and the partner organizations. This phase develops the leadership potential and entrepreneurial skills of the group through role plays and other managerial games.
2. Project Guidance Module: Helps trainees to scan the resources properly. This phase includes study of local markets, available skills, local resources and industry policy. Trainees then develop

vision and short- and long-term market-driven plans for their enterprises. At this stage, the trainees develop local resourcing strategies
for their enterprises and conduct a candid appraisal of their own
strengths and weaknesses. This exercise is helpful in developing
entrepreneurial discipline.

3. Training in Management Issues: This module consists of management issues like time management, proprietorship, and negotiation.

4. Shop-Floor Training: This module deals with the technicalities
   of operations and production process and helps trainees understand and learn how to handle technology. In this phase, they also
   meet successful and unsuccessful entrepreneurs, bankers, machine
   operators, and accounts and finance management. This phase gives
   trainees a first-hand feel of how real entrepreneurs work and under
   what constraints and opportunities and also validates their theoretical training so far.

5. Escort Phase: The trainees sum up the learning of all previous stages.
   After a thorough appraisal, gaps are identified and, at this stage,
   attempts are made to bridge the gaps identified. The escort service
   then helps the participants with practical aspects of establishing
   microenterprises including clearing all paper work, registering with
   the district work council, and dealing with the tax departments.
   Escort service essentially provides the initial push to help launch
   the microenterprise.

6. Follow-up Stage: This stage includes phased intervention as per
   the requirements of the trainee groups. During this phase, NEED
   organizes regular meetings with budding entrepreneurs to encourage them to involve more people from their communities in initiating self-supporting businesses.

NEED's founder, Mr Singh aspires that his programme should generate
more and more business leaders who impart their entrepreneurial skills
to others. Here are the statements of two EIGSEP trainees regarding the
impact of the programmer in their lives. Usha, an entrepreneur from
Lucknow, says:

> ... I came to know about NEED, which helps women to stand on their
> own feet. I immediately joined the training programme of NEED. The
> training was totally free and I got a monthly stipend of Rs 200 during
> training. First, I was trained in making jute bags. After training, I made jute
> bags at NEED and earned money. But since not having enough space for

keeping raw materials, finished products etc., I could not do this business at home although I was having a sewing machine

...So I started learning to make candles and *dhoopbatti* as per my request and agreed by NEED. Since I was determined, I learned very quickly and mastered making candles and incense, which made me stronger with an additional skill by the EIGSEP training programme. In addition, I got the chance to interact with other entrepreneurs, and also received field exposure, and the chance to identify inherent potentials, set entrepreneurial goals, techniques to manage an enterprise, concurrent exposure to market forces and information etc. ...I was so eager that during the time of my training itself, I brought the candle frame and started making candles at home. On completion of the training, I opened my own production unit at home. Even though I was trained, initially the process was tough for me, since I had no experience, and did not know how to market the products. With NEED's help, I learned how to find market linkages with suppliers, who would sell my products. I have done my own 'market survey' and also identified various shops where I can sell my products. Gradually, with the ongoing support and encouragement from NEED and with my own effort, my business began to flourish. NEED had shown me the right direction and helped me to convert the 'spark' in me to a 'fire'. Now I feel that I can stand on my own feet and I am independent.

Now with the earnings, I am able to provide food for the entire family and send my daughters to school. My status in the family has also changed dramatically. My husband and in-laws now respect me, since I am generating a substantial income. I have accepted the apologies of my in-laws, have forgotten the past and decided to move forward in my life. Even though I regret a lot that I was not fortunate enough to continue my education, I am sending my daughters to school. They should not have the same fate like me and face problems in their life. ...SHAKRI Self Help Group, taught me the importance of savings, which will help me during the time of adversities. Now I can face all my problems, social and financial, in a very confident manner. EIGSEP training programme has shown me a concrete way to begin a new, better life.

Sushila an entrepreneur from Lucknow also shares her experience.

I was passing through a phase of helplessness, confusion and without knowing what to do, but with all eagerness to do more and better in life. One day I came to know about NEED through a friend and had a subsequent meeting with NEED's Development Manager. I visited NEED and met Mr Anil K. Singh. In my meeting with him, he explained that the work would require a lot of moving around and might be too difficult for a woman of my age. He asked me whether I am prepared to do all that to be successful. I knew that it would take a long time to learn everything I needed to, but I was willing to try.

Sushila went back and talked to different people and decided to improve her sewing talents and to learn making jute bags. It was her choice to undergo the training programme. Her eldest son was pleased that she wanted to do it because it would bring more financial security to the family. On starting the training, she found herself very safe and protected in the new atmosphere. Being the eldest, she was given utmost respect by everyone. She was given a stipend of Rs 600 during the period of the training.

The training programme has helped Sushila upgrade her existing skills as well as learn new skills. It has brought a higher level of awareness and confidence in her. She was earning Rs 400 per month in making jute bags when she began the work. NEED gave her financial support. Soon she brought a sewing machine and started buying material by herself. She also became the member of SHAKTI, the Self Help Group of EIGSEP. Being a member of the self help group, she has come to know the importance of savings and managing all her problems in her domestic as well as entrepreneurial front in a properly planned and collective manner. Initially, she took a credit of Rs 1500 from her SHG, which she returned after sometime. After earning some money, she also opened a small business unit where she has been making a variety of jute bags and selling them. She also teaches other women. Today, through her growing business, Sushila earns her own living in a very respectful manner. Besides running her unit at home, she also continues to earn from stitching jute bags at NEED. This helps her to enhance her earnings. Side-by-side, she has got trained in learning *chikan* embroidery and other works. In the beginning, she started earning in the range of Rs 1000–Rs 1500 per month and had taken an interest-free loan of Rs 4000 from NEED. Now she has a business in *chikan* embroidery with 25 women working for her, and she also makes candles and incense. According to her, the total profits from all of this, deducting the costs of raw materials, transportation, and workers' wages is Rs 3000 per month. Her eldest son was able to contribute financially towards the family in a small way too. Now Sushila will pay back Rs 1000 per month to NEED. She says that the training has helped her to increase her knowledge and come to know the various ways of improving herself. This has placed her today in a position she never imagined.

Katy Rudder (2003)—a United Nations Fund for Women (UNIFEM) researcher has documented both qualitative and quantitative indicators of economic and socio-political empowerment and reduced vulnerability for EIGSEP participants:

Quantitative Indicators

Increased cash income: personally generated due to production, trading, or service provision

Improved level of subsistence: able to provide basic necessities (improved diet, lodging, clothing, able to purchase medicine); availability of surplus rations

Increased savings and assets: savings account, property jewellery, home improvements, 'luxury items'

Decreased dependency on moneylenders: reduced high-interest debt arrangements; borrowing more responsibly through low or no-interest loans, from self help groups

Increased business knowledge: in crafts, book keeping, business communications and management, in alliance-building with traders, bankers, and other entrepreneurs

Improvement in small business: evidence of entrepreneurialism, that is, reducing an exploitative middleman, initiating a change to more profitable product, improving work conditions (to a preferred location, time, or style), expanding the market (from close neighbours to people in the community of various classes, from areas within walking distance to distant markets, to other cities, and so forth), new strategies for increasing profit, and so forth

Has created 'safety nets' for her personal and her family's (physical, social, economic) security: work insurance, health and life insurance, health precautions (feeding herself as well as others, visiting the doctor before any health condition worsens), increased entrepreneurial exposure, investments, fixed deposits

Increased political participation: she has registered or voted knowledge of candidates; knowledge of reservation of seats for women, in Panchayati Raj Institutions; perception of the self help group as a political force

Has contributed to the recycling of resources in her community: replacing the neighbours dependency on exploitative middle-men, producing and selling locally, meeting the needs of their community; buying goods or hiring services from their NEED peer group

Gendered Quantitative Indicators

Increased physical mobility: number of trips to market or outside village; participation in SHG meetings or activities organized by NEED or others

Increased social networks and social mobility: outside the family; invited to functions outside her immediate family, class, or caste; indications of 'climbing the social ladder', gaining respect

Gendered Qualitative Indicators

Recognizes and has addressed personally-experienced prejudices and injustices: due to sex, age, religion, poverty, number of daughters, widowhood, illiteracy, divorce (that is, through discussion and behaviour that challenges unjust norms while maintaining positive/productive relations with the family and the community); identifying sources of support or resistance to address personal inequalities (NEED, individuals in family or community)

Perception of self-worth: perception of individual assets, personal responsibilities and capabilities; role/value as mother, wife, and daughter (daughter-in-law) and citizen

Sense of decreased dependency: on male relatives, on NEED; has developed support network among women in the community

Sense of increased bargaining power at home, in the market, and in the community: does she feel to be in a position to argue, to discuss, to bargain, to give advice, to have an opinion…; how often is her position accepted (with her husband, other family members, neighbours, traders); in what domains does she win her arguments

Sense of helping to develop community trust in women entrepreneurs: she changed people's negative perceptions of how capable women are in business

Perception among family and community of her work: Her work has changed the relationship with others. How does she/others define her work? Is it seen as central to family well-being, seen as supplanting to male relative income, or just as a temporary fancy

Increased interest in daughter's education/career/future: more days attended, intention to further educate, postponing marriage

Increased interest in daughter's exposure to the world: willingness to let daughter run errands, play outside the house, walk to school, or accompany or help her in work (outside of school hours)

Perception of increased personal leisure time: need and want for more free time and value of free time

Qualitative Indicators

Perception of family's well-being: Their definition of 'well-being'; opinion about their current standard of living in com-parison to past days

While evaluating EIGSEP outcome, Rudder (2003) observed, 'Although the microenterprise project has some negative unintended outcomes, women's experiences were overwhelmingly positive. Both the business training and the challenges of running a small business gave these women new skills and information, increased confidence, gave them an improved sense of self worth and opportunity to enjoy human rights previously not enjoyed'.

NEED and Fair Trade Advocacy

Group formation on the principle of Self Help and Microenterprise development alone can not solve the problems of women and the poor. NEED perceives that this is just the beginning and in order to have full justice, activists and NGOs need to form pressure groups for a fair trade practice. NEED itself has taken an initiative in this direction. Its fair trade activities have emerged out of questions of how far rural development processes should go in order to foster and nurture the entrepreneurial spirit of women in the poorest villages. Support and microcredit group formation are just the first stepping-stones on the long and rocky path to sustainable microenterprise development. Information provision alone does not usher the empowerment process of a human being. Similarly, credit alone does not facilitate the sustainability and growth of economic activities. There are many more specific issues which need to be addressed.

The core needs of emerging women entrepreneurs are not being provided by the prevailing commercial market forces. These have been identified as:

• A need for entrepreneurial skill, behaviour and practice training leading to capacity building and ownership
• Access to credit facilities for skill upgradation and other requirements for up-scaling
• Training in modern designs and production techniques
• Market access, information and awareness
• Fair working conditions, sustainable pay

To ensure that the emerging entrepreneurs can compete within the context of liberalizing market places, the provision of this infrastructure and resources becomes critical. Additionally, to ensure that the small scale producer or artisan is a beneficiary and not a victim of globalization, the regulatory, social, economic, and commercial environment in which the trade takes place needs to be addressed from a pro-poor perspective.

Fair trade marketing, advocacy and lobbying, at local, national and global levels are vital in providing these women producer groups the opportunity to generate sustainable livelihoods. Access to direct, fair, local and global markets helps them to earn enough from their work to be able to up-scale their production, increasing their income and improving the qualities of their own lives as well as that of their communities.

NEED's fair trade division exists to provide an extra dimension of support for the maturing women's producer groups, seeking to help sustain their production and crafts and maximize the revenue potential in the short term. By building their own community-engendered resource networks and centres, NEED aims to enable them to become increasingly self-sufficient, up-scale and ultimately mainstream their operations.

Intrinsic to this approach is that of NEED's marketing intervention that will ultimately lead to better lives for women—less drudgery, less stress, better nutritive value in food and less illness. This will lead to stronger local economies that retain money in the poor communities. In accordance with the international fair trade principles, NEED's fair trade division advocates and practices:

- The creation of opportunities for economically disadvantaged communities
- Transparency and accountability
- Capacity building and ownership maximization
- Promoting fair trade throughout channels of purchase and supply
- Gender equity
- Ideal working conditions
- Payment of fair wages
- Protection of the environment
- Protection of the rights of children

To pursue its initiative of fair trade practice, NEED is the member of the International Federation for Alternative Trade (IFAT), the Fair Trade Federation US and the Indian Fair Trade Forum (IFTF), New Delhi and a member of the Asia Fair Trade (AFT), Manila.

Capacity Building

Based on its professional experiences and experiments, NEED decided to publish learning documentation and conduct training programmes for the functionaries of other NGOs, governmental departments, banks and even the leaders of the formed SHGs. With this method of capacity-building intervention, NEED wants to spread its knowledge and vision to ensure benefits to as many deprived people as possible.

NEED's experience suggests that most members of the SHGs are not educated to such levels that they could maintain accounts properly or write the proceedings in a proper way. They also feel that proper maintenance of records and accounts is essential for the sustainability of the group. They feel that complete transparency must be maintained to avoid confusions and conflicts. Therefore, NEED has developed simplified registers to record the proceedings and write the accounts. These can be maintained easily without much skill. The two registers are:

1. Proceeding register for SHG.
2. Register for recording transactions for SHG.

    a. In the Proceedings register they have printed the following details:

- What is SHG?
- Why should a SHG be formed?
- For whom is the SHG meant for?
- SHGs: For how long?
- Developmental process of SHGs.
- What are the characteristics of an ideal SHG?
- What is saving?
- Why to save?
- How to save?
- Roles and responsibilities of the president, secretary, and treasurer.
- Format of by laws for the SHGs.

    b. Name and address of the SHG
    c. Objectives
    d. Goals
    e. Rules

- Eligibility of membership
- Number of members
- Management committee
- Roles and function of management committee
- Membership and saving

    f. Loans
    g. Conditions of membership disqualification
    h. Maintenance of accounts

- Passbook
- Proceeding register
- Accounts register
- Miscellaneous

- On the top of the page the names of the members who are present in the meeting are written. Then the page is divided into three columns as follows:

Sample 1   Simplified Register: Top of the Page

Sl. No.	Name	Signature

- The other side of the page is as follows:

Sample 2   Simplified Register: Proceedings Book

Date of meeting:
Place :

Proceeding of meeting, particulars of proposals and decisions taken:

3. Register for recording transactions contains:

- Table for calculating interest @ 2 per cent and fix installments with its help
- What to do to keep the SHG linked with the bank
- How to write the saving particulars of the members, entry of savings in pass book of members and accounts register specimen of the saving ledger of the group
- How to fill the individual loan ledger with the specimen of filled loan ledger
- How to fill the group's loan ledger with specimen
- Particulars of borrowings of group members
- Particulars of borrowings of outsiders from group
- Particulars of borrowings of group, from external resources (method and specimen)
- Consolidated ledger of borrowings from external resources
- Particulars of receipt and payments of group
- Method and specimen of filling particulars of receipt and payments of group

With their experience and expertise, NEED has been successful in forming successful and sustainable self help groups. There are a large number of cases recorded in the documents of NEED, which tell us how the groups have been empowered and how they have successfully tackled their problems. Some of the interesting observations and cases are cited later on in this case study.

NEED's Methodology: Some Feedback

Trickle Up is a non-profit voluntary organization that fights poverty by providing seed grants (not loans) of US$ 100 and business training to more than 10,000 aspiring microentrepreneurs worldwide every year. It has found that 80 per cent of its grantees continue in business a year later. Trickle Up identifies potential entrepreneurs with help from local organizations that are active in the regions of the project area and NEED is one such active organization. For private business assistance, the Trickle Up Grant Program is comprised of small grants that make it possible for individuals to purchase the tools, supplies, or raw materials needed to start their own business or possibly expand a small business to the next level of development (http://www.buckeyehills.org/assistance/trickleup). Based on NEED's office functioning and field observation, Rachel Kleinfeld, a representative of Trickle Up, New York, communicated:

> NEED is both a consultant and a direct development organization. As consultants, they train other NGOs and government officers in starting up self help groups, which they conceive of as far more than savings and loan groups. Their self help groups are just what the name implies, and are meant to be catalysts for social change. Income generation is a key part of the self help group's work. Through this constancy, NEED has launched over 20,000 self help groups. NEED also implements its own development projects in rural areas to the west of Lucknow, and out of NEED's own offices in the Lucknow suburbs. They have started about 70 self help groups, and have launched a number of income generation projects, including incense making, candle making, and jute bag sewing in a whole array of sizes and shapes. The most successful project is their jute bag wholesale work, where they make these bags for tea merchants to use as export containers. The market still has a high demand, and they are mainly held back by a lack of money to buy sewing machines for the women to work on and cycles for the men to bring the goods to the market. NEED

also engages in diverse rural development activities, such as sodic land reclamation and other agricultural, educational, and sanitation projects in the villages in which they are working. They work on these various projects through the self help groups, so that the villagers take control of their own development.

Joel and I spent a day in NEED's Lucknow offices, learning the scope of their work and explaining the Trickle Up Program. All morning women trickled into work in the sewing room attached to the modest offices. The women work together on bag orders and sew whenever they can get the time. All the women are very poor, and most walk to the office, often from many kilometres away, and would be greatly benefited by Trickle Up grants to purchase their own sewing machines. NEED stresses that the women should work on their own and helps them form their own linkages with buyers and distribution network, so the machines themselves are the real bottleneck.

Rachel Kleinfeld further stated,

I spent the next day in the field with N.D. (Nilanjana Das), the extremely able young woman who has been starting self help groups for the past year. We met with three different groups, one Muslim, two from lower castes, all functioning well as savings and loan groups. At one meeting, N.D. was confronted by suspicious husbands who wondered what this three-month-old group was: previous to these meetings, the women had only met together outside of their homes for the annual health clinics that came through the village. N.D. diffused the situation and explained the purpose of the self-help group to the men in such a way that they were enthusiastically behind it in the end, and asked what they could do to help. One man said in astonishment: 'Before, my wife never left the house, and could not save 10 paisa. Now she saves 20 rupees a month and is planning on working to supplement our family's income!' They then launched into a spirited male and female discussion of different income-generation projects, from packing lentils to sewing bags. On their own, they had come up with income generation as the first need the self help group had to address, so they could have some money for their own families and some additional funds to start village-wide development projects. In another village, I met both Muslim and Hindu groups. The Muslim women said that their first task was to start a school for girls, since none of the girls were educated, and none of the families would send them to the co-ed government school a few kilometres away, which was no good any-way. They wanted to start income generation projects that would create enough additional income for each family that they could afford to pay some tuition that would finance a teacher's salary. In the Hindu group, the one literate village women who kept records for all groups brought up the idea. They were enthusiastic, and said they would be willing to cooperate across religious and caste lines to bring such a school about! Income generation was, again, the main hold-up.

Trickle Up would be an obvious perfect fit for NEED, and Anil Singh was so enthusiastic that he wanted me to stress that the sooner he could start, the better! The group is excellent: very small, very low overhead (their offices are on the ground floor of Anil Singh's house, the sewing room used to be in their house area itself), used to receiving foreign funds, and extremely dedicated. Check out their website for more background: it was created for free by a German business student who came for an internship and has decided to stay with NEED and switch from business to social work as her vocation. Obviously, since all work is done through the self help groups, Trickle Up entrepreneurs would be linked in with all other development activities in these villages, and Anil Singh's understanding of micro-credit programmes available in India is top-notch. We heartily recommend that NEED be made a new TUP partner.

Arun R. Palakurthy from New York observed that people ignore social and political inputs and outcomes of microcredit which is an integral part of NEED's model. He states,

Volunteering for NEED changed the way I look at microfinance and rural development. In my college, I had read a lot of the academic literature on microfinance, and this had greatly shaped my views on the subject. I wanted to know about the overall loan portfolio, overall turnover of loans, outstanding balances, average loan size, etc. I was very interested in the purely financial aspects of the work that NEED was doing, but did not take into account the role of social and political inputs.

Throughout my initial time at NEED, Anil patiently answered my questions and encouraged me to go the field as often as possible. Every day, when I got back, Anil would challenge me to examine the problems I saw in the villages. What I gradually understood is that most of the problems I saw would not be solved by credit and microfinance alone. Providing credit to individuals for income generation was not going to create safe drinking water, adequate infrastructure, or end gender violence for the village as a whole. After spending time in the field, I started to understand the holistic approach Anil had been talking about—an approach that also looked towards building social and political empowerment.

I believe that Anil and NEED have developed a very comprehensive and holistic model. NEED uses SHGs not just to disburse credit, but also to create social and political empowerment for its members. While in the villages, I saw how hard the field staff worked to encourage women to address community and collective issues. I was struck by how vocal and outspoken the women were, and, I am still amazed by how much initiative and responsibility the women were able to take, with a little bit of help from NEED. There is now something like 12 non-formal education centres that are being run by the women themselves, and many women had met with local politicians push for the creation of better infrastructure.

If I had heard about this before coming to NEED, I probably wouldn't have believed it. But having seen how well NEED has worked to create social and political empowerment as well as distribution of credit makes me a strong believer in Anil's ideas. What now worries me is how little people talk about integrating microcredit with social and political inputs. In the rush to create profitable microfinance institutions that can access capital markets, important questions of how to create genuine empowerment are largely being ignored. I really hope that more people have an opportunity to hear Anil's ideas, and more importantly see them in action. Spending time in the villages seeing what NEED was doing was a really powerful experience.

I feel very fortunate to have had this experience and to have met the people I did. I am still overwhelmed by how nice everyone was. Everyone went out of their way to teach me and answer my questions. The many women I met in the villages were so eager to talk to me and ask me questions. The field staff made me feel included in everything that was going on, and extended the most genuine kind of friendship. What also impressed me was the dedication of the staff. They all consistently worked long days with very meager resources. Having worked in very well-funded institutions in the US, I feel that the NEED staff was able accomplish so much more with not even a tenth of the resources.

Recording personal experience with NEED and its EIGSP, Rudder recalled,

My research interests in women's empowerment initiatives in South Asia brought me to NEED via UNIFEM. As a graduate student in the departments of anthropology and public administration at the Maxwell School at Syracuse University, I sought a summer research project that would contribute to an existing women's empowerment project in India. As a UNIFEM South Asia intern, it was agreed that I should spend a month with NEED, collecting and documenting the stories of eight women who participated in NEED's UNIFEM-funded EIGSEP training in 1999.

With the help of Mani Yadav, my research assistant and interpreter, I had several interviews with each woman at her home, in the market or at NEED. We also interviewed NEED staff, some of the women's family members and a few of the people with whom they do business. My goal was to provide for NEED and UNIFEM a collection of case studies that would be useful for demonstrating how EIGSEP training impacts the lives of its participants. While we were looking for evidence of economic and social empowerment, we also hoped to identify potential problems or opportunities for maintaining their newly-developed independence.

Mr A. K. Singh introduced me to the 'NEED family,' its history, and the philosophies and strategies behind their work. He advised me on the design of the project and helped me put together a useful set of indicators that informed our line of questioning. Mrs. Pushpa Singh worked closely with me and Mani, accompanying us on all the initial interviews and trips to the market. Her guidance was critical for initiating long personal discussions with these women often about difficult topics, as all of the women were on good terms with Pushpaji.

All of the women that I met were very appreciative of their NEED training. Most of them had never earned money before, and each was very pleased with being able to now help take care of her family and herself. They were trained in one or all of the skills in *chikan* embroidery or candle, incense, and jute bag making. NEED also took the women to the city's bigger markets to buy raw materials and sell some of their products. For all of the women, starting a business meant leaving the familiarity of their home and interacting with significantly more people. Because of social norms that restrict women to home and family, the gains made by this part of training were, perhaps, the most exciting and challenging for the women. Learning to communicate with others in a business manner and feeling comfortable making their way around the maze of markets were two things the women reported as important new skills gained through NEED's training.

Furthermore, the women explained that they had gained a new confidence and sense of self worth from NEED's training and from their resulting success at running a business. NEED had selected these women, in part, because of their special hardships. All were living below the poverty line. Some were widowed; others were divorced or experiencing neglect and abuse. In our interviews, the women reported that after NEED training, they felt less dependent on their male family members and more respected by their family and community. They also experienced less domestic abuse and more cooperation from husbands.

The Learning

Mr Anil K. Singh was approached to share his vast field experience and insight on microenterprise development. His responses to our pointed questions are summarized below:

SS: 1. What are some personal and situational factors that lead to the success of enterprises?

AKS: Following are some of the key factors that account for success of microenterprises.

- Strong entrepreneurial sensitization and mobilization campaign
- Right kind of identification and selection process of products
- Market-led exposure and skill upgradation
- Strong service-driven approach to credit accessibility
- Institutional back-up support
- Gender sensitization for men
- Demonstrative intervention on enterprise setting process
- Creating a cadre of market entrepreneurs in the form of full-fledged career

SS: 2. What are some the common core components (structures, rules, guidelines) generally applicable to all successful models?

AKS: The core components of all successful models are:

- Mobilized and united small groups
- Formation of self help groups and cycling of saving and credit with start-up consumption, emergency, seasonal and social purposes
- Cultivating a rising demand for income generation through these saving and credit habits
- Entrepreneurial sensitization with rural achievement motivation needs
- Experience-based identification and selection of products, particularly on service and trading sectors
- Skill upgradation
- Market exposure
- Creating marketing entrepreneurs within the group itself

- Cultivating collective leadership with social discipline and responsibility
- Escort services and follow-ups.

SS: 3. What are the strategies adopted locally by self help groups to address the contextual realities of the locality in terms of resource mobilization, group formation, decision making, conflict resolution and income generation?

AKS: SHGs primarily work through

- Collective cohesion
- Leadership
- Transparent participation
- Discipline and above all Peer Pressure Groups with collective voice, verbs and visibility.

SS: 4. What are the approaches and tactics followed in the successful SHGs to operationalize the goals set forth the purpose?

AKS: Successful SHGs strategies include:

- Social value-driven experience based inputs
- The working committee on rotational leadership basis
- Collective freedom
- Daily prayer also places a significant role in their mindsets of their growth and development
- Experiencing the collective efforts for taking care of their many needs through money and non-money components
- Developing a sense of group solidarity and commitment, and mobility of the group

SS: 5. What are the methods and mechanism to replicate successful experiences of SHGs and microenterprise development in other areas?

AKS:

- Readiness to stay and station oneself in the villages
- Re-discovering the strength of entrepreneurial skill behaviour and practice from these rural poor based on their enriching long experience of working both in the house and fields

- Cultivating an immediate demand for marketing entrepreneurs from the rural area itself
- Developing a larger cohesive demand group in order to take the advantage of supply chain; Rotational leadership and Peer Pressure Strength

Case of Asma

The Kaluapur village is, one of the six gram sabhas of Lodhasa Nyaya Panchayat, situated at a distance of 2 kilometers from the development block, Mahmoodabad. There are 127 houses in all, of which 54 belong to Muslims, 26 to Scheduled Castes and 47 to other backward classes. The total population of the village is 789. Their source of livelihood is agriculture and they work as labourers. The education level is very low.

Before the formation of the group in the village, the condition of this village was very bad. There was no residence of the *pradhan* and neither there was an *anganbari*. Workers of NEED went several times to this village as it was felt that there was a need for forming a group so that work on development could begin. NEED workers kept on trying but there was no result. One day, a lady aged about 45 asked the workers to dispel her anxiety by answering whether NEED worked in context with medicines or the medical profession. The workers told her about NEED's mission. They said that medicines are required only when somebody falls sick but they have come up with an idea, employing which people do not fall sick. The lady introduced herself as Asma Begum and asked the NEED members to elaborate further. The workers told her that if they tell her alone it would remain limited to her, so they asked her to call some more ladies from her neighbourhood.

She took the lead and called 15–16 ladies from the neighbourhood. Some men also collected and stood at some distance with anxiety. In this meeting, the NEED members provided detail regarding SHGs, its objective, saving, formation process, and the benefits of SHGs. After listening to all this, 18 ladies agreed to join the group and they were given three days time for the formation of the group. On the third day when the NEED members reached the village, they found that three to four women were saying that the group was not going to work and so they would just collect the money and go away. The workers thought that all the efforts have gone in vain but Asma Begum handled the situation very efficiently and cleverly and encouraged 14 women to join the group.

Thus, on 6 September 2002, Kiran Self Help Group was formed and the group showed faith in Asma Begum and she was elected the president of the group.

Today the Kiran Self Help Group is counted among the good self help groups. There are 18 members in this group now; four more members have been included. They hold two meetings every month, that is, on the 6th and 20th of every month. They give priority to cultural works; hence, this has inspired other villagers to form another group *Unnati*, with 17 members. Asma Begum also went to Mumbai and Delhi to put forward the groups' rights.

Meanwhile, circumstances brought a crisis in Asma Begum's life, during which the SHG stood by her. Thus, her faith in the power of the SHGs has considerably increased. Asma Begum was leading a middle-class life with her whole family (husband, four sons, daughters-in-law and grandson), with three sons married. One day, her second daughter-in-law quarrelled at home and persuaded her husband to quit the family house and accompany her to her parental house without any prior notice. Acting very carefully, Asma freed her son from his in-laws. Soon after, to harass the family, the in-laws of her son falsely implicated her in a dowry case. In reality, Asma is completely against dowry.

Although notices and summons soon started coming from the court and the police, yet Asma behaved very patiently and bravely in this adverse situation. She discussed the problem with the group and then with the lady worker of NEED. She intended to go to Delhi and directly plead to the President of India. However, she was assured by NEED that if she was not guilty nothing would happen to her and that she would get justice. Asma did as she was advised to and met and requested the MLA of the area, Mr Narendra Verma, to help her. Mr Verma supported Asma, completely. Even during such a difficult situation, Asma did not feel lonely because the group members and NEED were always with her. Because of this, she felt proud to be associated with the NEED family. She gives full credit to the support of the SHG members and NEED for her high morale. Now Asma leads the voice of protest in the face of injustice in front of the *pradhan*, the S.D.M., bank officials, *sarpanch* or *pradhan* of the panchayat.

Case of Phool Bano

In Lodhasa Nyay Panchayat, at a distance of five kilometers from Mahmoodabad, there is a village Panchayat of Madaripur. There are three parts of this village in which six SHGs are working. One of them is Ekta Self Help Group in which there are 18 members. The group saves Rs 15 per month per member. The group was established on 9 September, 2002.

Phool Bano is a member of this group. She is 40 years old and very hard working. She is a mother of four daughters and her husband works as a barber in a temporary shop in Mahmoodabad. As there was no male child, her husband Ali Jaan started expressing an open desire for a second marriage. However, none of his other family members, including his father, mother, brother, sister-in-law as well as Phool Bano, agreed to Ali Jaan's aspiration. But in anticipation of the second marriage Ali Jaan had broken all ties with Phool Bano.

Hence the problem of subsistence of Phool Bano and her four daughters arose, the irony being that her youngest daughter is stricken by polio. However, Phool Bano did not lose courage and in one of the regular meetings she spoke out what was bothering her for long. She explained her problem and said, 'I am a member of the same NEED family to which all of you belong and now there is only way that I should stand on my feet. I have to make the future of my daughters. So, I want to start some business.' With her serious efforts she got the correct guidance. She decided that she would start a small bangle shop and along with that she started a cosmetics business. NEED supported her with funds that came from Trickle Up.

Today Phool Bano is all praises for NEED and says that if the group facilitated by NEED had not helped her, her family would have been ruined. She says, '*Bhalaa ho NEED sanstha ka jisne ki mere jaisi kitanii bahano kaa udhaar kiya hoga*' (God bless NEED which has helped numerous sisters like me). This group also serves as a model of communal harmony as Phool Bano is the only Muslim lady among the other 17 SC lady members and participates in all the Hindu festivals.

Tahrulnisha Freed from the Trap of the Moneylender

Tahrulnisha is a member of the Azad SHG of the Bhauri village, in the Mahmoodabad Block of Sitapur district. She is a mother of five, with three daughters and two sons. Prior to joining the SHG, she had borrowed Rs 700 from the village moneylender on an interest rate of Rs 10 per month, that is, 120 per cent per year. In the past two years, she had paid Rs 1900 as just interest, leaving aside the principal. She was in debt and wanted to come out of it. NEED had initiated a SHG in her village under the Poorest Areas Civil Society (PACS) programme funded by the Department for International Development (DFID). When Tahrulnisha came to know about the group, she decided to join it. Although she was not sure whether she would get help from the group as she believed that no one would support a Muslim lady when the majority of the members were Hindu. But when she witnessed the interaction and cohesiveness of the group members and the open support the members lend to each other, she gained confidence that she may receive support from the group.

In one of the meetings Tahrulnisha shared her problem with the group, and requested the group to help her in this case. After carefully listening to her plight, the Group decided to help her with the loan on the basis of her ability to save in the next six months and also wanted an assurance that she would continue her membership with the SHG even after borrowing from the Group.

Meanwhile, Tahrulnisha was receiving continuous threats from the moneylender. The group extended a loan of Rs 1000 to Tahrulnisha to pay back the moneylender in terms of principal amount and interest. Taharulnisha directly went to the moneylender for making the final settlement of the loan; but he did not accept the money and asked her to repay the entire amount with interest as per his records. She came back to the Group and narrated the incident. Then, the Group members went to moneylender together. They threw the money in front of the moneylender and threatened him that if he did not accept the money, they would inform the police. The moneylender quietly kept the money and closed Taharulnisha's debt account.

This way Tahrulnisha came out of the trap of the moneylender and started her life afresh. But she still owed Rs 1000 to the Group. An interest of 2 per cent was fixed for repayment which she feels she would be able to pay in time. NEED also told us that they came across many people who solicited help from the SHGs for getting rid of small loans and moneylenders.

Voices of the Group Members

- Through the Group, I realized that we need to empower women to have an empowered village community so that collectively, we can make our villages more beautiful and safer than the cities.

- Through the groups, now we are able to raise the issue of our rights. Otherwise, our voice was suppressed by men. Now we actively participate in the Panchayat activities.
- We still do not believe that through small thrift we have saved Rs 8000. Now we do not have to approach moneylenders for our small needs.
- I had stopped sending my daughter to school. After joining SHG, I came to know the importance of education. I have started her education again.
- Earlier, people used to discount us (women). Since we have organized the groups, we are respected not only at home but outside also.
- Earlier, we were not aware of vaccination. We came to know its importance after joining the group. Now if the Auxiliary Nurse and Midwife (ANM) does not come to village, we ourselves take our babies to hospitals.
- If we did not have the Group in our village, how would our village have developed or how would we have changed our mind set?
- The Group has provided a new direction to the girls by making them aware and providing education through Adolescent Girls' Camp.
- I have fulfilled my dream through the SHG. I have been able to show that we women can also do something. I became the president of a 19 strong women's group and got the opportunity to lead them. We formed the Mahila Mandal and got health management training from CARE. Now I will educate fellow villagers regarding health, hygiene, and sanitation and will keep the village away from diseases.
- We (women) got to know what we can do only after joining the Group. We could get rid of problems and diseases of our village by visiting and receiving help from the Block.
- Group has provided us with our voice.
- Earlier, my husband used to stop me from going to meetings. But now I save Rs 20 daily by learning sewing through NEED's training.
- We have earned freedom through the Group. We have gained self-confidence after a three days training from Lucknow.
- *Purdah* has reduced. We can express ourselves. Be it *thana* or *kotwali*.

- After the formation of SHG, we have developed such understanding among ourselves that we solve our problems ourselves rather than approaching the court and police.
- My son used to waste his time by roaming here and there. I had no money to help him start a business. With the support of NEED, I helped him in opening a saloon. Now he saves Rs 30 to Rs 50 per day.
- It is very easy to get a loan from the group. Earlier, we used to make repeated visits of the bank for small sums and they use to often refuse.

Conclusion

India, with more than 110 crore population, cannot provide employment to its eligible people in the organized sector. Thus, providing opportunities for self-employment is the most plausible route. Entrepreneurship development and training is necessary for promoting self-employment. This initiative is required both in the industrial sector as well as in the social sector. In fact, the issue of employment for the masses can be addressed by focussing on social entrepreneurship and SHGs. The initiative of NEED in promoting SHGs and training them to start microenterprises through a set of gender-sensitive training model called Entrepreneurship Linked Income Generation for Self Employment (EIGSEP). This training model consisted of six modules: motivation training, project guidance, training in management issues, operations and production issues, escort phase consisting of practical issues of enterprise formation, and follow-up stages. Evaluation of EIGSEP revealed success of the intervention in terms of improved quality of life measured through social and political empowerment, income generation, poverty reduction, and enterprise sustainability.

Reference

Rudder, K. 2003. A Case Study of UNIFEM Funded Intervention to Empower Women in India. Unpublished Master's Dissertation Paper, Department of Anthropology, Syracuse University.

A Resource-based Perspective to International Entrepreneurship

3

Deeksha A. Singh

Introduction

There is a growing consensus amongst researchers that the future prosperity of emerging economies is dependent on the liberalization of their economic systems and the consequent unleashing of hitherto-suppressed entrepreneurial energy (Hoskisson et al., 2000; Peng, 2001). Entrepreneurs in emerging economies face additional challenges in growing and sustaining new ventures which are not encountered by their counterparts in advanced economies. Less munificent institutional environment, poorly functioning labour and capital markets and dearth of experience in operating new ventures are some of the problems which complicate the matters for entrepreneurs in emerging economies. Yet, we see many a new firms from the emerging economies of the Asia Pacific region making their presence felt in the global market place.

There has been a sustained increase in the outward Foreign Direct Investment (FDI) from emerging economies, which has risen from US$129 billion in 1990 to US$869 billion in 2000 and to more than US$1 trillion in 2004 (UNCTAD, 2004). Emerging economies account for more than 10 per cent of the world's overall outward FDI, two third of which is accounted for by the countries of the Asia Pacific region excluding Japan. There are many examples in recent times of Chinese firms purchasing all or significant divisions of many developed country firms, such as Husky Oil in Canada, Rover in the UK and IBM's PC division in the US. Given that the firms in the emerging economies tend to be at a relative resource disadvantage compared to the big firms of the developed countries, their diversification into foreign markets poses a challenge to traditional international business and strategic management theories, which generally argue that firms are motivated to diversify into foreign markets when possessing firm-specific advantages that allow the firm to overcome the costs of being foreign. Therefore, there is a need to look at the issue of international entrepreneurship from the perspective of the firms from emerging economies. This paper attempts to provide an alternative framework based on a resource-based view to explain the rising phenomenon of international entrepreneurship from emerging economies.

In the following sections, we briefly review the literature on international business to establish the need of a new theoretical framework. This is followed by a resource-based explanation of international entrepreneurship of emerging market firms. Examples are given in support of the resource-based explanations followed by our recommendations for future exploration of this research stream.

Literature Review

If we trace the development of international business (IB) theories, the emergence of IB as a separate field can be partially attributed to the refusal of traditional economics scholars to recognize the growing phenomenon of businesses across borders in the decade of the fifties. Prior to the sixties, there was no established theory of international business. However, there were some limited attempts to study the cross border activities of firms in terms of the theory of capital movements (Iversen, 1935), single country empirical studies on the factors affecting the location of foreign investment (Southard, 1931; Dunning, 1958) and in terms of recognition of benefits of common ownership of cross border horizontal activities (Penrose, 1956). This neglect motivated some scholars from the economics stream and the business stream to provide explanations for international activities of firms. Noticeable amongst these are the product life cycle model (Vernon, 1966), stages model (Johanson and Vahlne, 1977), internalization theory (Caves, 1971; Buckley and Casson, 1976) and the eclectic paradigm of internalization (Dunning, 1993).

However, most of these explanations have been developed keeping in view the internationalizing activities of large MNEs of developed countries and there seem to be a neglect of the growing phenomenon of internationalization of small and newly-developed firms from emerging economies. The existing IB theories may not be adequate to explain this phenomenon. For example, the proprietary assets approach which is the central tenet of many of current IB theories may not apply to emerging economy MNEs as these MNEs are poor in traditional resources, such as technical know-how, market goodwill, finances, and so forth (Caves, 1996). The stages model is not satisfactory as many of these MNEs start off as international firms from the onset in response to the opportunities provided by globalization itself. The eclectic theory or the Ownership Locational License (OLL) framework as well as the internalization theory are also not adequate due to their emphasis on market failure and internalization incentives of the proprietary assets owned by the firm. If we believe these to be largely the main stream IB theories, we indeed need a new theory for explaining the international entrepreneurship by the emerging economy firms.

The perspective I would take to explain the rise of such firms is heavily based on the resource-based view (RBV) of the firms (Barney, 1991). I believe that the RBV combined with the theories of organizational learning and the insights gained from the studies on international new ventures (INVs) can adequately explain the rise of MNEs from the emerging economies of the Asia Pacific region.

Resource-based View (RBV) and International Entrepreneurship

Resource-based view (RBV) of firms has become a dominant and influential theoretical perspective in the strategy and international business area. According to RBV (Barney, 1991), firms are a bundle of resources, some of which are valuable, rare, difficult to imitate, and non-substitutable. Such resources give a sustainable competitive advantage to firms over others in their competitive domain. RBV has been applied in various domains of strategy research, such as the core competence of firms and capability perspective.

RBV is not new to IB researchers. In a citation study of the *Journal of International Business Studies* and other six mainstream strategy journals, Peng (2001) reported 61 articles using RBV framework to explain IB questions. Clearly RBV is not a totally new approach and can be applied to the current phenomenon. However, much of the emphasis of the RBV approach has been on how firms prolong their competitive advantage by extending their underlying resource base. The issue of how firms actually acquire such resources which can provide a competitive advantage to them has not been adequately addressed. This issue is particularly important as many of the emerging economy firms do not start off high on traditional resources. However, they make up for it by different kinds of resources, which reduce their reliance on traditional resources as well as help them in gaining access to traditional resources.

The core of my arguments is that even though emerging economy firms may not have the traditional proprietary advantages enjoyed by big MNEs, they have different kinds of resources, which satisfy the criteria of being rare, valuable, inimitable, and non-substitutable. It is these resources which provide the competitive advantage to these firms over the domestic firms in foreign markets. They not only help the firms in overcoming the additional costs of doing business abroad (Hymer, 1960), but also help them in developing capabilities for global competitiveness.

In this sense, my arguments based on RBV are an extension of the internalization theory (Buckley and Cason, 1976; Caves, 1996) as well as the eclectic perspective (Dunning, 1993). RBV helps us identify and define the types of resources these firms may have. While the emphasis in transaction cost (TC) based explanations is on explaining the role of internalization in avoiding market failure, the emphasis in RBV is on the nature of resources which make it more efficient to use them within the firm rather than by alternate arrangements. For established firms of developed countries, such resources include capital (and its cheap and easy availability), market goodwill (partially associated with these belonging to advanced nations), technological superiority, and so forth. While many of the emerging market firms are undoubtedly weak on these resources, they have some other types of resources, such as superior organizational practices (Tallman, 1991, 1992; Zaheer, 1995), administrative heritage (Bartlett and Ghoshal, 1989), superb capabilities and tacit knowledge (Peng et al., 2000; Peng and York, 2001; Liesch and Knight, 1999), or even the capabilities of the management team (Hitt et al., 1997) amongst many other things.

The important difference between the existing predominantly TC-based explanations and the proposed RBV-based explanations lie in the way TC and RBV look at the resources. While the focus of eclectic paradigm and TCE is on the exploitation of resources across borders, RBV focusses on exploitation as well as development of resources (Madhok, 1997) for international competitiveness. Looking at the organizational and governance decisions, much of the arguments based on the transaction cost considerations look at foreign entry as a static decision. RBV considerations take into account the global scheme of things for the MNE (Hill et al., 1990). Rather than taking each entry decision as a one-time decision, RBV takes into account the dynamic view of learning and capability building from previous entries (Kogut, 1997). This helps explain the complex web of interrelationships formed by the dragon MNEs.

In the section below, I elaborate on the above points and present some examples and propositions.

RBV in the Context of Emerging Economy Entrepreneurs

Resources of Emerging Economy Firms

MNEs from emerging economies of the Asia Pacific Region (APR) have special resource configurations because of their home countries' economic development level, resources, and market structure. The developing world has the highest population density, so there is an abundant labour resource. Because of high competition in the labour market, the wage level is relatively low, providing firms with an inexpensive labour resource. In addition, the unique institutional environment in which they operate, availability of cheap factor inputs, government backing, entrepreneurial vision of the founders, flexibility and nimbleness due to small size, international orientation of their entrepreneurs and their social capital help these firms a great deal in their internationalization efforts. The success of firm, such as Acer and Ranbaxy can be attributed to the ability of entrepreneurs to create innovative and nimble organizations which can achieve *much more with much less.*

Many of the Indian pharmaceutical firms started very late (in the nineties). These were started by individuals who had earlier worked with MNEs and had technical expertise. These entrepreneurs took advantage of the opportunities provided by the inadequate patent laws of their domestic countries and started off by making slight process modifications which gave the same end product. Once the entrepreneurs established a foothold for themselves in the domestic market, they started sensing opportunities in the foreign markets. However, since they could not sell the copied medicines, they took up manufacturing of those molecules that had gone off patent. Due to the cheap technical manpower, these firms could sell these bulk drugs to other developed countries as well as developing countries at a fraction of the prices charged by the big MNEs. Further, to upgrade their technical capabilities, they took up the jobs of contract manufacturing for big MNEs. This provided them with a platform to start their own in-house research and development activities. Presently, many of such pharmaceutical firms have quite a noticeable presence not only in the developing markets but also the markets of the US and Europe. Dr Reddy's, one such Indian firm, is even planning to shift its headquarters to the US to stay closer to its future market!

Another example could be that of the Indian Space Research Organization (ISRO); ISRO has an expertise in manufacturing and launching satellites. It is aggressively active in a market presently populated by a handful of private players and big government agencies, such as NASA. The question that may be asked is how is ISRO able to compete against the Western agencies in the highly competitive space market even though it greatly lacks financial resources as well as critical technologies, both of which are very crucial for success in this domain. ISRO's success lies in its capability to manufacture various components for as cheap as 1/100 times the cost incurred by its Western counterparts.

There are similar examples of Korean, Taiwanese and Chinese firms, which started off without the traditional proprietary-based resources, but have been able to create a niche for themselves in the global market place. In the initial stages, the growth of these firms could be through a network of relations and linkages, which does not just provide them with the initial market opportunities and technical expertise in some cases, but also a chance for learning. Such learning may be a source of competitive advantage in the long run. Clearly the very ability to identify such opportunities and generate these capabilities constitutes the ownership specific advantages for such firms.

Based on the above discussion I put forth the following propositions:

Proposition 1: Emerging Economy Firms have Different Types of Resources (Cheap Labour, Government Backing, Visionary Entrepreneurs, and Support of Strong Diaspora, etc.) than Advanced Economy Firms

In the following section, I elaborate on each of these aspects individually.

Lower Labour Costs: We have argued earlier that the emerging economy firms generally have lower labour costs. As per one of the surveys in early nineties, an experienced software engineer earned about US$10,000 a year in India, which is only about 20 per cent of the level of salary of a person with comparable skills in the US (Vijayan, 1996). The wage difference between the developing and developed countries may be more apparent in other labour intensive industries, such as textile, toys, electronics, and so forth. Although the wage level in some emerging economies is increasing, it is still lower than that in the advanced countries.

Such a resource is rare, inimitable, and non-substitutable for the emerging economy firms. Even though firms from advanced economy may reduce their costs by outsourcing, this will only result in a comparatively better position as compared to other firms from advanced countries.

Proposition 2: Emerging Economy Firms Engaged in Activities where they can Leverage Lower Labour Costs have Greater Chances of Success in the International Market Place than their Counterparts who do not have Such Resources

It is important to emphasize that the lower labour cost in itself does not provide a sustainable competitive advantage. In the long run, other firms may develop technologies reducing the cost component substantially. In addition, as the industry develops and becomes lucrative, the costs are expected to go up. Lower labour costs can only provide initial impetus in getting a foothold in the international market place. Once a firm establishes itself, it will have to develop traditional resources, such as technological and market capabilities. The positive benefits of lower labour costs can get enhanced when coupled with the traditional resources as has been seen in the case of software and pharmaceutical firms of India.

Proposition 3: Technological and Marketing Skills Enhance the Advantages Obtained from Lower Labour Costs for Emerging Economy Firms and Increase their Chances of Success in International Market Place

Role of Government: Role of government in the development of such firms and establishment of their international operations could be a source of valuable resource for such firms. It is argued that the home country environment plays a very important role in the internationalization process of firms (Wan and Hoskisson, 2003). It is also generally argued that the business environment of emerging economies is not particularly munificent for internationalization. A look at the global indicators confirms this notion. However, if we carefully study the specific environment in which a particular business operates, we can see a different pattern. Thus, while it is true that the munificence of the environment plays an important role, it is not entirely true that the environment in developing countries is not munificent. In fact, the environment is highly munificent for the business which internationalize from a particular country (software and pharmaceutical from India, textiles from China, and so forth). Governments view such ventures as a symbol of national pride and go all the way to listen to their needs and demands. Recent advances of some of the Chinese firms in the global market place can be attributed to this unique resource. Use of cheap labour by Korean firms and English fluent labours for Indian firms are some examples pointing towards the institution specific resources utilized by these firms to their advantage.

Proposition 4: Emerging Economy Firms with Active Government Backing have Better Chances of Success in International Market Place

Role of Entrepreneur's Social Capital: Oviatt and McDougall (1994) placed a great deal of emphasis on the individual level internationalization experience on early and rapid internationalization. The entrepreneurs of such firms have a great deal of international experience as well as social capital. These people were in many cases earlier employees of the MNEs and were extremely competent in doing what they started off. These entrepreneurs could sense the problems of MNEs associated with being big and inflexible. They created nimble organizations which were global in their outlook since the beginning and yet did not face the rigidities which came naturally to the big MNEs. Being new and small was their advantage rather than disadvantage. Such an experience played a very crucial resource in the internationalization of these firms.

However, entry into foreign markets require a considerable amount of knowledge. Researchers have argued that it may be difficult for small firms to have access to such knowledge (Liesch and Knight, 1999). However, such knowledge is not always proprietary and many a times publicly available through government agencies, export intermediaries, and so forth, or even through friendly firms (such as, sister affiliates in a business group). This could be one of the reasons why newcomers as well as latecomers can leapfrog in their internationalization efforts. Entrepreneur's social capital plays a big role in obtaining such knowledge without incurring much cost.

Proposition 5: Entrepreneur's Social Capital has a Strong Positive Influence in the Success of International Activities of Emerging Economy Firms

Conclusion

This study presented a resource-based explanation for the rise of international entrepreneurship from emerging economies. I argued that the existing theories do not adequately deal with this issue and there is a need to develop a new perspective. In doing so I proposed that the emerging economy firms possess unique resources, such as cheap labour, government backing, visionary entrepreneurs, the support of a strong diaspora, and so forth, which are not possessed by their counterparts in the developed economies. However, these resources can only provide initial impetus in the internationalization efforts. For long-run success, emerging economy firms will have to focus on developing strong technological resources and market good will. The value of the resources will get enhanced in the presence of technological and market-based resources.

To summarize, the RBV-based explanation with insights from learning and the International New Venture (INV) literature can adequately explain the phenomenon of the rise of international entrepreneurship from emerging economies. Such explanations are TC-based explanations as the role of market failure is not over emphasized here. Internalization is done to make better use of the certain firm specific resources, rather than due to concerns of market failure.

References

Barney, J. B. 1991. 'Firm Resources and Sustainable Competitive Advantage', *Journal of Management*, 17(1): 99–120.

Bartlett, C., and S. Ghoshal. 1989. *Managing across borders*. Boston: Harvard Business School Press.

Buckley, P. J. and M. C. Casson. 1976. *The Future of the Multinational Entreprise*. London: Macmillan.

Caves, R. E. 1971. 'International Corporations: The Industrial Economics of Foreign Investment', *Economics*, 38: 1–27.

———. 1996. *Multinational Enterprise and Economic Analysis*. Cambridge: Cambridge University Press.

Dunning, J. H. 1958. *American Investment in British Manufacturing Industry*. London: George Allen and Unwin.

———. 1993. *Multinational Enterprises and the Global Economy*. Reading: Addison-Wesley.

Hill, C., P. Hwang and W. C. Kim. 1990. 'An Eclectic Theory of the Choice of International Entry', *Strategic Management Journal*, 9: 93–104.

Hitt, M., R. Hoskisson and H. Kim. 1997. 'International Diversification: Effects on Innovation and Firm Performance in Product-Diversified Firms', *Academy of Management Journal*, 40(4): 767–798.

Hoskisson, R. E., L. Eden, M. L. Chung and M. Wright. 2000. 'Strategy in Emerging Economies', *Academy of Management Journal*, 43(3): 249–267.

Hymer, S. 1960. *The International Operations of National Firms: A Study of Direct Investment*. PhD thesis. MA: MIT press.

Iversen, C. 1935. *Aspects of International Capital Movements*. London and Copenhagen: Levin and Munksgaard.

Johanson, J. and J. Vahlne. 1977. 'The Internationalization Process of the Firm', *Journal of International Business Studies*, 8: 23–32.

Kogut, B. 1997. 'The Evolutionary Theory of the Multinational Corporation', in B. Toyne and D. Nigh (eds), *International Business: An Emerging Vision*, pp. 470–488. Columbia, SC: University of South Carolina Press.

Liesch, P. and G. Knight. 1999. 'Information Internationalization and Hurdle Rates in Small and Medium Enterprise Internationalization', *Journal of International Business Studies*, 30(2): 383–394.

Madhok, A. 1997. 'Cost, Value, and Foreign Market Entry Mode: The Transaction and the Firm', *Strategic Management Journal*, 18(1): 39–61.

Oviatt, B. and P. McDougall. 1994. 'Toward a Theory of International New Ventures', *Journal of International Business Studies*, 25(1): 45–64.

Peng, M. W. 2001. 'The Resource-based View and International Business', *Journal of Management*, 27: 803–829.

Peng, M. W., C. Hill and D. Wang. 2000. 'Schumpeterian Dynamics Versus Williamsonian Considerations: A Test of Export Intermediary Performance', *Journal of Management Studies*, 37(2): 167–184.

Peng, M. W. and A. York. 2001. 'Behind Intermediary Performance in Export Trade: Transactions, Agents, and Resources', *Journal of International Business Studies*, 32(2): 327–346.

Penrose, E. T. 1956. 'Foreign Investment on Growth of the Firm', *Economic Journal*, 60: 220–235.

Southard, F. A. Jr. 1931. *American Industry in Europe*. Boston: Houghton Mifflin.

Tallman, S. 1991. 'Strategic Management Models and Resource-based Strategies Among MNEs in a Host Market', *Strategic Management Journal*, 12(Summer Special Issue): 69–82.

———. 1992. 'A Strategic Management Perspective on Host Country Structure of Multinational Enterprises', *Journal of Management*, 18(3): 455–471.

UNCTAD. 2004. *World Investment Report 2004: The Shift Towards Services*. Geneva: United Nations Conference on Trade and Development.

Vernon, R. 1966. 'International Investment and International Trade in the Product Cycle', *Quarterly Journal of Economics*, 80: 190–207.

Vijayan, Jaikumar. 1996. 'Look out, Here Comes India', *Computerworld*, 30(9): 100.

Wan, W. P. and R. E. Hoskisson. 2003. 'Home Country Environments, Corporate Diversification Strategies, and Firm Performance', *Academy of Management Journal* 46(1): 27–46.

Zaheer, S. 1995. 'Overcoming the Liability of Foreignness', *Academy of Management Journal*, 38(2): 341–363.

Developing Entrepreneurial Workforce for Sustainable Growth of the Small Scale Sector

4

V.P. WANI

The small scale sector has acquired a prominent role in the socioeconomic development of the country during the past five decades. It has contributed to the overall growth of the gross domestic product as well as in terms of employment generation, removal of regional imbalance, and export. Therefore, after independence, the government provided numerous incentives and protection plans to this sector. This has resulted in the growth of this sector; however, simultaneously, sickness in this sector has become a matter of great concern. The changing economic scenario due to liberalization has also posed challenges and has opened up the opportunities for the small scale sector. The challenges are in the form of a shorter product life-time cycle, fast changing technology, entry of multinationals, and awareness of the customer due to deep penetration of media. This is the fact that these units are facing numerous problems resulting to their sickness. This has necessiated them to be competitive for their sustenance.

On the other hand, the opportunities have come in the form of access to a better technology, availability of a variety of raw materials and components, impetus to quality, efficiency, and opportunities to restructure and diversify. To face these challenges and grab the opportunities, an entrepreneur has to adopt innovative product process, productivity improvement techniques and effective technology management for sustainability of the unit. In this context, the paper examines the factors responsible for growth and sickness to small scale industrial units. It also proposes the model with a strategic approach for developing entrepreneurial capabilities among engineers. The objectives are to foster an increasingly entrepreneurial culture that helps the students and the faculty to understand the fundamentals and feasibility of forming technology enterprise to help them establish and manage sustainable ventures and to accelerate the commercialization of technologies developed.

Introduction

In recent years, the development of entrepreneurship programs for engineering students has gained considerable momentum. Through entrepreneurship, an engineer can bring a technical revolution that can meet the challenges. Simultaneously, the mushroom growth of engineering institutions will be producing thousands of engineers per annum. The addition of thousands of engineers per year will increase the unemployment problem for the students. This increasing unemployment problem has forced the policy makers in India to explore new avenues in the small scale sector and take necessary steps to encourage engineering students towards self-employment/entrepreneurship in their early career.

Engineering has undergone significant changes in the recent past. The lead-time in education, in general, and in the course of engineering in particular, is long and unless we plan ahead reasonably and accurately, we would be unable to fulfil our obligations effectively. In the changing environment where the world is becoming a global village, the study of engineering must not only teach the fundamentals of engineering theory, experimentation, and practice, but also be relevant, attractive, and connected. It should cover the essential ingredients conducive to preparing students for a broad range of careers and life-long learning. The essential ingredients include the willingness to take calculated risks—in terms of time, equity, or career, the ability to formulate an effective venture team, the creative skill to marshal needed resources; and fundamental skills of building a solid business plan; and finally the vision to recognize opportunity where others see chaos, contradiction, and confusion (Kuratko and Hodgetts, 2004).

Prosperity and the Embeddedness of Entrepreneurship

When discussing the driving forces of prosperity and employment generation, entrepreneurship comes out as a prominent and strategically important issue. In combination with the ideas about new regional economies and new information and communication technologies, entrepreneurship serves as a universal key that provides within itself fruitful paths into the future. Different approaches coexist and an academic discussion on entrepreneurship is trying to develop typologies of different concepts (Martinelli, 1994). Listening to many recent talks about entrepreneurship, we notice that references are made in turn to the sector of small- and medium-sized enterprises, to venture creation and to self-employment. In this sense, the rising self-employment is regarded as a stimulus towards fresh social and economic blood in the economy and, of course, innovation and the restructuring of actors and organizations are always needed (Acs and Audretsch, 1990a, 1990b). Rao and Pareek (1982), describe entrepreneurship as a creative and innovative response to the environment. Such responses can take place in any field of social endeavour—business, industry, agriculture, education, social work and the like. Doing new things or doing things that are already being done in a new way is therefore a simple definition of entrepreneurship.

Essentials of Entrepreneurship

As per Drucker (1998), there is far more to entrepreneurship than systematic innovation—the very foundation of entrepreneurship as a practice and discipline is the practice of systematic innovation. Purposeful systematic innovation begins with the analysis of the sources of the new opportunities and innovators must analyze all opportunities. Finding those opportunities, and exploiting them with focussed practical solutions, requires disciplined work. As viewed by Kickul and Gundry (2000), due to the rapid acceleration of technology the ability to respond quickly to changes as well as to forge new relationships with the other firms are the needs of the time. Considering the dual role of a small entrepreneur, as entrepreneur and multifarious manager, Bhat (1999) feels the development of entrepreneurs to make him:

- Highly knowledgeable with great vision and dynamism
- Knowledgeable regarding the different incentive schemes offered to Small Scale Industry (SSI) and procedures thereof
- Understand the rules, regulations, and law of the land in starting/ running the unit
- Aware of the entrepreneurial values and competencies for successful entrepreneurship
- Acquainted with technical and managerial skills and
- Train him to identify and seize the opportunity

Babson College and the Arthur M. Blank Centre for Entrepreneurship explains entrepreneurship as identifying an opportunity regardless of the resources currently available and executing on opportunity for the purpose of wealth creation in the private, public, and global sector. The centre has given the essentials of entrepreneurship as follows:

- Opportunity focussed: recognition, assessment, and shaping
- Creative resource marshalling
- The entrepreneurial mind
- The entrepreneurial team and a team locus of control
- Extended enterprise management
- Creativity
- Communication
- Leadership

Entrepreneurship and the Small Scale Sector

In developing countries like India, the SSI is a potent way by which maximum employment can be generated with comparatively low investment. It is also helpful in the removal of regional imbalance in industrial development. The performance of the SSI sector in terms of critical parameters, such as number of units, production, employment generation and export are significant. This sector in India contributes about 40 per cent of the national industrial production, 35 per cent of the total national exports and provides employment to over 18.6 million people (Prasad, 2001). Even in developed countries like the USA, employments by small firms contributed 53 per cent of the total employment during the period 1976–1990. Birch (1979) showed how this new force of small entrepreneurial companies had created some 80 per cent of the new jobs in the United States from 1969 to1976.

Contemporary transformation of the business environment, due to liberalization, privatization, and globalization, has increased competitive pressure on the small scale enterprises in India. They are facing an entirely new paradigm of competitive threats:

1. Major shift in product and process technology
2. Changes in preference from the customer segment, and so forth

Under the changed circumstances, the ability to generate and utilize knowledge is the only way to sustain oneself. Technological innovation is a key to survival and growth for small scale enterprises in India (Wani et al., 2002b). Technical entrepreneurship plays a pivotal role in the process of industrialization. It can make a contribution to industrial development through innovations in product development, improvements in productivity, production process and systems. Therefore, the technical education integrated with the systematically-planned entrepreneurial input can be useful in developing an engineer as an entrepreneur. This education can play a vital role in the development of technical entrepreneurship for a sustainable growth of the SSI sector in India. The engineer as an entrepreneur can make a significant contribution to industrial development through innovations in product/process development, increased productivity, production process, and systems (Wani et al., 2004a), with the application of the knowledge he gained.

Significance of the Small Scale Sector

In India, small and medium-sized enterprise (SME) termed as small scale unit (including the tiny sector) is defined by the criteria of capital investment. This is unlike many other countries where a different criterion is used for identifying small and medium scale units (Mukharjee, 2001). Small enterprises serve as the seedbed of entrepreneurship (see Table 4.1) due to the following features:

1. It creates more employment opportunities with comparatively low capital investment
2. SSI unit is generally local resources/demand based
3. Location flexibility, resulting in horizontal growth and removal of regional imbalance
4. This sector gives quick returns and has a shorter gestation period;
5. These units help to maintain/retain traditional skills and handicrafts

Table 4.1   Contribution of SMEs Worldwide

Country	Share of				Criteria for recognition
	Total Estt.	Output	Employment	Exports	
India	95%	40%	45%	35%	Fixed assets
USA	98%	n.a.	53%	n.a.	Employment
Japan	99%	52%	72%	13%	Employment and assets
Taiwan	97%	81%	79%	48%	Paid up capital, assets and sales
Singapore	97%	32%	58%	16%	Fixed assets and employment
Korea	90%	33%	51%	40%	Employment
Malaysia	92%	13%	17%	15%	Shareholders' fund and employment
Indonesia	99%	36%	45%	11%	Employment

Source: *Laghu-Udyog*, Volume XXVI, No. 6 to 8, January–March 2002.

Ever since Independence, the Government has consistently encouraged this sector as is evident from the policies framed from time to time. This sector received much attention during 1977 when a centrally sponsored scheme known as 'District Industries Centre' was launched throughout the country with the purpose of providing all necessary services at the centre under the single roof (Wani et al., 2004a). In India, the performances of the small scale sector in terms of critical parameters, such as number of units, production, employment generated and export during the last decade is as indicated in Table 4.2.

Table 4.2   Year-wise Growth of SSI Units in India

Year	No. of units (in million)	Production (Rs in billion)	Employment (in million)	Export (Rs in billion)
1990-91	1.94	1553.40	12.53	96.64
1991-92	2.08	1786.99	12.98	138.83
1992-93	2.24	2093.00	13.40	177.85
1993-94	2.38	2416.48	13.93	253.07
1994-95	2.57	2939.90	14.65	290.68
1995-96	2.72	3562.13	15.26	364.70
1996-97	2.85	4126.36	16.00	392.49
1997-98	3.01	4651.71	16.72	439.46
1998-99	3.12	5275.15	17.15	489.78
1999-2000	3.22	5784.70	17.73	Not available

Source: *Laghu-Udyog*, Volume XXV, April–September 2001

In India, the small scale sector has been constantly out-performing the large-scale sector on the crucial parameters of growth in production and growth in employment. The basic accent of India's policy for the small scale sector has been defensive, aiming to protect the small scale sector from the dynamics of the competitive growth. The changing economic and liberalized scenario has removed this protection. In this process (Raje, 2000), the liberalized policy has posed certain challenges and provided opportunities to the small scale sector. The challenges are in the form of increased competition and reduced protection due to lowering of tariffs and market determined rates of interest. On the other hand, opportunities have come in the form of access to better technology, availability of variety of raw materials and components, impetus to quality, efficiency and opportunity to restructure and diversify. Further, the challenges posed before the small scale sector are as follows:

1. Increased competition (both domestic and international) in most of the spheres of manufacturing activities including those in the rural area
2. Penetration of branded consumer products in rural area from large-scale units
3. Deep penetration of media—increased awareness of consumers leading to:

   • Quality consciousness;
   • Preference for branded products;

- Wider choice of brand/products and services to satisfy similar needs;
4. Limited scope for quality price trade off;
5. Increased purchasing power among the rural populace/masses.

Sickness in the Small Scale Sector

In spite of this growth and development, it is a fact that small scale sector has not been developed to its fullest potential. This sector is beset with a number of problems, which have impeded the complete development of this sector. The sickness in this sector is widespread and growing at a fast rate, resulting in huge losses of different kinds. It is because of this reason that the units in this sector were operating in a sheltered market and a majority of them paid little attention to technology upgradation, quality improvement, and cost reduction during the last several decades. Due to the regime of quotas, control and licensing, this policy has given rise to setting-up industrial units with the only aim of making windfall gains, irrespective of the fact that an individual is quality conscious or not. This resulted in a large number of units becoming sick with little scope for any improvement in the future. The Reserve Bank of India has defined a weak unit as one, which has shown accumulated losses equal to or exceeding 50 per cent of its peak net worth for the immediately preceding five years, and suffered a cash loss in the immediate preceding year (http://www.smallindustryindia.com/sido/ar2001.htm).

Sickness in the small scale sector is a matter of great concern and debate. Sickness in the industrial sector results in locking-up of resources, wastage of capital assets, loss of production and increasing unemployment. In addition, it affects the circulation of the bank credit. As per the Reserve Bank of India, the magnitude and nature of sickness and its growth in the last 10 years is reflected in Table 4.3.

Developing Entrepreneurship for a Sustainable Growth of the Small Scale Industry (SSI) Sector

It is a fact that if a person with enough entrepreneurial zeal is provided with proper education and training, sustainable entrepreneurship can

Table 4.3   Sickness in the SSI Sector in India

As at the end of the year	Sickness unit details		Potentially viable unit details	
	No. of units	Outstanding amount (Rs in crore)	No. of units	Outstanding amount (Rs in crore)
1991	2,21,472	2792.00	16,140	693.12
1992	2,45,575	3100.67	19,210	728.90
1993	2,38,176	3432.97	21,649	798.79
1994	2,56,452	3680.37	16,580	685.93
1995	2,68,815	3547.16	15,539	597.93
1996	2,62,376	3721.94	16,424	635.82
1997	2,35,032	3609.20	16,220	479.31
1998	2,21,536	3856.64	18,686	455.96
1999	3,06,221	4313.48	18,692	376.96

Source: Annual Report of SIDO 1999–2000 (Aranha et al., 2002).

Note: These units include village industries as well.

be developed. Bhat (1999) supported this fact when he carried out experiments in the two towns of Andhra Pradesh in collaboration with the Small Industries Extension Training Institute, Hyderabad. Although, it is a universal fact that the education and training of potential entrepreneurs has a significant bearing on the successful pursuits of entrepreneurship, yet the question arises as to what training inputs are needed for potential entrepreneurs (Wani et al., 2002a). Entrepreneurs of SME sector have to discharge the twin functions of 'entrepreneur' and a multifarious 'manager' so as to make them:

- Highly knowledgeable and dynamic
- Fully aware of the different schemes/incentives being offered to SME sector and procedures thereon
- Understand the different laws, regulations and procedures to be followed in the establishment of a unit
- Develop entrepreneurial vision, attitude and motivation, and making them understand what behavioural competence are important for successful entrepreneurship
- Understand how important it is to submit to financial discipline
- Educated about the different stages of growth of an enterprise, and how to face the uncertainties and to meet competition

- Understand how to forge good relations with different individuals and organizations looking after industrial development
- Understand how to seize an opportunity and thereof in the conduct of market survey studies and preparation of project cum feasibility report
- Marshal and utilize the knowledge as well as resources in an effective way for the success of the industrial venture.

Secondly, in the context of globalization and liberalization, the industries are to respond to the emerging calls of quality assurance as well as cost-effective strategies of production and services. The management of new enterprises and establishments has therefore, to respond to the management of technological growth and innovation. This challenge of growing competition has necessitated a high degree of application capability and innovative spirit among the entrepreneurs. Innovation is to be initiated by entrepreneurs by seizing an opportunity in the changing situation by discovering how to:

- Make sure that all innovations create customer delight and meet quality standards;
- Bring innovativeness into every important and crucial process from planning to communication feedback system;
- Find paradigm to keep on the cutting edge of change;
- Study the past, analyze the present, and forecast the needs of the customer as well as the technology in the unit for its sustainability;
- Establish a shared vision that involves all members of the unit in fostering and achieving important innovation synthesis of opportunities of the market place with both the capabilities and the need of stockholders.

Necessity of Developing Engineers as Entrepreneurs

To face the challenges posed to the small scale sector due to the changing environment, entrepreneurs have to adopt innovative products/processes, productivity improvement techniques and effective technology management (http://www.education.nic.in/htmlweb/techedu.htm).

Kelmer and Wanghman (1995) considered technology process as important, but the ability to utilize and capitalize on the advantage of technology through invention and innovation subsequently achieving through synergy, is considered more important in the running and survival of the unit.

Sanghi (1996) rightly described the role of technical entrepreneurship as being pivotal in the process of liberalization. It can make a contribution to industrial development through innovations, new product/process development/improvement in productivity, and so forth. Technicians and technocrats can easily play the role of innovators comparatively because they have characteristics, such as propensity to adapt to new knowledge more rapidly. Technologists and technicians who learn sufficient science and engineering acquire capabilities to know the why and how of various theories and can design products and services based on their knowledge and skill competencies (Baburao, 1995). In the fast changing technological environment, the role of technical entrepreneurship has assumed a central place. Moreover, as per Baburao (1999), the favorable factors that affect the development of a technical person into an effective entrepreneur, after proper education and training, can be as follows:

(i) Ability to grasp opportunities which offers economic advantage
(ii) Ability to analyze/diagnose the problems of an enterprise and devise remedial measures at the right time
(iii) Ability to work out economics of production/service and evolve competitive strategies
(iv) Ability to give fillip to ancillarization
(v) Technical and analytical capabilities helpful in preventing accidental breakdown problems, thus reducing expenditure on trouble shooting
(vi) Ability to forecast the changes in technology and respond accordingly
(vii) Ability towards self-propelled performance rather than externally propelled developments
(viii) Ability to effectively transfer technology from laboratories to industries

Engineers as entrepreneurs can meet the challenges of the emerging scenario of liberalization, privatization, and globalization with key elements of competition rather than protection.

How Entrepreneurial Engineers Are

In order to assess the entrepreneurial concept and entrepreneurial capability of engineering students, a survey was conducted among the engineering institutions in and around the state of Haryana. The hypothesis set was that the engineering students do possess the entrepreneurial concept and capability, and it was set to identify as to how it affects the selection of career options by students. In the survey, the criteria followed were that the students should be of the final year, belonging to the mechanical engineering discipline, and possessing the choice of option self-employment or wage-employment as career option.

The institute-wise engineering students were categorized on the basis of the students' choice of self-employment as career option, and students opting wage-employment as a career option (see Table 4.4). The institute-wise entrepreneurial characteristics and entrepreneurial capability of the students of both categories has been detailed below.

Observations

1. The number of students selecting self-employment as career option is lower as compared to the number of students opting wage-employment as career option.
2. The entrepreneurial characteristic of the students is on higher side as compared to their entrepreneurial capability.
3. The entrepreneurial characteristic of the students opting for self-employment is on a comparatively higher side than students opting wage-employment as career option.
4. The entrepreneurial capability of the students opting for self-employment is on the higher side than students opting wage-employment as career option.

Analysis of the Survey in Response to the Faculty in Engineering Institution

It is a fact that the engineering student's concept and capability depends on the input of the faculty. In order to assess their input, a survey was conducted among the faculty of the same institutions, of which the earlier survey was conducted for students. The survey tried to find out the knowledge of the faculty; receptive mind/learning attitude of the faculty; input by the faculty for developing effective engineers, and

Table 4.4 Students' Entrepreneurial Characteristics and Capability Data

Institute option	Self-employment option			Wage-employment option		
	No. of students	Characteristics	Capability	No. of students	Characteristics	Capability
RECK	25	0.9013	0.6577	22	0.4712	0.6077
RECH	15	0.8989	0.6605	20	0.4767	0.6231
SLIET	14	0.9101	0.6772	21	0.4809	0.5965
COTP	19	0.8048	0.6652	25	0.4733	0.5503
RADAUR	19	0.9000	0.6672	23	0.4746	0.6099
KAITHAL	09	0.8787	0.6214	25	0.4686	0.5974
JIND	18	0.8732	0.6219	27	0.4737	0.5823
SKIET	19	0.8842	0.6043	20	0.4741	0.5986
MULLANA	25	0.8983	0.6396	15	0.4822	0.5938
NILOKHERI	15	0.9137	0.6456	31	0.4618	0.6141
AMBALA	19	0.9039	0.6481	24	0.4747	0.5462
% of options		43.78			56.22	

industrial exposure and also the input of faculty for developing engineers as entrepreneurs. The institute wise data related to the above points is given in Table 4.5.

Table 4.5   Institute-wise Faculty's Response Analysis

Sl. No.	Name of the institution	Knowledge	Continuous learning	Developing effective engineers	Industrial/ Entrepreneurial exposure
	Degree Institutions				
1.	REC Kurukshetra	0.9084	0.7561	0.8473	0.6491
2.	REC Hamirpur	0.9138	0.7487	0.8692	0.6461
3.	Radaur	0.8629	0.7714	0.8571	0.6191
4.	HCTM Kaithal	0.8771	0.7333	0.7786	0.5571
5.	JIET Jind	0.9171	0.7714	0.8643	0.5476
6.	SLIET Longowal	0.9000	0.7800	0.8400	0.7133
7.	SKIET Kurukshetra	0.8950	0.7667	0.7688	0.5750
8.	MMEC Mullana	0.9143	0.7524	0.7429	0.5524
9.	COT Pantnagar	0.9040	0.8444	0.8500	0.6133
	Diploma Institutions				
10.	Nilokheri Polytechnic	0.8977	0.8000	0.7556	0.5852
11.	Ambala Polytechnic	0.9022	0.7926	0.7722	0.5778

The header spanning: "Factors regarding teachers that affect the capability of the student"

Observations

1. The knowledge of the faculty is on a higher degree with respect to the rest of the factors/inputs.
2. Faculty input for developing the personality of the students as engineer is a second preference.
3. The learning attitude/receptive mind of the faculty is a third preference.
4. The industrial exposure and entrepreneurial awareness of the faculty comes as the least important factor among all.

Proposed Model for Developing Engineers as Entrepreneurs

The students have the willingness to opt for self-employment as a career option and need to be developed by proper input during their training in engineering. The faculty input affects the entrepreneurial capability of the students. The entrepreneurial characteristics of a student is an inherent characteristic which cannot be changed. However, the entrepreneurial capability of the student selecting self-employment as career option can be improved by a proper input of the faculty during their training in engineering. The input of the faculty will depend on its qualification and knowledge, learning attitude, input for developing engineers, and entrepreneurial awareness plus industrial exposure of the faculty. These are the factors affecting qualitative input in the engineering education. Thus, it can be said that the entrepreneurial capability of a student is directly proportional to the input of the faculty provided during engineering education.

In engineering education, the theoretical lectures should be followed by practical lessons, relevant to the theory taught. Then an open-ended real industrial problem should be given to the students. This exercise will be helpful in giving the students an exposure to develop an understanding of engineering as well as face its uncertain nature. An open interaction with entrepreneurs and acquaintance with real life industrial problems can help to instill in engineering students the capability to face the uncertainties and unforeseen problems more tactfully and determine the viable solutions for sustainable development. This will also help in giving industrial exposure to the faculty.

Entrepreneurial awareness needs to be made mandatory in the curriculum of engineering education so as to facilitate students (interested in self-employment as a career option) to gain an awareness and broad outline of the area (see Figure 4.1). The entrepreneurial development programme

Figure 4.1   Role of the Institution in Entrepreneurship Development

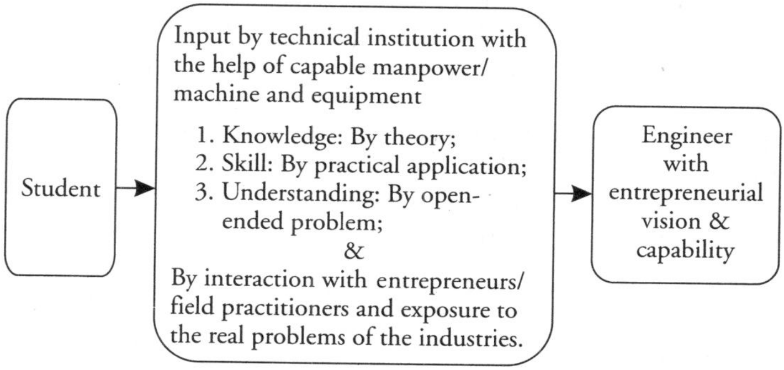

should not be only theoretical, that is, lectures and theory paper. Rather, it should be theoretical at the first level and then practically oriented. Thus, the complete curriculum of the entrepreneurship development programme should be adopted as follows:

(i) Pre-operational drill;
(ii) Operational drill;
(iii) Post-operational drill;
(v) Functional and structural parameters; and
(v) Competence building for decision-making.

The first three stages will be for technical competence building and the remaining ones for managerial competence building for the participants of the programme. The detail coverage of the proposed entrepreneurial development programme (Wani et al., 2002c) would be as in Table 4.6.

Table 4.6   Steps and Processes in the Entrepreneurship Development Programme

Step	Process
Pre-operational drill	• Identification of Entrepreneur • Individual's decision to choose self-employment as career
Operational drill	• Opportunity recognition • Product identification • Self-confidence building • Techno-commercial aspects of a unit
Post-operational drill	• Vetting of techno-economical viability of unit • Vetting of project report from the financial institutions • Technical sustainability of the unit
Functional and structural parameters	• Land/Shed allotment for the unit • Resource generation for the unit • Technical know-how for the unit • Rules, Regulations of the land
Competence building for decision-making	Development of: • Leadership qualities, • Decision-making ability,

(Table 4.6 continued)

(*Table 4.6 continued*)

Step	Process
	• Labour management skills,
	• Finance management skills,
	• Sales, marketing and purchase management skills,
	• Shop-floor management skills.

This programme would make the students aware about the steps in technical entrepreneurship as follows:

1. To be well-versed with the product/process line is not sufficient; process know-how and know-how to operate the machine/equipment is a must, too.
2. To have sufficient shop floor experience to guide operational staff at different levels.
3. To be familiar with raw material requirement alternatives, their specifications, availability, quality, source of supply price, and so forth.
4. To have knowledge of quality requirements of products, and measures for improving quality.
5. To have knowledge of marketing channels, distribution networks, agency practices, transport intricacies, and economies of packaging and presentation.
6. To be well-versed in taxation and other regulatory rules.
7. To maintain accounts, and store inventors in an efficient way.
8. To have the willingness to put up with bureaucratic regulations, external environmental turbulence, and the ability to move with the wind.
9. To have the ability to identify the opportunity and avail opportunity benefits.
10. To develop quality expertise, shrewdness, resourcefulness and perseverance.
11. To follow the five *P* principles, that is, Planning, Preparation, Persuasion, Patience, and Perfection for running industrial ventures successfully.
12. To be physically and mentally tough in order to withstand neck-to-neck competition from similar units and business rivals.

The entrepreneurship development programme to be conducted should incorporate these factors. With these, the proposed entrepreneurship development programme to be run at technical institutions can be categorized into five phases as in Table 4.7.

Table 4.7 Entrepreneurship Development Programme in Engineering Institutions

Programme phase	Focus to be made on	Input/Action during programme
Selection of the right prospective entrepreneur.	The Entrepreneur	Entrepreneurial characteristics and capability test of student.
Motivation of an individual to become an entrepreneur.	The Entrepreneur	Awareness about incentives, avenues, and schemes in the field, interaction with entrepreneurs followed by visits to their unit achievement motivation programme.
To start the unit.	Venturing process: steps in marshalling the resources, that is, men, m/c's, material, money, land, services and technology, and so forth, and product/market assessment.	Industrial potential survey, market survey for assessment of product demand, market terms and conditions. Preparation, presentation of the techno economic feasibility project report followed by group discussion.
To run the unit.	Running a business/ venture; awareness of internal and external factors affecting the unit's performance.	In plant study, interactions with the successful/unsuccessful entrepreneurs. Giving an open-ended problem in industrial training as an exercise. Report preparation involving the techno-commercial aspects and presentation.
To expand the unit.	Unit, market, and customer.	Case study, written report, formal presentation, and discussion.

The said entrepreneurship development programme will be useful for:

(i) Building entrepreneurial vision among engineers;
(ii) Effective industry institute interaction;

(iii) Industrial exposure to the faculty;

(iv) Entrepreneurial awareness to the faculty;

(v) Effective utilization of infrastructure available at engineering institutes.

In a nutshell, it will be helpful in developing an engineer most effectively as per the requirements of the industry either in a *self-employment* or in a *wage-employment* career for an engineering student.

Conclusion

In the small scale engineering industry, entrepreneurial success and failure depend not only on what entrepreneurs know but also on what they can do with what they know. Since they are often working in areas of uncertainty and change, their comfort and insight with intuitive judgements and actions are as important as their deliberative decisions and implementation.

The objective of this paper was to identify the entrepreneurial capability of engineering students. It is clear that the engineering students who are under the guidance of a faculty that has industrial exposure can develop engineers as entrepreneurs.

1. Engineering students possess entrepreneurial characteristics and capabilities. For improving the latter, efforts need to be made to improve the input given to students during an engineering education.

2. The faculty of the engineering institution needs to provide entrepreneurial awareness and industrial exposure to realize the industrial problems and requirements of the industry.

3. There is a definite relationship between the entrepreneurial capability of a student and input of faculty through engineering education. Improving the industrial exposure/entrepreneurial awareness and learning attitude of the faculty can increase the entrepreneurial capability of the engineering student.

The engineer-turned entrepreneur can have a long-term positive implication on various corners of the society as follows:

• Engineering Institutions: Lead to better revenue generation; effective utilization of expertise and facilities at the industries and institutes; more relevant curriculum and effective R&D inputs due to feedback from the end users; better placement of students, resulting in better intake of students to those institutions.

- Engineering Students: The effective industry-institute interaction will make students aware of the real industrial problems. This will be helpful in their knowledge enhancement, skill improvement, and better understanding of the application of knowledge and skill in the real industrial world, thus increasing the avenues in self-employment and employability in the wage-employment sector.

- Industrial Developmental Agencies: The entrepreneurship awareness camps at the doorstep of the engineering institutions can inculcate in students an urge to consider self-employment as a career option. Moreover, the small industries service institutes and the so called industrial consultancy organizations can play a catalytic role among the SSI sector and academic institutions. Thus, the SSI sector can take the benefit of the research carried out in academic institutions for smooth technology transfer and commercialization.

- Government and Policy Makers: Unemployment problem can be sorted out to a large extent in addition to the sustainable industrial growth.

- Industrial Sector: This sector can get engineering workforce with better understanding of industrial problems, thus can reduce the expenditure on-the-job training.

References

Acs, Z. and D. B. Audretsch. 1990a. *Innovation and Small Firms*. Cambridge: MIT Press.
———. 1990b. *The Economics of Small Firms: A European Challenge*. Dordrecht, The Netherlands: Kluwer Academic Publishers.
Annual Report for 1999–2000 of Small Industries Development Organization Government of India. Available online at http://www.smallindustryindia.com/sido/ar2001.htm.
Aranha Jose Alberto, Bueno J. A. Pimenta, Luiz Carlos Scavarda do Carmo and Marcos A. Da Silveira. 2002. 'Entrepreneurship in the Engineering Curriculum: Some Initial Results of PUC Rio's Experiment', Proceedings of the ASEE 2002 Conference, Berlin (Germany).
Arthur, M. Blank Centre for Entrepreneurship and Babson College. Available online at http://www.babson.edu/babson/babsoneshipp.nsf/public/E3.

Baburao, G. 1995. 'Entrepreneurial Education in Technical School', *The Hindu.*

————. 1999. 'Promotion of Technical Entrepreneurship: Role of Humanities and Social Sciences', *Journal of Engineering Education:* 7–11.

Bhat Khursheed. 1999. 'Small Entrepreneurial Education: Approach and Methodology', *Abhigyan,* XVII(4): 35–44.

Birch, D. 1979. '*The Job Generation Process*'. Washington, D.C.: Economic Development Administration of the U.S. Department of Commerce.

Drucker Peter F. 1998. 'The Discipline of Innovation', *Harvard Business Review,* November–December: 149–157.

Growth of Engineering and Technology in India. Available online at http://www.education.nic.in/htmlweb/techedu.htm.

Kelmer, J. and D. W. Wanghman. 1995. 'Determining the Relevant Factors in the Success Strategies of Small Enterprises', *Journal of Entrepreneurship*: 215–236.

Kickul, Jill and Lisa, K. Gundry. 2000. 'Pursuing Technological Innovation: The Role of Entrepreneurial Posture and Opportunity Recognition among the Internet Firms', *Frontiers of Entrepreneurship Research.* Available online at: www.babson.edu/entrep/fer/papers2000/.

Kuratko, D. F. and R. M. Hodgetts. 2004. *Entrepreneurship: Theory, Process Practice.* Mason, OH: South Westorn Publishers.

Martinelli, A. 1994. 'Entrepreneurship and Management', in N. J. Smelser and R. Swedberg (eds), *The Handbook of Economic Sociology,* pp. 476–503. Princeton and New York: Princeton University and Russell Sage.

Mukharjee, Neela. 2001. 'World Trade Organization and Small and Medium Enterprises from a Developing Country's Perspective—A Study of Indian Small-scale Industries', *Laghu-Udyog,* XXV to XXVI(1 to 2): 36–48.

Prasad, C. S. 2001. 'The Third Census of SSI Units', *Laghu-Udyog,* XXV to XXVI: 14–20.

Raje, Vasundhara. 2000 'Taking SSI towards New Millennium—Message of Hope', *Laghu-Udyog,* XXIV to XXV: I–VI.

Rao, T. V. and U. Pareek. 1982. *Developing Entrepreneurship—A Handbook.* New Delhi: Learning Systems.

Sanghvi, A. N. 1996. 'Promotion of Technical Entrepreneurship through Technical Education', *The Indian Journal of Technical Education,* 19(2): 42–44.

Wani, V. P., T. K. Garg and S. K. Sharma. 2002. 'Effective Technological Innovation Necessity for Sustainable Development of Small Scale Enterprises in India', (July) International Conference on SME's in a Global Economy. University of Wollongong, Wollongong NSW Australia.

————. 2004a. 'Effective Industry Institute Interaction for Developing Entrepreneurial Vision among Engineers for Sustainable Development of SMEs in India', Intl. *Journal of Technology Transfer and Commercialization,* 3(1): 38–55.

————. 2004b. 'Developing Technoentrepreneurial Workforce for Effective Technological Innovation Necessity for Sustainable Development of SSIs in India', *International Journal of Entrepreneurship and Innovation Manage-ment,* 7: 23–38.

Does Human Resource Factor Matter in Achieving Energy Efficiency in Small Industry Clusters?
An Empirical Study

5

N. NAGESHA

Small scale Industries (SSIs) which often exist in the form of clusters are a vital component of the Indian economy on several counts. Energy being an indispensable input, enhancing its utilization efficiency not only helps in improving the competitiveness of SSIs through cost reduction but also aids in alleviating the energy linked to environmental pollution. The level of energy efficiency in an SSI depends not only on the production technology adopted but also on other non-technology factors. This paper analyzes such factors including entrepreneurial and human resource factors, in the context of two energy intensive SSI clusters. The analysis of empirical data from 42 iron foundries and 41 textile dyeing units located in two South Indian states establish the significance of non-technology factors and identifies the key variables in achieving energy efficiency. Multiple regression analysis is used for assessing the significance of four *a priori* identified factors, such as, Technical Factor (TF), Economic Factor (EF), Human Resource Factor (HRF) and Organizational and Behavioural Factor (OBF), in explaining the variation in energy efficiency levels within a given cluster. Further, the key variables affecting energy efficiency are identified using Analysis of Variance (ANOVA [sequential sum of squares method]) models. The results show that HRF is the most significant factor in explaining the variations in energy efficiency levels in the selected SSI clusters, with the identified key variables complementing it. The outcome of the study underlines the need to involve non-technology factors in the prevailing technology centred, energy-efficiency improvement initiatives in the small industry sector for discernible improvements in the long run.

Introduction

Energy, environment and sustainable development (SD) are closely inter-connected subjects attracting a growing attention in research and policy-making circles of the contemporary world. Energy, the capacity to do work, is the 'life blood of modern economy' as every human being uses it in one form or the other each day; with that the use of energy lies at the core of modern industrial society. The environment comprises the biosphere: the thin skin on the earth's surface on which life exists; the atmosphere: the geosphere and all flora and fauna. SD is 'a development which meets the needs of the present without compromising the ability of future generations to meet their own needs' (UNIDO, 1998). The concept of SD involves three important dimensions, such as, environmental, economic, and social. In other words, a development which is environmentally, economically and socially sustainable, is an SD.

There is an interaction among energy, environment, and SD in an economy. As most of the environmental problems are associated with the use of energy and the fact that without it, economic development becomes difficult, there is an 'energy trilemma' involving energy consumption, economic development, and environmental impact (Khan, 1992). It is very difficult to come out of this vicious circle especially for developing countries, with their expanding economic activities causing amplified energy consumption. Demand for energy in a growing economy stems from diverse sectors, such as agriculture, industry, commerce, transport, and domestic needs. Of these major sectors, the industrial sector is the largest energy consumer in most of the developing countries (Ross, 1997). At the global level, the industrial sector is the largest energy consumer accounting for about 32 per cent of the total energy use (IEA, 2004).

The industrial sector has emerged as the major energy-consuming sector in India as well, with a share of about 42 per cent of the total energy consumption (Reddy and Balachandra, 2003). Even though the Indian industrial sector comprises both small- and large-scale enterprises, the former accounts for a lion's share of the total industrial units. As per the prevailing definition in India, an industrial undertaking is called the SSI unit if the original investment in fixed assets, that is, plant and machinery is up to Rs 10 million (in case of hosiery and hand-tool categories up to Rs 50 million) (DCSSI, 2002). The SSI sector is of strategic importance in the Indian economy in view of its contribution to employment generation, production, GDP, and exports. In 2004–2005, the SSI sector comprised 11.85 million units, employed more than 28 million people and generated Rs 3,990 billion worth of production (MoF, 2005). The export by this sector stood at Rs 860 billion during 2002–2003. The SSI sector has created a diversified and prominent presence in the Indian economy by producing over 7,500 products and accounting for about 7 per cent of GDP, 40 per cent of industrial production and 34 per cent of national exports (MoSSI, 2004).

The SSI growth in India is characterized, among others, by its concentration in different parts of the country in the form of clusters (Abid Hussain, 1997; UNIDO, 2001). In fact, over 400 modern small industry clusters and 2000 rural and artisan clusters exist in the country. These clusters contribute about 60 per cent of the manufactured national exports and account for a significantly high share in employment generation (SIDO, 2004). The SSI sector, being a vital component of the Indian economy, is also a major consumer of energy input. Even if the energy use at the individual level of SSIs is trivial, the total consumption by their clusters and the sector as a whole is likely to be of a sizeable quantum in view of the large number of SSI units and clusters operating in the country. However, SSIs are found wanting in energy utilization efficiency and environmental aspects like pollution control (LUS, 1997). Highly energy-intensive SSIs belonging to steel, paper and pulp, textile, cement, sugar, and so forth, cause both global and local pollution due to their inefficient energy use. Studies have shown that SSI firms not only produce more waste per unit of output but also, at an aggregate level, account for at least equal if not more pollution than their large-scale counterparts (UNEP, 1998; Visvanathan and Kumar, 2002; Kathuria and Gundimeda, 2002). Analyzing energy efficiency in the SSI clusters assumes significance as they are under unprecedented pressure to improve their competitiveness, apart from reducing environmental pollution for their survival and growth in the liberalizing Indian economy. However, it is crucial to note that the level of energy efficiency in an SSI unit depends not only on the production technology adopted but also on a whole lot of non-technology factors including quality of human resources and entrepreneurship. In this backdrop, the current paper analyzes the various non-technology factors affecting energy efficiency in two energy intensive SSI clusters located in South India by making use of the empirical data pertaining to them.

Factors Influencing Energy Efficiency: Review of Literature

Based on the available literature, it appears that the energy and environment related aspects of SSIs in India have not attracted the researchers and policy makers in the past to the desired extent. Although there are a few studies on SSIs regarding 'grain-mills', 'foundries', 'brick/tile units', and so forth, yet it is found that most of these studies and initiatives undertaken to improve energy efficiency or environmental performance in SSIs have predominantly adopted a technocratic approach. Such initiatives lacked a holistic perspective necessary for comprehensively addressing the problem (Dasgupta, 1999). Further, there are not many energy-efficiency-related studies in literature involving non-technical factors in the analysis of energy use.

According to Weber (1997), energy consumption belongs to the realm of technology whereas energy conservation belongs to the realm of society. Since efficiency improvement is a part of the energy conservation strategy, a whole lot of social factors are relevant in addition to the manufacturing technology in the energy efficiency analysis. Particularly, it is true for studies conducted in clusters of specific industries using more or less similar production technologies. Baranzini and Giovannini (1996) link energy consumption to four major factors such as, technological, economic and financial, institutional, and cultural. They observe that the technical factors based on energy-using equipment and economic and financial factors in terms of income and relative energy prices have attracted much attention in the past. Further, they feel that the institutional factors comprising information campaigns, infrastructure, property rights, and so forth, and cultural factors involving attitudes, behaviours, lifestyles, and so forth, must be understood better in order to attain a significant improvement in the energy efficiency.

Another study conducted by the University of Kiel (University of Kiel, 1998) on small and medium-sized enterprises (SME) of certain European countries emphasizes on the importance of organizational and behavioural aspects of SMEs in achieving energy efficiency. Through empirical investigations it concludes that energy efficiency depends to a large extent on the existing company culture and on the engagement of firm internal key actors and their interaction within the organization. Furthermore, the findings underline the paramount importance of external actors to trigger energy-related activity in SMEs and to foster a lasting implementation of efficiency measures, which points at promising domains for policy intervention. Dasgupta (1999), after analyzing some initiatives of energy efficiency and environmental improvements in Indian SSIs, is of the opinion that a technocratic top-down approach for energy efficiency improvement is not comprehensive. Advocating a bottom-up participatory approach, she emphasizes the need to address other non-technical factors associated with energy efficiency, such as resource use efficiency, waste-management, poor work practices, layout, house-keeping, and so forth.

Bala Subrahmanya and Balachandra (2002 and 2003) have analyzed energy consumption and environmental pollution of a few SSI clusters in Karnataka from a managerial perspective. They have identified labour skill levels, owner qualifications, and technology levels as the important factors in explaining the energy use and environmental pollution. Further, they advocated the promotion of energy efficiency in SSIs through a 'cost cutting' or 'profit maximizing' strategy. Thus, it appears from a theoretical angle that non-technical factors do play a role in energy efficiency analysis. We have kept this in mind while developing a hypothetical framework for analyzing the various factors influencing energy efficiency in the two SSI clusters under reference.

Objectives, Scope and Sampling

The overall objective of the current paper is to analyze the non-technology factors, including entrepreneurial and human resource factors, influencing energy efficiency in the selected SSI clusters. The scope of the study is limited to an iron foundry cluster and a textile dyeing cluster, which are highly energy intensive. The strategy behind selecting these two industries is that as per the National Industrial Classification (ASI, 2002), while foundry represents the basic goods industry, textile belongs to the consumer goods industry. The clusters are located at Belgaum and Tirupur in the South Indian states of Karnataka and Tamil Nadu, respectively. The study is based on the primary data pertaining to 42 iron foundries and 41 textile dyeing units from the respective clusters, selected on a 'Random Sampling' basis. The required sample size (Kothari, 2001) for the study is computed using the equation (1). Energy-efficiency indicated by Specific Energy Consumption (SEC: Energy used in MJ per unit of product) is adopted as the criterion variable for estimating the sample size. Table 5.1 gives the details of sample size calculations.

$$n = \{Z^2.N.\sigma_p^2\}/\{(N-1).e^2 + Z^2.\sigma_p^2\} \tag{1}$$

where

n = size of the sample required for a given precision and confidence level;

N = finite population size

Z = standardized variate at a given confidence level (1.96 for 95 per cent confidence level)

e = acceptable error or the precision required (about 5 per cent of the mean value)

σ_p = standard deviation of the population (estimated through pilot study)

Table 5.1   Sample Size Estimation in the Foundry and Textile Clusters

Sl. No.	Product cluster	Population size	Estimated SEC through pilot study			Required (executed) sample size
			Mean	e	σ_p	
1.	Iron Foundry	100	5800 MJ/ton	290 MJ/ton	1000 MJ/ton	32 (42)
2.	Textile Dyeing	280	40 MJ/kg	3 MJ/kg	10 MJ/kg	38 (41)

Source: Calculations based on field data.

Considering the uncertainty of the exact population size and the limitations of field survey, data is collected from a slightly higher number of SSIs (42 and 41) than required (32 and 38). The primary data required for the study is gathered by canvassing a structured questionnaire. The questionnaire covered various aspects pertaining to SSI enterprises like:

unit profile/material input/production details/energy consumption/output/wastage/technology details/investment/and human resource and entrepreneurial aspects.

Factors Influencing Energy Efficiency: A Hypothetical Model

One of the most noticeable features of energy efficiency (SEC: Specific Energy Consumption) in the Indian SSI clusters is its wide variation among the SSI firms within a given industry (Ramachandra and Subramanian, 1993; TERI, 1998, 1999a and 1999b; Bala Subrahmanya and Balachandra, 2002 and 2003). This is true even in the present study, though energy use technology adopted in a given cluster remained almost similar. This means that the variation in energy efficiency in the cluster cannot be attributed to production technology *per se*. This motivated us to interpret the efficiency variation through non-technology factors. Thus, we developed a hypothetical framework of factors influencing energy efficiency as depicted in Figure 5.1.

The factors are formulated on the basis of the earlier indicated literature followed by discussion with the experts. The interactions with some progressive entrepreneurs in the clusters and also with officials of SSI development institutions assisted in this endeavour. We arrived at four factors *a priori* which are likely to influence energy efficiency in the clusters: Technical Factor (TF), Economic Factor (EF), Human Resource Factor (HRF), and Organizational and Behavioural Factor (OBF). It is hypothesized that the variation in energy efficiency may be explained by a combination of these factors. The important variables under these factors are also shown in Figure 5.1 and their logical connection with energy efficiency is briefly presented in the following paragraphs.

Despite the adoption of mostly the homogeneous energy use technology within the clusters under study, there were still differences in terms of age of plant and machinery, quality of energy used, and certain process-specific variables. They are mostly connected directly or indirectly with the technology of manufacturing the product, and hence are grouped under Technical Factor (TF). The age of plant and machinery is an important variable, as generally, the efficiency level tends to get worse with the age. The energy efficiency also tends to be higher with better quality

Figure 5.1   Factors Influencing Energy Efficiency: A Framework

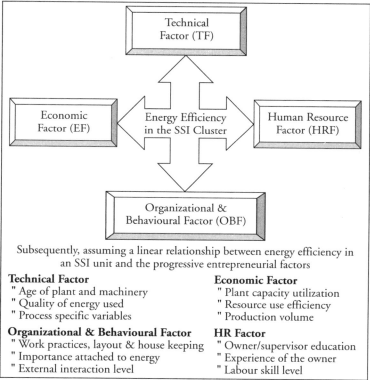

Subsequently, assuming a linear relationship between energy efficiency in an SSI unit and the progressive entrepreneurial factors

Technical Factor
" Age of plant and machinery
" Quality of energy used
" Process specific variables

Economic Factor
" Plant capacity utilization
" Resource use efficiency
" Production volume

Organizational & Behavioural Factor
" Work practices, layout & house keeping
" Importance attached to energy
" External interaction level

HR Factor
" Owner/supervisor education
" Experience of the owner
" Labour skill level

Source: Proposed hypothetical framework.

of energy used. For example, during a process, the usage of electricity leads to better utilization efficiency than fossil fuels, such as coal or oil. The type of manufacturing process used determines the material and energy consumption level due to usage of different machines and techniques.

The role of the Economic Factor (EF) in achieving efficiencies in production is well established. We try to capture the effect of this factor in energy use through variables, such as capacity utilization, resource (other than energy) use efficiency and production volume. There are evidences in literature showing higher capacity utilizations leading to better energy efficiency. The efficiency of utilizing other material resources causes variation in the energy requirement for further processing these resources, thus affecting energy efficiency. For example, more scrap/rejection/rework will have a considerably negative effect on the energy efficiency due to wastage of energy consumed during their production. With the large production volume, it is possible to realize 'economies of scale' which indirectly contribute positively to energy efficiency.

The contribution of the Human Resource Factor (HRF) in achieving better efficiency needs no emphasis. Particularly in SSIs, which generally depend on the entrepreneurial ability for its survival and growth, the HRF is of prime importance. Besides, as SSIs are mostly labour-intensive, the skill level of employed labour also merits due attention. The HRF consists of variables, such as the quality of labour, managerial and technical ability, and business experience of the owner. Highly-skilled labour force can reduce wastage and effectively perform the job in the best possible manner. It is believed that higher the educational level of owners/managers/supervisors, higher will be their capabilities in terms of planning, decision-making, implementing, innovating, and so forth, with respect to the overall operation of the unit. This again affects the overall efficiency of the operation including the energy. The owner's business experience does count a lot in energy efficiency, especially in SSIs, in view of their critical role in taking long-term and technology oriented decisions.

The proposed fourth factor such as, Organizational and Behavioural Factor (OBF) encompasses variables like work practices, layout and housekeeping, importance attached to energy related issues, and the external interaction level of the organization. This factor is expected to capture the variation in attitudes and organizational aspects among SSIs within a given cluster. The best work practices, neat layout and good housekeeping, such as proper insulation for heat loss, regular overhaul and maintenance, and so forth, will positively contribute towards energy efficiency improvement. The attitude of SSI entrepreneurs/supervisors/workers towards energy in terms of the importance that they attach to energy-related issues in the day-to-day functioning is seemingly important for efficiency improvement. A progressive entrepreneur with a positive attitude and social accountability may use the government policies, regulations and programmes to improve the overall performance of his firm, especially related to energy and environment. The general interaction level of the SSI firms with other units within or outside the cluster, industry associations, R&D institutions, participation in seminars/conferences and so forth, help the SSIs in upgrading the knowledge and skill of their manpower thus resulting in an improved energy efficiency, among other benefits.

As each variable under a given factor is likely to capture a particular dimension, the cumulative values of all the included variables are worked out to represent a factor. However, a variable is included under the respective factor only if it meets the basic requirement of showing some significant association with energy efficiency. Though all the above-explained four factors are expected to influence energy efficiency in SSI clusters, the extent of their influence and significance may vary from one cluster to the other. We seek to validate the foregoing hypothetical framework by analyzing the empirical data pertaining to the two SSI clusters under reference. We adopt the 'multiple regression' technique in the following form to achieve this objective:

$$\eta = f \; (TF, EF, HRF, OBF) \qquad (2)$$

or $\quad \eta = b_0 + b_1 \, (TF) + b_2 \, (EF) + b_3 \, (HRF) + b_4 \, (OBF) + u \qquad (3)$

where
   η = energy efficiency (SEC–Specific Energy Consumption)
  TF = Technical Factor score
  EF = Economic Factor score
HRF = Human Resource Factor score
OBF = Organizational and Behavioural Factor score
   u = random component
  b_0 = constant (intercept)
b_1, b_2, b_3 and b_4 = coefficients of the above factors

In multiple regression analyses, it is assumed that the dependent variable is a quantitative measure with normal distribution and equal variance for all combinations of independent variables. It is not assumed that the independent variables are normally distributed or even that they are quantitative measurements (Overall and Klett, 1972). It is perfectly acceptable to use qualitative or categorical variables as independent variates, provided they are logically or empirically derived ordinal scale measurements (Overall and Klett, 1972). Considering this, the application of multiple regression analysis in the present case appears to be justified from a statistics standpoint. If the overall model explains a considerable amount of variation in the energy efficiency (SEC), we consider that our hypothesis of these four factors influencing SEC is acceptable. Then, we assess the ability of the individual factors in explaining variation in energy efficiency through their standardized beta coefficients in the multiple regression models.

Measurement and Scaling of Variables

We identified around 15 variables and classified them under four categories. Further, three levels are created for each variable, considering their 'central tendency' and 'dispersion' within the cluster based on the empirical data. In other words, variable values are derived on a scale of 1 to 3. Level 3 (with a score of 3) indicates the most favorable situation for energy efficiency and is represented by group 3. Similarly, level 1 is the least preferred state (with a score of 1) and comes under group 1. Level 2 is the intermediate level indicated by group 2. Then, each of the sampled SSI firms is classified appropriately in any of these three groups under every variable. By expressing all the variables in a common scale of 1 to 3, an equal weightage is assumed for each of the variables within a factor. However, a variable gets included in the respective factor group, only if it shows significant correlation with energy efficiency—otherwise it is omitted. As a result, there is no uniformity among the four factors, in terms of the number of variables used to arrive at their factor scores.

The grouping criteria for variables in the iron foundry cluster are presented in Table 5.2. In the TF category, the 'quality of energy' is based on the price of coke, as it accounted for about 80 per cent of energy use in the cluster. Moreover, different grades of cokes are used in the foundries of this cluster, which can be better captured by its cost. Since in the Electric Induction Furnace (EIF), the heat loss is minimum compared to Cupola, they represent a better process with higher energy efficiency. The 'rejection rate' in the EF category refers to the scrap/rejected castings due to defects, such as blow/pin holes, sand/slag inclusions, shrinkage cavities, sand fusions, shifting of parting lines, irregular surfaces, and so forth. In many such cases, the defective castings may have to be scrapped and re-melted representing wastage of all the inputs used in the course of production, thus suggestive of the level of 'resource use efficiency'. Under the HRF, it is believed that a professionally qualified owner is relatively in an advantageous position in terms of understanding and implementing better tools and techniques for energy efficiency improvements. Also, those who have actual practical work experience in the similar industry

Table 5.2 Variable Grouping for Obtaining Factor Scores in the Iron Foundry Cluster

Factor	Variable	Group 3	Group 2	Group 1
Technical Factor (TF)	Age of plant and machinery	Up to 10 years	Between 10–20 years	Above 20 years
	Quality of energy (Proxy: Cost of energy per tons of coke)	Above Rs 20,000	Between Rs 17,500–20,000	Below Rs 17,500
	Process specific variable (Based on metal melting furnace)	Firms using only EIF	Firms using both EIF and Cupola	Firms using only Cupola
Economic Factor (EF)	Plant capacity utilization	Above 70%	Between 50–70%	Below 50%
	Resource use efficiency (Proxy: Rejection rate)	Below 5%	Between 5–10%	Above 10%
	Annual production volume of casting	Above 500 tons	Between 250–500 tons	Below 250 tons
Human Resource Factor (HRF)	Owner/Supervisor qualifications	Professional/Master's degree	College education	School education
	Business experience of the owner	Previous work experience	Family occupation	No previous experience
	Labour skill level (Skilled/Unskilled)	Above 1.50	Between 0.75–1.50	Below 0.75
Organizational and Behavioural Factor (OBF)	Work practices, Layout and House-keeping	Very Good	Good	Average
	Interaction level of the organization	High	Medium	Low
	Importance attached to energy aspects	Very important	Important	Moderately important

Source: Grouping based on empirical data.

before starting their own SSI firms, are likely to have an edge over the others on all aspects of production including efficient energy use. Deciding the skill level of labour force objectively in the SSIs is a difficult task. This prompted us to adopt skilled to unskilled labour ratio as its measure. We obtained information from the owners regarding the number of employees performing relatively skilled functions along with those who perform unskilled activities to arrive at this ratio.

The variables under OBF are qualitative and hence complex to assess. During the course of the field study, we noticed that the general features of the SSI firms were related to: overall environment in and around the firm, the factory layout, the building design features, ventilation, lighting, house-keeping, status of plant and machinery, maintenance of tools and equipments, overall appearance, and so forth. Then, based on these aspects, the firms are accordingly graded as very good, good, and average. As far as the interaction level is concerned, our questionnaire solicited information about both formal and informal interactions of SSI firms. Interactions with local industry associations, professional colleges, research institutions, participation in seminars, conferences, exhibitions, and so forth, are obtained. Additionally, data pertaining to the training of workers, discussion with professionals, consultants, suppliers, customers, and so forth, are also gathered. Subsequently, firms indulging in more formal interactions are grouped under high, more informally interacting under medium and the less interactive ones under low interaction group. The questionnaire directly asked the SSI entrepreneurs to indicate the importance they attach to energy aspects in the day-to-day functioning of their firm, on a 3 point scale marked with 'Moderately important', 'Important', and 'Very important' on it.

The variable classification in the textile dyeing cluster is provided in Table 5.3. In the TF category, the 'quality of energy' is not a relevant variable because there was no appreciable variation in the prices of firewood, which is the main energy carrier in the cluster. Nonetheless, it was found that two process-related variables merited inclusion in this factor category.

The textile industry is one of the largest industrial users of process water. As the 'quantity of water used' indirectly affects the total steam required for raising the temperature of the 'liquor' required in dyeing, it has a bearing on the energy efficiency too. Similarly, the Open Winch based dyeing process requires relatively higher energy than the Soft Flow dyeing. Hence, we have included both these variables under TF to capture

Table 5.3 Variable Grouping for Obtaining Factor Scores in the Textile-dyeing Cluster

Factor	Variable	Group 3	Group 2	Group 1
Technical Factor (TF)	Age of plant and machinery	Up to 10 years	Between 10–20 years	Above 20 years
	Process specific variable (based on the water used per case)	Below 7,500 litres	Between 7,500–10,000 litres	Above 10,000 litres
	Manufacturing Process	Firms using only SFM	Firms using both SFM and Winches	Firms using only Winches
Economic Factor (EF)	Plant capacity utilization	Above 80%	Between 70–80%	Below 70%
	Resource use efficiency (Proxy: Rework rate)	Below 5%	Between 5–10%	Above 10%
	Annual production volume of casting	Above 9,000 cases	Between 4,500–9,000 cases	Below 4,500 cases
Human Resource Factor (HRF)	Owner/Supervisor qualifications	Professional/Master's degree	College education	School education
	Business experience of the owner	Previous work experience (>10 years)	Family business/ Prev. experience (<10 years)	No previous experience
	Labour skill level (Skilled/Unskilled)	Above 1.50	Between 0.75–1.50	Below 0.75
Organizational and Behavioural Factor (OBF)	Work practices, Layout and House-keeping	Very Good	Good	Average
	Interaction level of the organization	High	Medium	Low
	Importance Attached to Energy Aspects	Very important	Important	Moderately important

Source: Grouping based on empirical data.

differences in SSIs within the cluster on these two counts. There is no appreciable difference in variable grouping criteria under EF and OBF compared to the iron foundry cluster. However, in the HRF category, it is found that an overwhelming majority of the entrepreneurs had 'previous work experience'. There were only a few owners who are either new or running their family business. In view of this, we slightly changed the grouping criterion as given in Table 5.3.

Results of Multiple Regression in the Two SSI Clusters

Following the grouping criteria in the two clusters, values are assigned on a scale of 1 to 3 under each variable, for all the sampled SSI firms. Then, correlation analysis is performed between each of the variables and energy efficiency (SEC) to ascertain their usefulness in explaining the variation in SEC. Eventually, only those variables which have a significant correlation with energy efficiency (SEC) are included in a particular factor group. Then, the cumulative variable scores are obtained to arrive at the respective factor scores to be used in the multiple regression models. As already discussed in the beginning, we are attempting to explain the variation of energy efficiency (SEC) within a cluster by a set of four factors. Expressed in a more formal way, we are testing the following hypothesis:

Null hypothesis H_0:   There is no relationship between energy efficiency (SEC) and the considered set of four factors in the cluster (i.e.: $b_1 = b_2 = b_3 = b_4 = 0$).

Alternative hypothesis H_1:   There is a linear relationship between the considered set of four factors and energy efficiency (SEC) in the cluster (i.e.: $b_1, b_2, b_3, b_4 \neq 0$).

Iron Foundry Cluster

In the foundry cluster, while TF, EF, and HRF contained two variables each, the OBF involved all the three variables based on the preliminary correlation analysis between each variable and the SEC. The TF comprised 'age of plant and machinery' and 'energy cost' (proxy for quality of energy). The process variable represented by 'metal melting method' did not prove to be statistically significant in explaining the variation in SEC. In the EF category, 'production volume' turned out to be insignificant while 'plant capacity utilization' and 'resource use efficiency' were found significant. In HRF, the variables 'labour skill level' and 'owner/supervisor education' are found to be significant while 'business experience of the owner' did not merit inclusion. This perhaps indicates the relatively higher technology and knowledge requirement of iron foundry. But, the insignificant effect of 'owner experience' on energy efficiency may be attributed to the probable substitution of qualified managers/supervisors in firms with less experienced ownership. Under OBF, all the variables are found to contribute towards explaining the variation of energy efficiency. Hence, TF, EF and HRF scores ranged from 2 to 6, and OBF scores from 3 to 9 in the regression analysis.

The multiple regression result for the iron foundry cluster is exhibited in Table 5.4. The initial model with all the four factors included, had a percentage variance (R^2) of about 63 per cent and all the coefficients of independent variables were different from zero, disapproving the null hypothesis. However, the coefficients of OBF and TF were not significant enough to be included in the final analysis. The final model consists of HRF and EF with significant beta coefficients as given in Table 5.4. The adjusted R^2 of about 64 per cent with statistically significant 'F' is an indication of rejection of the null hypothesis. Two of the hypothesized factors, if not all, possess a linear relationship with energy efficiency (SEC)

Table 5.4   Multiple Regression Results in the Iron Foundry Cluster [Dependent Variable: Energy Efficiency (SEC)]

TF	EF	HRF	OBF	Constant	Adj. R^2	F	N
–	–0.392	–0.427	–	9.327	0.640	37.488**	42
	(–2.619)*	(–2.717)*		(22.331)**			
	[–0.419]	[–0.434]					

Source: Output of regression analysis using SPSS.

Notes: Entries within the parentheses and square brackets indicate the 't' value and 'standardized beta coefficient', respectively.

   ** and * indicate significance at the 0.00 and 0.01 level, respectively.

in the iron foundry cluster. Negative sign of the factors indicate their positive association with energy efficiency (as SEC is a measure of inverse of energy efficiency). The relevant assumptions of regression are corroborated by carrying out appropriate statistical tests.

Regarding the relative impact of EF and HRF on energy efficiency, there is nothing much to choose between the two factors (based on the standardized beta coefficients). Human resource factor obtaining marginally higher coefficient may indicate the relatively higher technical knowledge requirement in this industry. But it is important to note that EF in the form of capacity utilization and resource use efficiency are also important for achieving energy efficiency in this industry. Though TF and OBF also have some influence on energy efficiency, their effect was not found as statistically significant.

Textile-dyeing Cluster

After carrying out the correlation analysis between SEC and each of the variables, it was found that while TF and EF consisted of one variable each, OBF had two variables and HRF covered all the three variables. In the TF category, except 'quantity of water used' the other two variables 'age of plant and machinery' and 'manufacturing process' did not find any statistical significance in explaining the variation of SEC. This is likely to be due to the direct association of water consumption and energy used (in the form of steam) to raise its temperature. Again, in the EF category, only 'plant capacity utilization' proved to be significant while 'production volume' and 'resource use efficiency' turned out to be insignificant. In this cluster, the proxy for 'resource use efficiency' largely refers to rework percentage rather than complete rejection.

Thus, although some amount of extra resources is spent for correcting the defects, yet it is not the extent of completely rejecting the entire product as in iron foundries. In HRF, all the variables are found to contribute in explaining the variation of energy efficiency. Under OBF, the variables 'importance attached to energy' and 'work practices, layout and house keeping' are found to contribute towards explaining the variation of energy efficiency. But, the 'interaction level' of the organization did not prove statistically significant. This is perhaps due to better interaction level prevailing in almost all the units of the cluster. Thus any exclusive energy benefit may not be attributable to the level of interaction in this cluster.

In the end, TF and EF scores ranged from 1 to 3, OBF scores varied from 2 to 6 and HRF attained the scores from 3 to 9 in the regression analysis.

The multiple regression result for the textile dyeing cluster is exhibited in Table 5.5. Seven of the total 41 SSI firms surveyed, adopted the 'cold process' in dyeing, with radically different SEC (Specific Energy Consumption) from the remaining firms and hence are excluded from this analysis. The preliminary model with all the four factors included, had an R^2 of about 72 per cent and all the coefficients of independent variables were different from zero, suggesting the rejection of the null hypothesis. However, the coefficient of OBF was not significant enough to be included in the further analysis. The final model encompasses HRF, EF, and TF with significant beta coefficients. The adjusted R^2 of about 72 per cent along with the statistically significant 'F' value is a pointer to the approval of the alternative hypothesis that these three factors, if not OBF, possess a linear relationship with energy efficiency (SEC) in the textile dyeing cluster. The pertinent assumptions of regression analysis are authenticated by appropriate statistical tests.

Table 5.5   Multiple Regression Results in the Textile-dyeing Cluster [Dependent Variable: Energy Efficiency (SEC)]

TF	EF	HRF	OBF	Constant	Adj. R^2	F	N
−3.202	−5.686	−5.322	−	94.092	0.725	29.964***	34
(−1.961)*	(−2.997)**	(−5.151)***		(15.695)***			
[−0.190]	[−0.321]	[−0.568]					

Source: Output of regression analysis using SPSS.

Notes: Entries within the parentheses and square brackets indicate the 't' value and 'standardized beta coefficient', respectively.

***, ** and * indicate significance at 0.00, 0.01 and 0.05 levels, respectively.

Among the three final factors included in the regression, HRF is well ahead of the other two factors suggesting its highest influence on energy efficiency variation in the cluster (based on the standardized beta coefficients). This cluster demands higher professional knowledge, both technological and managerial which is reflected in the larger coefficient of HRF. But it is vital that EF continues to be important for achieving energy efficiency with a minor role for TF as well. Again, the influence of OBF on energy efficiency is found statistically insignificant even in this cluster.

Identifying Key Variables Influencing Energy Efficiency

So far, we have analyzed energy efficiency of the clusters considering four different factors. As a step further, we shall now focus on the variables which are used in building up these factor scores to find their individual effect on energy efficiency. Apart from this, there is also a possibility of variables exhibiting some interactions among themselves. Interactions indicate the extent to which the effect of one variable differs according to the levels of another variable. Since the variables are mostly qualitative and they may also have interaction effects, it is felt that the Analysis of Variance (ANOVA) models are better suited for the purpose. Thus, ANOVA is carried out in order to determine the important variables within a cluster and their interaction effects, if any, in explaining the variation in energy efficiency.

Univariate Analysis of Variance

Analysis of variance models are versatile statistical tools for studying the relation between a dependent variable and one or more independent variables. They neither require making assumptions about the nature of the statistical relation nor the independent variables to be quantitative. There are three regression-based least square methods for analyzing experimental or observational data (Overall and Klett, 1972). Method 1, called 'complete linear model analysis', is simply a conventional least squares multiple-regression solution in which each effect, whether it is the main effect or interaction, is adjusted for relationship to all other effects in the model. Method 2, termed 'experimental design analysis' takes into account the experimental-design hierarchy of main effects and interactions, adjusting each effect for all others at an equal or lower level and ignoring higher order effects. Method 3, named 'sequential sums of square' involves an initial ordering of the effects and then estimating each effect adjusted for those preceding it in the ordering and ignoring those following it. Method 3 can be used if a logical *a priori* ordering exists among the hypotheses to be tested. For example, if certain classification variables have a logical priority in a theoretical or causal sense, their main effects can be tested, disregarding secondary factors and then the effects of secondary factors tested after adjusting for the primary factors (Overall and Klett, 1972).

In the present case, the Method 3 has been used for the analysis of variance because of the following reasons. It is possible to arrive at an *a priori* ordering of variables influencing energy efficiency levels based on the relative importance. The relative importance of individual variables is assessed through their beta coefficients in a preliminary multiple regression analysis. The intention is to test, first, the effect of variable which is expected to be strongest in influencing energy efficiency and subsequently, the weaker effects to determine whether they add anything to the efficiency. Further, the design developed in this study is likely to be an unbalanced one. In other words, the variables in the design are likely to have an unequal number of observations in each of the three levels. As the variable levels are decided on a logical basis and the number of observations under each variable level is derived from the field survey data, it is difficult to obtain an equal number of SSI firms in each level of a variable. Additionally, Method 3 can also be used with less concern over dependencies among the classification variables (Overall and Klett, 1972). The General Linear Model (GLM) univariate procedure (Type I) of the Statistical Package for Social Sciences (SPSS) is used in carrying out the ANOVA analysis.

The ANOVA Model

The familiar ANOVA model for the two-way case (Overall and Klett, 1972) with interaction is presented here for simplification. Let A and B be the two variables under study. Then the model is given by:

$$X = \mu + \alpha_i + \beta_j + \alpha\beta_{ij} + \varepsilon_{ijk} \qquad (4)$$

where

X = dependent variable

μ = grand mean

α_i = the main effect of variable A at the ith level (deviation of row means about the grand mean)

β_j = the main effect of variable B at the jth level (deviation of column means about the grand mean)

$\alpha\beta_{ij}$ = the interaction effect when variable A is at the ith level and variable B is at the jth level (deviations of the cell means about row and column effects)

ε_{ijk} = Random error: $n(0, \sigma^2)$ and independent

$\quad$ i = 1, ..., a

$\quad$ j = 1, ..., b

$\quad$ k = 1, ..., n

Restrictions; $\Sigma\alpha_i = \Sigma\beta_j = \sum_i\alpha\beta_{ij} = \sum_j\alpha\beta_{ij} = 0_{ij}$

Results of the ANOVA Analysis in the Two SSI Clusters

The results of the ANOVA analysis to identify the key variables in the SSI clusters are discussed below.

Iron Foundry Cluster

Initially, in an effort to ascertain the key variables influencing energy efficiency, we carried out a multiple regression with the nine variables which were used for building the four groups of factors in this cluster. However, the regression output revealed only three significant variables in explaining the variation in energy efficiency levels, such as: labour skill level, capacity utilization and resource use efficiency, with a decreasing order of priority. This preliminary ordering is based on the beta coefficients of these variables in the regression equation. Thus, the ANOVA model included only these three variables with potential interaction effects to explain variation in SEC. All the variables had three levels based on the grouping criteria given in Table 5.2. The three variables considered in the analysis with initial ordering, type of classifications made and number of SSI firms coming under each level of the variables are provided in Table 5.6.

The result of the ANOVA analysis is presented in Table 5.7, which mainly contains the information on the total sum of squares (total variance in the dependent variable), sum of squares accounted by the main effects of considered variables, unaccounted variance (error term) and percentage variance (R Square) explained by the model. Only the variables and interactions with significant effects (at least at the 10 per cent level) are shown in the table. The model has a moderate ability to explain the variation in energy efficiency considering its adjusted R^2 of 0.538. In this cluster most of the SSI firms used the conventional Cupola furnace

Table 5.6   Variables for ANOVA in the Iron Foundry Cluster

Variables	Levels	Classes	No. of SSI firms in the class interval
Labour Skill Level	Low	1.00	17
	Medium	2.00	12
	High	3.00	13
Capacity Utilization	Low	1.00	09
	Medium	2.00	19
	High	3.00	14
Resource Use Efficiency	Low	1.00	10
	Medium	2.00	21
	High	3.00	11

Source: Empirical data analysis.

Table 5.7   Univariate ANOVA Results in the Iron Foundry Cluster
[Dependent Variable: Energy Efficiency (SEC)]

Sources of variation	Sum of squares	Degrees of freedom	Mean sum of squares	F	Significance of 'F'
Labour Skill Level	31.489	2	15.745	23.003	0.000
Capacity Utilization	8.465	2	4.233	6.184	0.006
Model Sum of Squares	42.900	15	2.860	4.178	0.001
Sum of Squares due to Error	17.796	26	0.684		
Total Sum of Squares	60.696	41			
R Square	0.707				
Adjusted R Square	0.538				

Source: Output of ANOVA analysis using SPSS.

with coke for metal melting and there was not much of a difference in terms of attitude towards energy efficiency or knowledge level of owners/supervisors, and so forth. Further, the ANOVA model comprising only two significant variables also contributed towards achieving a modest value of R^2. Out of the three considered variables, the effect of 'resource use efficiency' turned out to be insignificant in explaining the variation in SEC among the SSI firms, after accounting for the variation accounted by 'labour skill' and 'capacity utilization'. However, 'labour skill level' accounts for a considerable amount of variation in SEC, and 'capacity utilization' also significantly affects SEC even after adjusting for the variations caused in the former. But, none of the interactions among variables turned out to be significant. Although it is inappropriate to read too much from the ANOVA results in view of the large amount of unexplained variations by the model, it appears that the 'labour skill level' and 'capacity utilization' are important variables which need to be focussed upon for improving the energy efficiency in this cluster. The reason behind 'labour skill level' playing a significant role may be attributed to the fact that mould preparation, metal pouring, and post-pouring operations in this cluster require relatively higher labour skill and ultimately affect SEC. Similarly, higher 'capacity utilization' means, among others, more frequent firing of the furnace, minimizing the initial heat loss to the furnace walls, reduced preheating of ladles, and so forth.

Textile Dyeing Cluster

To recognize the key variables causing variation in energy efficiency, we carried out a preliminary multiple regression with seven variables which were used for building four groups of factors in this cluster. The regression output projected three variables: labour skill level, business experience of the owner, and plant capacity utilization as significant variables in that order. Again, the *a priori* ordering is based on the beta coefficients of these variables in the regression equation. Hence, the ANOVA model involved these three variables along with possible interaction effects to explain variation in SEC. Each variable has three levels based on the grouping criteria given in Table 5.3. The three variables considered in the analysis with initial ordering, type of classifications and number of SSI firms included under each level of the variables is given in Table 5.8.

Table 5.8   Variables for ANOVA in the Textile-dyeing Cluster

Variables	Levels	Classes	No. of SSI firms in the class interval
Labour Skill Level	Low	1.00	15
	Medium	2.00	9
	High	3.00	10
Business Experience of the Owner	Low	1.00	5
	Medium	2.00	13
	High	3.00	16
Plant Capacity Utilization	Low	1.00	6
	Medium	2.00	9
	High	3.00	19

Source: Empirical data analysis.

The result of the ANOVA analysis in this cluster containing similar details as in the previous ANOVA table is presented in Table 5.9. The model has an adjusted R^2 of 0.715, thus indicating its effective ability to explain the variation in SEC. All the three variables considered in the analysis proved to be significant, though no significant interaction is observed among them. As in the iron foundry clusters, 'labour skill level' is again found to account for maximum variation in SEC among the textile dyeing firms in the cluster. Unlike in the previous two clusters, the 'business experience of the owners' is found to explain the substantial amount of variation in SEC, even after adjusting for the variations accounted by the 'labour skill'. Further, the 'plant capacity utilization' also explains a significant amount of variation in energy efficiency after allowing for the other two preceding variables.

Table 5.9   Univariate ANOVA Results in the Textile-dyeing Cluster [Dependent Variable: Energy Efficiency (SEC)]

Sources of variation	Sum of squares	Degrees of freedom	Mean sum of squares	F	Significance of 'F'
Labour Skill Level	2577.096	2	1288.548	23.659	0.000
Business Experience of the Owner	1505.839	2	752.919	13.825	0.000
Plant Capacity Utilization	641.754	2	320.877	5.892	0.011
Model Sum of Squares	5374.817	16	335.926	6.168	0.000
Sum of Squares due to Error	925.861	17	54.462		
Total Sum of Squares	6300.677	33			
R Square	0.853				
Adjusted R Square	0.715				

Source: Output of ANOVA analysis using SPSS.

Labour skill is important because energy-related tasks like maintaining liquor bath temperature, operation and maintenance of steam boilers, and so forth, require technical skill. The textile dyeing cluster has more technology content apart from higher capital requirement. This means that in this cluster, the owners have a relatively superior role to play in various aspects of running their business, including achieving energy efficiency. This is perhaps reflected by the variable 'business experience of the owners', which turned out to affect the energy efficiency level significantly. The SSI firms managed by owners with higher business experience have shown better energy efficiency in this cluster. Higher capacity utilization helps in better application of steam generated in the boilers (most energy consuming activity) for dyeing in the winches/soft flow machines, as it cannot be stored for a long time.

Summary and Conclusion

In the beginning of this paper, a hypothetical framework of four non-technology factors influencing energy efficiency was proposed. This included Technical Factor (TF), Economic Factor (EF), Human Resource Factor (HRF), and Organizational and Behaviour Factor (OBF) apart from the identification of three vital variables under each factor. The empirical data was used to derive the cumulative factor scores through the respective variable values. The hypotheses of these factors influencing energy efficiency levels in the clusters are tested by separate multiple regression models. While HRF and EF emerged significant in the iron foundry cluster, TF was also found significant in addition to HRF and EF in the textile dyeing cluster for explaining the variation in energy efficiency. Then we focussed on the variables used in building-up the factor scores in an attempt to identify key variables and their possible interactions in energy efficiency improvement. We performed univariate ANOVA in both the clusters in order to accomplish this goal. In the iron foundry cluster, only two variables, such as, 'labour skill level' and 'capacity utilization' emerged important without any significant interaction term. Similarly, in the textile dyeing cluster, three variables, such as, 'labour skill level', 'owners' business experience', and 'capacity utilization' were considered as statistically significant with no interaction term meriting attention.

Thus, the empirical data analyses establishes that 'technology' is not the only concern, but other factors related to human resource, economic, organizational and behavioural aspects of the SSI firms are also vital in energy efficiency improvement. Further, the regression results at the factor level are complemented by ANOVA results involving variables. The fact that HRF proved to be the most significant factor influencing the energy efficiency level in both the clusters is of particular relevance. This emphasizes the need to involve non-technology factors in the prevailing technology-centred energy-efficiency improvement initiatives in this sector for discernible improvements in the years to come.

It is widely believed that entrepreneurs are the backbone of small industries, considering the role played by them in the survival and growth of these enterprises. Being major stakeholders of SSIs, the success or failure of these firms largely pivots around the entrepreneurs. Given this, the human resource characteristics of SSIs in terms of entrepreneurs' education, business experience, and the skill level of employed labour force assume significance. The improvement in the quality of human resource needs to involve all of them. Firms with more skilled labour force and professionally qualified owners with practical work experience have achieved better energy efficiency. Thus, enhancing the quality of human resource in SSIs by imparting specialized and periodic training to workers to improve their skill set should be emphasized. Additionally, advanced managerial and technical training for the entrepreneurs to tackle complex issues like technology, energy efficiency, and environmental pollution, and so forth, is likely to produce desired results in the long run. Thus, 'capacity building amongst entrepreneurs as well as workers', as spelt out in the new SSI policy, needs to be considered on a priority basis in the years ahead.

References

Abid Hussain. 1997. 'Report of the Expert Committee on Small Enterprises', Ministry of Industry, Government of India, New Delhi.

Annual Survey of Industries (ASI). 2002. *A Database on the Industrial Sector in India: 1973–1974 to 1997–1998'.* Mumbai: EPW Research Foundation.

Bala Subrahmanya, M. H. and P. Balachandra. 2002. 'An Exploratory Study of Environmental Pollution by SSI Sector in Karnataka'. Research Project Report. Mumbai: Indira Gandhi Institute of Development Research.

———. 2003. 'A Study of Energy Consumption Pattern and Potential for Energy Efficiency in Small Industry Clusters of Karnataka', Research Project Report. New Delhi: Central Statistical Organization, Ministry of Statistics and Programme Implementation, Government of India.

Baranzini, A. and B. Giovannini. 1996. 'Institutional and Cultural Aspects of Energy Consumption Modeling', in Swiss National Science Foundation, Zurich, (ed.), *Structural Transformation Process towards Sustainable Development in India and Switzerland—Synthesis and Case Studies,* pp. 53–56. Zurich, Switzerland: INFRAS Publication.

Dasgupta, N. 1999. 'Energy Efficiency and Environmental Improvements in Small-Scale Industries: Present Initiatives in India are Not Working', *Energy Policy,* 27(13): 789–800.

Development Commissioner Small Scale Industries (DCSSI). 2002. *Small Scale Industries in India—An Engine of Growth.* New Delhi: Ministry of Small Scale Industries, Government of India.

International Energy Agency (IEA). 2004. 'Key World Energy Statistics', *Energy Statistics Division of IEA*: 36–39, Paris.

Kathuria, V. and H. Gundimeda. 2002. 'Industrial Pollution Control: Need for Flexibility', in K. S. Parikh and Radhakrishna (eds), *India Development Report 2002*, pp. 140–155. New Delhi: Oxford University Press.

Khan, A. M. 1992. 'Energy Systems: End Uses', *Proceedings of Workshop and Conference on Global Change and Environmental Considerations for Energy System Development.* Bangkok, Thailand: Asian Institute of Technology.

Kothari, C. R. 2001. *Research Methodology: Methods and Techniques.* New Delhi: Wishwa Prakashan.

Laghu Udyog Samachar (LUS). 1997. Journal of Small-scale Industries, Ministry of Small Scale Industries, Government of India, New Delhi.

Ministry of Finance (MoF). 2005. *Economic Survey 2004–2005.* New Delhi: Economic Division, Government of India.

Ministry of Small Scale Industries (MoSSI). 2004. *Annual Report 2003–2004.* New Delhi: Government of India.

Overall, J. E. and C. J. Klett. 1972. *Applied Multi-Variate Analysis.* New York: McGraw-Hill.

Ramachandra, T. V. and D. K. Subramanian. 1993. 'Analysis of Energy Utilization in the Grain Mill Sector in Karanataka', *Energy Policy*, 21(6): 644–655.

Reddy, B. S. and P. Balachandra. 2003. 'Integrated Energy Environment Policy Analysis—A Case Study of India', *Utilities Policy*, 11(2): 59–73.

Ross, M. 1997. 'Energy Efficiency' in A. Bisio and S. Boots (eds), *Encyclopedia of Energy and Environment*, Vol. I: 530–567. New York: John Wiley & Sons Inc.

Small Industry Development Organization (SIDO). 2004. Available online at: http://www. smallindustryindia.com/sido/sido.htm, accessed: November 2004.

The Energy and Resources Institute (TERI). 1998. *Energy Conservation Plan for the SSIs Located in Noida (UP).* Project Report. Submitted to DCSSI (Development Commissioner—Small Scale Industries), Government of India, New Delhi.

———. 1999a. *Action Research Programme in Foundry Sector (TA1).* Project Report Submitted to SDC (Swiss Agency for Development and Corporation), New Delhi.

———. 1999b. *Action Research Project on Brick Kilns.* Project Report No: 98IE41, New Delhi.

United Nations Environment Programme (UNEP). 1998. *Sustainable Business: Economic Development and Environmentally Sound Technologies.* London: Regency Corporation Ltd. Publication.

UNIDO. 1998. *Sustainable Industrial Development.* Vienna: United Nations Industrial Development Organization.

———. 2001. *General Review Study of Small & Medium Enterprise (SME) Clusters in India.* Geneva: United Nations Industrial Development Organization.

University of Kiel (UoK). 1998. *Inter-Disciplinary Analysis of Successful Implementation of Energy Efficiency in the Industrial, Commercial and Service Sector.* Department of Psychology, University of Kiel.

Visvanathan, C. and S. Kumar. 2002. 'Policy Interventions to Promote Energy Efficient and Environmentally Sound Technologies in SMI', Regional Energy Resources Information Center, AIT, Thailand.

Weber, L. 1997. 'Some Reflections on Barriers to the Efficient Use of Energy', *Energy Policy*, 25(10): 833–835.

Effect of Market Turbulence and Market Focus on the Firm's Performance in Small and Medium Scale Manufacturing Firms

6

SANJAY S. GAUR AND HARI VASUDEVAN

The purpose of the study was to ascertain the effect of market turbulence and market focus on the performance of small and medium scale manufacturing firms in India. The study ascertains that firms perform better during the time of market turbulence. The study also shows that the components of market focus like customer orientation and competitor orientation of the firm are not directly related to the firm performance. However, the study found that during the time of high market turbulence, firms with better market focus, that is, which are more customer oriented and competitor oriented perform better.

Economic reforms of the early nineties brought significant changes in the environment in which Indian businesses operate today. The Indian economy is now integrating with the global economy and thus making the business environment more vibrant and competitive. As a result, several developments like emphasis on manufacturing technology, elimination of trade barriers, removal of control on foreign exchange, eradication of license requirements for industries, devaluation of Indian currency, and trade and tax benefits have taken place (Singh, 2003) and are still underway. These reforms have attracted a multitude of multinational firms that offer Indian consumers a variety of products and services. Due to this, Indian firms are compelled to achieve world-class manufacturing capabilities to compete in the market place and the competition is widespread across all segments/sectors of the industry.

Miller and Friesen (1982) have observed that the performance of firms often came in response to the market, competitors or other external environmental influences. Moreover, Lipparni and Sobrero (1994) have concluded that the firms which are customer oriented will survive. The level of environmental turbulence, as a result of the reforms, is of critical importance for survival and continued growth of manufacturing firms, particularly in the small and medium scale manufacturing firms. As the economic reform policies have provided multinational firms with an opportunity to access the Indian market with their wide range of products and services, the Indian firms can no longer afford to serve a fixed set of customers with staple preferences. Miller and Friesen (1982) have observed that more dynamic and hostile the environment, the greater the need for performance. When the competitor's products change rapidly or when the needs of the customer fluctuate, firms need to perform better. For entrepreneurial firms particularly, environmental characteristics like market turbulence are expected to relate to performance. According to Miller and Friesen (1982), entrepreneurial firms are often found in dynamic and hostile environments because their venturesome managers prefer rapidly growing and opportune settings—settings which may have high risks as well as high rewards. Such firms may even be partly responsible for making the environment dynamic by contributing innovative strategies for product performance. John (1998) suggested that small and medium scale manufacturing firms, in particular, need to concentrate on better customer satisfaction for better financial benefits as the environment is more dynamic and hostile in this sector. His study deals with the entrepreneurial orientation and focusses on three dimensions: risk taking, innovation, and proactiveness. The effect of market turbulence influencing the outcome in these types of firms is realistic and probable considering the environment in which they operate.

Also, over the last few decades, marketing academics and practitioners have suggested that a business should adopt market-focussed practices to improve its performance in order to derive advantages in the market place. Writers like Peters and Waterman (1982) have recognized the 'closeness to customers' as an important characteristic of a successful firm. Hooley and Lynch (1985) have also established 'marketing excellence' as an important feature of highly successful firms. In studying the classifications of different firms with diverse strategic orientations, Day and Nedungadi (1994) found that the competitor centred businesses tended to draw a direct comparison with their close competitors on some salient factors, such as cost and price, which is in line with the observation made by Porter (1985). Competitor centred firms focus on beating the competitors by responding quickly to their competitors' move. Thus, they have to change their strategic and tactical manoeuvres as soon as the major competitors act out a new scheme (Oxenfeldt and Moore, 1978). This, in turn, drives the performance required in manufacturing the product and delivering them to the customers.

Day and Wensley (1983) pointed out that beyond customer orientation the explications of the marketing concept did not do enough justice to competitor orientation. As if to remedy the problem, Narver and Slater (1990) added competitor orientation as a behavioural component in addition to customer orientation in their study on market orientation. Competitor orientation requires that the firm closely analyzes and monitors the major competitor's strategic intents and tactical moves associated with their strengths and weaknesses (Aaker, 1988). In fact Narver and Slater (1990) defined the market orientation concept as 'the organization culture that most effectively creates the necessary behaviours for the creation of superior value for buyers and thus continuous superior performance for the business'.

Derozier (2001) has coined the term 'market focus' in lieu of market-orientation in her thesis titled, 'Marketing Creativity in New Product Development: The role of Market Orientation, Technology Orientation and Inter-functional Coordination'. In this work, customer orientation and competitor orientation have been considered as two components of market focus. Therefore, the construct of market focus is similar to the construct of market orientation. Market focus is expected to have an effect on performance because a modification to the marketing mix is required to satisfy the dynamic preferences of a given set of customers (Kohli and Jaworski, 1990). Therefore, managerial perception of an increasingly dynamic market environment could influence Indian firms to emphasize the development of a market focus (Golden et al., 1995). According to Singh (2003), theoretical market-focussed postulates and empirical evidences are in paucity in emerging economies like India. There are especially no studies on the market focus and performance link pertaining to small and medium scale industry in India. We would, therefore, be guided by the literature available on the studies done in the developed countries.

Specifically, this paper fills the gap in the existing literature by exploring the effects of market turbulence on the performance of firms. This study is designed to contribute further to the existing literature in a number of ways: first, it empirically tests the market turbulence and performance link and second, it attempts to examine whether the relationship between the market turbulence and performance varies in case of firms that have high customer orientation and high competitor orientation. Additionally, the study enriches our knowledge of market focus in a developing economy like India, which has been a focal point for scholars and managers alike in the last two decades (Singh, 2003).

This paper first reviews the literature pertaining to market turbulence, market focus and firm performance. Hypotheses were formulated to test the model. The remainder of the paper reports the findings of the empirical investigation on these hypotheses. Finally, it shows the managerial implications of the research findings followed by a discussion on the limitations and summary are presented.

Background to the Study

In a manufacturing firm, a typical product is manufactured mainly by material shaping and/or material removal techniques. Material removal techniques involve wastage of material and material shaping techniques require part-specific tooling, which are expensive and take a long time to develop. These manufacturing activities fulfil the physical needs of end users, as the products provide utility or satisfaction to human/living beings. Manufacturing can thus be defined as the set of activities leading to and including the transformation of materials into physical products needed by end users or intermediaries using productivity enhancing tools, machines and methods (Ravi et al., 2002). In general, the manufacturing processes consume a high amount of various resources: material, energy, and labour. They are economical only when the end requirement is large and this results in better performance of the firm in the market. Therefore, the role of fulfilling the customer's wants and desires and subsequently enlarging the customer base through overall performance has become crucial in such firms.

As explained earlier, reforms have ensured that India has increasingly become a key player in the world economy, as it is one of the most important emerging markets in the world with a tremendous potential for a sustained, high rate of economic growth. The impact of reform on industries, international trade, and financial areas is noticeable. For example, the economic reform policies enticed a number of multinational firms with a wide range of products and services now available to Indian consumers. Since the market focus concept is widely a part of the developed world and largely suited to these societies which are affluent and have a high rate of consumption, it is logical to expect that the arrival of foreign firms in India has influenced Indian managers to adopt foreign business paradigms in order to compete with foreign firms. For instance, innovations were adopted, technologies were upgraded, customer services were increased, and so forth. Such examples can be multiplied. Hence, the market-focussed trend in businesses saw an increase in spending by the customers. As a consequence, these spending activities contributed significantly to higher economic productivity. The good performance and results achieved by many Indian firms have generated a considerable amount of interest of the international business institutions in the Indian economy (Kriplani and Clifford, 2000). India, with a population of over a billion, has a sizeable chunk of qualified entrepreneurs involved in manufacturing activities amidst the unprecedented economic growth. India also has a big market of such high consumers.

Research in market focus has been given a boost in the last two decades as a result of two phenomenal studies by Kohli and Jaworski (1990) and Narver and Slater (1990). Also, for many years, researchers have concluded that a market focussed approach to business will result in better corporate performance (Kotler, 2000). Researchers who have attempted to study the link between market focus and business performance in various firms include Kohli and Jaworski (1990), Narver and Slater (1990), Ruekert (1992), Wong and Saunders (1993), Greenley (1995), Hunt and Morgan (1995), Raju et al. (1995), Pelham and Wilson (1996), Appiah-Adu and Ranchod (1998), Bhuian (1998), Deng and Dart (1999) and Harris and Ogbonna (2001) to name a few. These studies on market focus have indicated that there exists a positive relationship between market focus and performance of firms. In fact, they have concluded that market focus influences performance. Further, a study by Kohli and Jaworski (1993) indicates that a higher degree of market focus actually results in higher overall performance of the firm. A number of measures of the effect of market orientation have been employed in these studies which include rate of interest (ROI), sales profitability, financial profitability, sales volume, sales increase rate, market share, customer orientation rate, product quality, and so forth. The emerging, turbulent Indian economy can provide appropriate grounds to test the impact of market turbulence on performance and also the effect of market focus on the performance of firms.

Also, the impact of economic reforms has ensured that manufacturing firms are required to optimally use their resources to profitably manufacture and market products. For survival and growth, they are required to develop sustainable competitive advantage in complex market conditions. They need to perform better than the competition in those aspects that are important to their potential customers. Today's customers expect a higher level of product and service quality than ever before because they have more choices and possess better knowledge about the product/service options. Miller (1992) has observed that the challenge for any firm in seeking to remain competitive is to determine what its customers want and whether they are satisfied with the firm's products/services. This thinking is in line with marketing philosophy as marketing suggests that the long term purpose of a firm is to satisfy the needs of its customer for the purpose of maximizing corporate profits (Kohli and Jaworski, 1990). For this, firms need to adopt a proactive attitude in pursuing business and also be responsive to customer needs and market changes. Day (1994), in his study, concluded that firms that are better equipped to respond to market requirements and to anticipate changing conditions will enjoy long-run competitive advantage and superior profitability. In this context, it is pertinent to understand that practitioners and academicians have for long agreed with the view of Drucker (1954) that creating a satisfied customer is the only justifiable definition of a business purpose. Further, Kotler (2000) observed that the key to achieving organizational goals is to be more effective and efficient than one's competitors in identifying and satisfying the needs of target markets. Miltenburg (1995: 13–27) has argued that in order to meet the requirements of the modern day, manufacturing managers are required to provide better products and a wider choice, a lower cost and at a faster rate.

Market Turbulence

In a highly competitive market, a firm needs to be competitor oriented as well to identify the competitors' strengths and weaknesses, develop competitive advantages and anticipate the competitors' reactions. Consequently, the required level of competitor orientation of a firm must be closely linked with the competitive level of the markets in which the firms operate (Gatignon and Robertsen 1991; Kohli and Jaworski 1990). In particular, in a turbulent and competitively intense market, the management must pay greater attention to costs partly because of the greater pressure on prices (Porter 1980).

One of the features of economies, particularly of globalizing economies, is increased market turbulence caused by the arrival of multinational firms that provide customers with a range of products and services. Therefore, under the climate of market turbulence and competition, a firm must identify the customers' changing needs and preferences and respond accordingly (Steel and Webster, 1992). Competition leads to a hostile environment, which is characterized by competitors who attack each other aggressively on numerous dimensions, for example, pricing, promotions, distribution and product development (Golden et al., 1995). Further, the ever-changing economic conditions have provided suppliers and distributors with opportunities to outsource resources. This gives rise to even more intense competition in the market, because now a business pays close attention to the competitors' costs and strategies and is aware of their competitive moves. This agility leads to acquiring a competitive advantage by developing an appropriate strategy (Kotler, 1987). On the contrary, a business with a monopoly in the market may perform well, irrespective of changes instituted to satisfy customer preferences (Houston, 1986). The implication is that the benefits offered by a market focus should be greater for firms operating in a highly competitive sector than for their counterparts in less competitive sectors.

Market Focus

As explained earlier, going by the definition of Narver and Slater (1990), market focus can be defined as 'the organization culture that most effectively creates the necessary behaviours for the creation of superior value for buyers and thus continuous superior performance for the business'. The following sections give a brief description of customer orientation and competitor orientation.

Customer Orientation

Customer orientation has a prominent stature in literature. The reason for this may be related to the marketing concept which places top priority on satisfying customer needs and the marketing concept is the foundation of market focus (Kohli and Jaworski, 1990). Customer orientation dictates that firms must be centred around consumers. Thus, market focussed firms must go beyond merely discovering and meeting expectations. Customer orientation requires that market focussed firms have an extraordinary calibre to glean new insights into consumers' evolving needs and satisfy their current and latent needs.

More importantly, a customer oriented firm is likely to develop sustainable competitive advantage from an in-depth understanding of the key elements along the buyers' value chain and their dynamics over time (Day and Wensley, 1988), which enables the firm to create and deliver superior customer value (Aaker, 1989; Slater and Narver, 1994). Addressing customer needs and sustaining them can only be achieved through better performances in the manufacturing of the product.

Competitor Orientation

Competitor-centred firms focus on beating the competitors by responding quickly to competitors' move. Thus, they have to change their strategic and tactical manoeuvres as soon as the major competitors act out a new scheme (Oxenfeldt and Moore, 1978). This in turn drives the performance required in the manufacturing the product and delivering them to customers. Competitor orientation requires that the firm closely analyzes and monitors the major competitor's strategic intents and tactical moves associated with their strengths and weaknesses (Aaker, 1988).

Conceptualization and Hypotheses

Today, the multinational firms' entry everywhere with their wide range of products and services implies that the Indian firms can no longer afford to serve a fixed set of customers with stable preferences. Environmental characteristics like market turbulence ensure that firms need to improve their performance. This is the rate of change in the composition of customers and their preferences. The level of market turbulence is of critical importance to survival and continued growth of firms. A firm that is oriented to the markets is required to satisfy dynamic preferences of a given set of customers (Kohli and Jaworski, 1990). Therefore, managerial perception of an increasingly dynamic market environment could influence firms to emphasize on better performances (Golden et al., 1995).

The ability to adapt and respond to the evolving needs of customers is critical to business success in a constantly changing business environment. In such conditions, company executives may develop activities to identify and fulfill customers' needs and monitor their competitors. It has been found that the perceived market turbulence is positively related to a firm's level of customer orientation and better performance. This is due to the firm's desire to minimize uncertainty, and to emphasize the importance of market segmentation in such markets (Davis et al., 1991). On the contrary, in a stable environment, where customer types and preferences do not change frequently over time, a little adaptation to the marketing mix is required to satisfy customer needs, resulting in a lower degree of market focus while being profitable (Appiah-Adu and Ranchod, 1998).

The level of market turbulence, as a result of reforms, is of critical importance to performance and thereby survival and continued growth of Indian manufacturing firms (Singh, 2003). Market turbulence implies changing strategies in the face of changing customer needs and the extent to which managers are willing to strive for performance in relation to environmental dynamism that is prevailing in the market. Therefore, the first hypothesis to be tested is:

H1a: Firms perform better during the time of market turbulence.

As mentioned earlier, 'Entrepreneurship may be a key orientation among firms, especially small and medium firms, struggling with the forces of globalization. Firms with strong entrepreneurial orientation appear to be more inclined to leverage marketing strategies for entering new product markets and coping with more complex environments'. The small and medium scale manufacturing firms have a typical entrepreneurial orientation. Entrepreneurial orientation is associated with opportunity seeking, risk taking, and decision action catalyzed by a strong leader or an organization possessed of a particular value system (Gary Knight, 2000). Entrepreneurial orientation also connotes autonomy and competitive aggressiveness. 'It is through the entrepreneur's ability to build a varied set of linkages with the external actors, around a nucleus of firm specific competence and skills, that competitive advantage is reached and sustained' (Lipparini and Sobrero, 1994).

The ability to adapt and respond to the evolving needs of customers is critical to business success in a constantly changing business environment in India. In such an environment, business heads of small and medium scale manufacturing firms may develop activities to identify and fulfill customer's needs and monitor their competitors. This is due to the firm's desire to minimize uncertainity and add to emphasize the importance of market focus in such markets (Davis et al., 1991). Otherwise, in a stable environment where customer types and preferences do not change very frequently, a little adaptation to the marketing mix will be sufficient to satisfy customer needs. Therefore, the next hypotheses to be tested are:

H1b: Customer orientation is positively related to firm performance.
H1c: Competitor orientation is positively related to firm performance.

Although it is logical to expect that the economic changes have caused the business environment to be more turbulent in terms of changing preferences of customers, yet it may be noted that increasing and maintaining a magnitude of market orientation is a complex process that requires a considerable expenditure of time and money. Therefore, even if there is a temptation to become market-oriented in the face of market turbulence, managers may like to wait and see if the environmental conditions are sufficiently long-lasting for their businesses to be cost-effective before they can attempt to adjust their level of market focus, given the complexity of achieving the right market focus (Slater and Narver, 1994). Moreover, previous studies have found market focus to be positively related to performance under different level of market turbulence (Appiah-Adu and Ranchod, 1998; Slater and Narver, 1994; Greenley, 1995).

As explained earlier, market focus is a means of developing a competitive advantage because it enables a firm to understand customer needs and accordingly offers products and services that meet those needs. Although market focus is an important means of obtaining competitive advantage, yet there are others like the technological changes in a turbulent market. Firms working with nascent technologies may be able to obtain a competitive advantage via technological innovation, there by diminishing, but not eliminating, the importance of market focus. In contrast, firms working with mature technologies are poorly positioned to use technology to obtain competitive advantage and must rely on market orientation to a great extent. Hence, market focus implies changing strategies in the face of changing customer needs and competitor actions; it leads us to the hypothesis:

H2a: During the time of high market turbulence, firms which are more customer oriented perform better.

H2b: During the time of high market turbulence, firms which are more competitor oriented perform better.

Our conceptual model incorporating the above hypotheses is presented in Figure 6.1.

Figure 6.1 Study Hypotheses

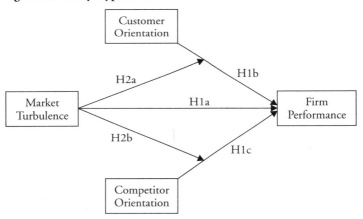

Methodology

Data Collection and Sample

The data for this study was collected by administering questionnaires in person. A face-validity test was initially conducted with a group of business heads of small and medium scale manufacturing firms in Mumbai. A total of 400 respondents were initially contacted on phone requesting the appointment for personal interviews. 290 responses were received from Mumbai and Pune of which 277 were found useful. The respondents were asked to mark their responses on a point Likert-type scale for the variables like market turbulence, market focus, and performance.

Subjective measures of performance are frequently used in marketing research and have been found to be reliable and valid (Singh, 2003). The sample consisted of 100 per cent manufacturers involved in manufacturing industrial products and services. Firms having annual turnover of up to Rs 100 crores were included.

Construction of the Scales

Market Turbulence

This calls for changing strategies and production capabilities to enable firms to stay abreast with changes in the market. It assesses the degree of change in customer's needs, products/services, and so forth. A hostile environment, need for changing strategies and production capabilities to stay abreast with changes in the market in a state of flux are some of the characteristics involved. We have used a 7-point Likert-type scale for measuring the market turbulence (MT) as adopted from Jaworski and Kohli (1993).

Market Focus

For the purpose of this study based on the earlier discussion on the concept of market focus, the market orientation scale developed by Narver and Slater (1990) in the USA was used. This scale has received widespread support in literature for its reliability and validity. The scale consisted of six items for customer orientation (CO) and four items for competitor orientation (CPO) measuring them on a 7-point Likert-type scale. The business head of the small and medium scale manufacturing firms were asked for their perceptions of the two components of market focus, that is, customer orientation and competitor orientation.

Firm Performance

Performance measurement is an important issue in the areas of management science as these measurements provide managers with insight into planning, control and the improvement of firm performance. In this study, we are measuring performance as a subjective measure that best describes a firm's turn over in last three years (TO3YEARS) on a 7-point Likert-type scale ranging from 1 'very substantially increased' to 7 'very substantially decreased'. This scale was adapted from Gilgeous and Gilgeous (2001).

Data Analysis

Analytic Approach

We tested the above hypotheses separately on three models. In Model 1, we only included the direct effect relationships as given by H1a, H1b, and H1c. In Model 2, we incorporated the interaction between customer orientation and market turbulence (H2a) and in Model 3, we incorporated the interaction between competitor orientation and market turbulence. In all three models we included the measurement models and structural model in a single *Structural Equation Modelling* (SEM) framework using maximum likelihood estimation. We included the interaction terms in separate models to reduce the total number of parameters to be estimated. SEM analysis is very sensitive to small samples and the adequate sample size is directly proportional to the number of parameters to be estimated.

As a rule of thumb, the number of cases should be around 10–15 times the number of parameters to be estimated. Incorporating all the paths in one model would have made the testing very unstable.

Our baseline model (Model 1) is shown in Figure 6.2. As we can see market turbulence comprised five factors:

(a) In our kind of business, customers' product preferences change quite a bit over time.
(b) Our customers tend to look for new products all the time.
(c) We are witnessing demand for our products and services from customers who never bought them before.
(d) New customers tend to have product-related needs that are different from those of our existing customers.
(e) We cater to much the same customers that we used to in the past.

Customer orientation consists of:

(a) Our business objectives are driven primarily by customer satisfaction.
(b) We constantly monitor our level of commitment and orientation to serving customer's needs.
(c) Our strategy for competitive advantage is based on our understanding of customer's needs.

Figure 6.2   Model 1

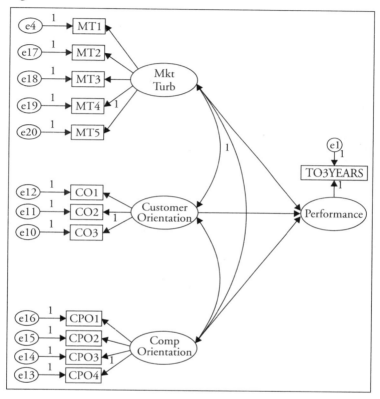

(d) Our business strategies are driven by our beliefs about how we can create greater value for customers.

(e) We measure customer satisfaction systematically and frequently.

Competitor orientation consists of:

(a) Our sales people regularly share information within our business concerning our competitors' strategies.

(b) We rapidly respond to competitive actions that threaten us.

(c) Top management regularly discusses competitors' strengths and strategies.

(d) We target those customers where we have an opportunity for competitive advantage.

For testing the interaction effect between customer orientation and market turbulence, we developed a composite measure of market turbulence by averaging across the five items and multiplied this composite score with each of the three items of customer orientation. We used a composite measure in place of multiplying individual items as that, which would have resulted in 15 items for interaction term, thereby increasing the number of parameters to be estimated substantially. In addition, developing a composite measure of market turbulence is justified due to high validity and reliability of scale as is explained by high model fit of Model 1 (discussed later). This model is shown in Figure 6.3. We tested

Figure 6.3 Model 2

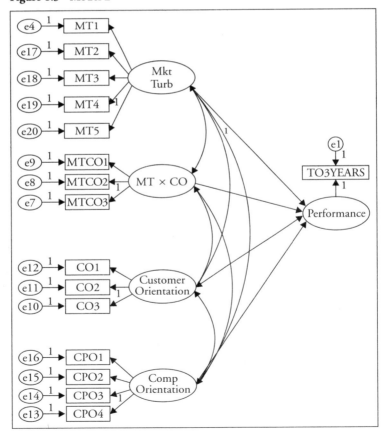

the interaction between market turbulence and competitor orientation in a similar manner as shown in Figure 6.4.

Figure 6.4 Model 3

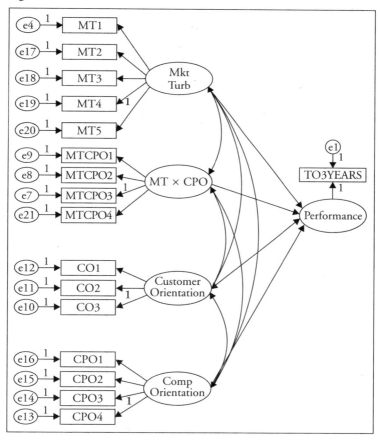

Results and Discussions

The first step in testing an SEM framework is to assess for an overall model fit. Since chi-square test is very sensitive and is not always very reliable, especially in case of assessing the model fit in SEM (Hair et al., 1998), we used a variety of other fit indices such as Root Mean Square Residuals

(RMR), Goodness-of-Fit Index (GFI), Adjusted Goodness-of-Fit Index (AGFI), Tucker-Lewis Index (TLI), Incremental Fit Index (IFI), Comparative Fit Index (CFI), and so forth, following the research standards. These values are reported in Table 6.1 for all the three models. Looking at the fit indices, we can see the model fit is excellent. RMR is low for all the models and all other indices are consistently above 0.90 or 0.95. As per Bentler's (1992) guidelines, this is an excellent fit.

Table 6.1   Model Fit Indices

Model	χ^2 (d.f.)	RMR	GFI	AGFI	NFI	IFI	TLI	CFI
Model 1	89 (60)	0.074	.953	.929	.910	.969	.959	.968
Model 2	148 (95)	0.152	.937	.910	.964	.987	.983	.987
Model 3	182 (110)	0.134	.928	.900	.961	.984	.980	.984

Validity and Reliability of Scales

Convergent validity is established if the overall model has a good fit and all the individual factor loadings are high and significant at 0.01 level (Gefen et al., 2000). We found each of the measurement paths to be highly significant along with an excellent fit for the model. Discriminant validity among the latent variables is shown without question if the inter-correlations are less than 0.60 (Carlson et al., 2000). Table 6.2 lists the inter-correlations between the latent variables for both the models. The highest value is much below the critical value of 0.60, giving robust support to discriminant validity.

Table 6.2   Inter-factor Correlation Coefficients for Base Model (Model 1)

Latent variables		Estimate	S.E.	P
Market Turbulence	<—> Customer Orientation	0.071	0.032	0.029
Market Turbulence	<—> Competitor Orientation	0.263	0.058	<0.001
Customer Orientation	<—> Competitor Orientation	0.197	0.052	<0.001

To establish convergent and discriminant validity conclusively, we conducted two additional analyses on the base model (Model 1). First, a more detailed test was performed using a constrained analysis method (Sharma, 2000), which involves setting the correlation between one pair of variables (for example, customer orientation and competitor orientation) to unity (1.0) and running the model again. A chi-square difference test is used to compare the results from the constrained and original models (Anderson and Gerbing, 1988). Discriminant validity is evidenced if the chi-square difference is significant (supporting the original model). We did this for all the pairs of latent variables for both the models, and found the original unconstrained model to be significantly better than the constrained models. The fit indices for the original model were also better.

Second, following Gefen et al. (2000), we ran alternate models in which we combined two (or more) latent variables into one and then compared the resulting chi-square to that of the original model (with the sub constructs modeled separately). Here again, the original model proved to be a better fit than any of the alternate models, giving conclusive proof of discriminant and convergent validities.

We tested the reliability of the three scales of MT, CO and CPO using the Cronbach alpha coefficient. The value of Cronbach alpha coefficient for MT scale with five items was 0.772. The same for CO scale with three items was 0.615 and for CPO scale with four items was 0.840. The alpha value is less than the cut off of 0.70 for CO scale, but the lower value was accepted since with a less number of items in a scale, it is not uncommon to get low alpha values. The other two scales crossed the cut off criterion.

Hypotheses Testing

We looked at the regression weights for the directional paths. The path estimates along with the corresponding standard error and p values are shown in Table 6.3. In Model 1, we can see that the path from market turbulence (MT) to performance is positive and significant ($\beta = 0.291$, $p = 0.01$). This supports Hypotheses 1a that during the times of market turbulence, firms generally perform better. The other two paths were not significant; therefore H1b and H1c were not supported. Next we look at the coefficient of the interaction term in Model 2. The interaction between MT and customer orientation (CO) was positive and significant ($\beta = 0.029$, $p = 0.05$) giving support to Hypotheses 2a. During the times of market turbulence, firms with higher CO have better financial performance. Finally, we look for the interaction between MT and competitor orientation (CPO) in Model 3. The interaction coefficient is positive and significant ($\beta = 0.039$, $p = 0.05$) giving support to Hypotheses 2b. During the times of market turbulence, firms with higher CPO have better financial performance.

Table 6.3   Path Coefficients for Hypotheses Testing

	Estimate	S.E.	P
Model 1			
Performance ← Mkt. Turb.	0.291**	0.121	0.01
Performance ← Customer Orientation	0.001	0.151	0.99
Performance ← Comp. Orientation	−0.089	0.081	0.27
Model 2			
Performance ← Mkt. Turb.	0.027	0.035	0.44
Performance ← Customer Orientation	0.004	0.151	0.97
Performance ← MT × CO	0.029*	0.015	0.05
Performance ← Comp. Orientation	−0.071	0.078	0.36
Model 3			
Performance ← Mkt. Turb.	−0.028	0.074	0.70
Performance ← Customer Orientation	−0.008	0.154	0.96
Performance ← Comp. Orientation	−0.048	0.074	0.52
Performance ← MT × CPO	0.039*	0.02	0.05

Notes: * Significant at 0.10 level; ** Significant at 0.05 level.

Conclusion

This research finding, based on the sample, suggest:

(a) Firms perform better during the time of market turbulence.
(b) The market focus of a firm is not directly related to firm performance.
(c) During the time of high market turbulence, firms which are more customer oriented and more competitor oriented perform better.

In addition, this research study has contributed to the existing limited scholarly work in several ways: from an empirical point of view, it has established that the scales used (for market turbulence and market focus) in developed countries like the USA was reliable and valid in the context of small and medium scale manufacturing firms in India. Further, given the scarcity of empirical evidence in the Indian industrial literature, the study bridges the gap between the Western and developing economies management literature. Finally, our findings add further to the limited efforts to extend our emerging knowledge of the effect of market turbulence and market focus on the firm's performance to non-Western firms, particularly in the Indian context.

Managerial Implications

There are few implications that emerge from this study. It is evident that firms perform better during market turbulence. Therefore, it is essential that business heads of small and medium scale manufacturing firms understand the nature of such markets to position their firm and take necessary steps for improving performance. It is also important to commit adequate resources for the necessary market focus so as to make the firm perform better. It is important to establish whether the market turbulence conditions are enduring enough for managers to modify the market focus to suit their firms. It may be useful to plan market focus as a long-term strategy of investment, provided managers could overcome the temptation and commercial pressure associated with achieving short-term results.

Limitations

Like any other research, this research study also has its limitations. For example, the respondents were asked to score subjectively on a 7-point Likert-type scale; these types of evaluations are subject to personal bias and judgement errors. However, financial constraint necessitated the use of this methodology. Future research may also include objective data and may collect data from multiple respondents in each firm, which will increase the reliability and validity. The data was collected from firms in Mumbai and Pune only and therefore, it is not conclusive to generalize the research findings in the larger Indian context. Nevertheless, the findings of the study do shed some light on understanding the effect of market turbulence and market focus on the performance of small and medium scale manufacturing firms.

Summary

Given the importance of competitive markets and related activities in a turbulent economy like India, the issue of market turbulence and market focus will continue to attract the attention of practitioners and academics alike. Moreover, understanding the markets within such an economy remains a major challenge. Nonetheless, the study supports that even in turbulent markets, the market focus facilitates better firm performance.

References

Aaker, D. A. 1988. *Strategic Marketing Management*. Second edition. New York: John Wiley and Sons, Inc.

————. 1989. 'Managing Assets and Skills: The Key to Sustainable Competitive Advantage', *California Management Review*, 31(2): 91–106.

Anderson, J. C. and W. D. Gerbing. 1988. 'Structural Equation Modeling in Practice: A Review and Recommended Two-Step Approach', *Psychological Bulletin*, 103(3): 411–423.

Appiah-Adu, K. and A. Ranchod. 1998. 'Market Orientation and Performance in the Biotechnology Industry: An Exploratory Empirical Analysis', *Technology Analysis and Strategic Management*, 10(2): 197–210.

Bentler, P. M. 1992. 'On the Fit of Models to Covariances and Methodology to the Bulletin', *Psychological Bulletin*, 112(3): 400.

Bhuian, S. 1998. 'An Empirical Examination of Market Orientation in Saudi Arabian Manufacturing Firms', *Journal of Business Research*, 43(1): 13–25.

Carlson, D. S., K. Michele and J. W. Larry. 2000, 'Construction and Initial Validation of a Multidimensional Measure of Work-Family Conflict', *Journal of Vocational Behavior*, 56(2): 249–276.

Davis, D., M. Morris and J. Allen. 1991. 'Perceived Environmental Turbulence and Its Effects on Selected Entrepreneurship and Organizational Characteristics in Industrial Firms', *Journal of Academy of Marketing Science*, 19(1): 43–51.

Day, G. S. 1994. 'The Capabilities of Market Driven Organizations', *Journal of Marketing*, 58(4): 37–52.

Day, G. S. and P. Nedungadi. 1994. 'Managerial Representations of Competitive Advantage', *Journal of Operations Management*, 58(April): 31–44.

Day, G. S. and R. Wensley. 1983. 'Marketing Theory with a Strategic Orientation', *Journal of Marketing*, 47(4): 78–89.

————. 1988. 'Assess Advantage: A Framework for Diagnosing Competitive Superiority', *Journal of Marketing*, 52(2): 1–20.

Deng, S. and J. Dart 1999. 'The Market Orientation of Chinese Enterprises During a Time of Transition,' *European Journal of Marketing*, 33(5/6): 631–654.

Derozier, C. 2001. *Marketing Creativity in New Product Development: The Role of Market Orientation, Technology Orientation and Inter-functional Coordination*. Ph.D. thesis. Texas Tech University, Lubbock, Texas.

Drucker, P. 1954. *The Practice of Management*. New York: Harper and Row.

Gary Knight. 2000. 'Entrepreneurship and Marketing Strategy: The SME under Globalisation', *Journal of International Marketing*, 8(2): 120–145.

Gatignon, H. and T. S. Robertson. 1991. 'Innovative Decision Process', in the Thomas S. Robertson and Harold H. Kassarjian, (eds), *Hand book of Consumer Behaviour*, pp. 316–348. Englewood Cliffs, New Jersey: Prentice-Hall.

Gefen, D., D. Straub and M. Boudreau. 2000. 'Structural Equation Modeling and Regression: Guidelines for Research Practice.' *Communications of the Association for Information Systems*, 7(7): 1–78.

Gilgeous, V. and M. Gilgeous. 2001. 'A Survey to Assess the Use of a Framework for Manufacturing Excellence', *Integrated Manufacturing Systems*, 12(1): 48–58.

Golden, P A., P. M. Doney, D. M. Johnson and J. R. Smith. 1995. 'The Dynamics of a Market Orientation in Transition Economies: A Study of Russian firms', *Journal of International Marketing*, 3(2): 29–49.

Greenley, G. 1995a. 'Forms of Market Orientation in UK Companies', *Journal of Management Studies*, 32(1): 47–66.

———. 1995b. 'Market Orientation and Company Performance: Empirical Evidence From UK Companies', *British Journal of Management*, 6(1): 1–13.

Hair, J. F., R. Anderson, L. T. Ronald and C. B. William. 1998. *Multivariate Data Analysis*. Upper Saddle River, New Jersey: Prentice Hall International.

Harris, L. and E. Ogbonna. 2001. 'Strategic Human Resource Management, Market Orientation and Organizational Performance', *Journal of Business Research*, 51(2): 157–166.

Hooley, G. and J. Lynch. 1985. 'Marketing Lessons From the UK's High Flying Firms', *Journal of Marketing Management*, 1(1): 63—74.

Houston, F. S. 1986. 'The Marketing Concept: What it is and what it is not', *Journal of Operations Management*, 50(April): 81–87.

Hunt, S. and R. Morgan. 1995. 'The Comparative Advantage Theory of Competition', *Journal of Marketing*, 59(April): 1–15.

Jaworski, J. and K. Kohli. 1993. 'Market Orientation: Antecedents and Consequences', *Journal of Marketing*, 57(3), July: 53–70.

John, D. 1998. 'Relationship Marketing: Its Key Role in Entrepreneurship', *Journal of Business Venturing*, 9(2): 75–101.

Kohli, A. and B. Jaworski. 1990. 'Marketing Orientation: The Construct, Research Propositions and Managerial Implications', *Journal of Marketing*, 54(April): 1–18.

———. 1993. 'MARKOR: A Measure of Market Orientation', *Journal of Marketing Research*, 30(4): 467–477.

Kotler, P. 1987. *Competitive Advantage*. New York: The Free-Press.

———. 2000. *Marketing Management: Analysis Planning Implementation and Control.* New Jersey: Prentice-Hall.

Kriplani, M. and M. L. Clifford. 2000. 'India Wired', *Business Week*: 82–88. February 21.

Lipparni, A. and M. Sobrero. 1994. 'The Glues and Pieces: Entrepreneurship and Innovation in Small Firm Networks', *Journal of Business Venturing*, 9(2): 125–140.

Miller, D. and P. H. Friesen (1982), 'Innovation in Conservative and Entrepreneurial Firms: Two Models of Strategic Momentum', *Strategic Management Journal*, 3(2):1–25.

Miller, T. 1992. 'A Customer Definition of Quality', *Journal of Business Strategy*, 13(1): 4–7.

Miltenburg, J. 1995. *Manufacturing Strategy: How to Formulate and Implement a Winning Plan*. Portland, Oregon: Productivity Press.

Narver, C. and F. Slater. 1990. 'The Effect of Market Orientation on Business Profitability,' *Journal of Marketing*, 54(4), October: 20–35.

Oxenfeldt, A. R. and William L. Moore. 1978. 'Customer or Competitor: Which Guideline for Marketing?' *Management Review*, (August): 43–48.

Pelham, A. and D. Wilson. 1996. 'A Longitudinal Study of the Impact of Market Structure, Firm Structure, Strategy and Market Orientation Culture on Dimensions of Small-Firm Performance,' *Journal of the Academy of Marketing Science*, 24(1): 27–43.

Peters, T. and R. Waterman. 1982. *In Search of Excellence: Lessons from America's Best Run Companies*. New York: Harper and Row Publishers Inc.

Porter, E. 1985. *Competitive Advantage: Creating and Sustaining Superior Performance.* New York: The Free Press.

Porter, M. E. 1980. *Competitive Strategy.* New York: The Free Press.

Raju, P., S. Lonial and Y. Gupta. 1995. 'Market Orientation and Performance in the Hospital Industry', *Journal of Health Care Marketing*, 15(4): 34–41.

Ravi, B., T. Pushpa, K. T. Ravi, J. Manish, Jalan Manish and G. Rahul. 2002. 'Made in India: The Past, Present and Future of Indian Manufacturing Industry', Mumbai: National Manufacturing Policy Draft, Indian Institute of Technology, Bombay.

Ruekert, R. 1992. 'Developing a Market Orientation: An Organizational Strategy Perspective', *International Journal of Research in Marketing*, 9(4): 225–245.

Sharma, S. 2000. 'Managerial Interpretations and Organizational Context as Predictors of Corporate Choice of Environmental Strategy', *Academy of Management Journal*, 43(4): 681–697.

Singh, S. 2003. 'Effects of Transition Economy on the Market Orientation–Business Performance Link: The Empirical Evidence from Indian Industrial Firms', *Journal of Global Marketing*, 16(4): 73–96.

Slater, S. and J. Narver. 1994. 'Does Competitive Environment Moderate the Market Orientation-Performance Relationship?', *Journal of Marketing*, 58(1): 46–55.

Steel, W. and L. Webster. 1992. 'How Small Enterprises in Ghana Have Responded to Adjustment', *The World Bank Economic Review*, 6(3): 423–438.

Wong, V. and J. Saunders, 1993, 'Business Orientation and Corporate Success', *Journal of Strategic Marketing*, 1(1; March): 20–40.

Student Expectations of Entrepreneurs
A Survey

7

FRANCIS JOSE

B ased on a survey conducted among postgraduate students in Chennai, this paper closely looks at what college students expect from entrepreneurs, in terms of the personality traits they need to possess, and the interrelationships that these characteristics have with the varied demographic profiles of the student community. 128 respondents provided two estimates. (1) about the level of entrepreneurial qualities that entrepreneurs need to posses and (2) rating themselves on these qualities. Nine such qualities were thus evaluated in two contexts. This paper proposes two different methodological treatments for these evaluations. The first one, a surprising insight, is termed 'reverse effect' of evaluation, and is explained theoretically in this paper. Two perceptions of entrepreneurial personal qualities like 'confidence' and 'ruthlessness' are especially investigated as 'reverse-effect' evaluations of qualities to be possessed by entrepreneurs. Tests of difference on the 18 qualities among students in their varied backgrounds reflect sociological trends and mind patterns, which primarily reflect the hidden needs and ambitions that the young educated Indians have about entrepreneurship. The methodological propositions and other insights gathered from the study analysis suggest that entrepreneurial qualities like confidence, enthusiasm, intelligence, honesty and creativity can be inculcated and furthered in the society. These qualities will help governments and social institutions identify and develop specific strategies to enhance the global and societal consciousness of our entrepreneurs. These efforts will make entrepreneurs become more competitive, and should help them to be more useful and productive members of a society on the merit of their qualities.

Objectives and Background

The personal qualities of entrepreneurs are often observable traits reflected in their daily lives and involvement with society, media and work life, apart from the personal dreams and aspirations they have about life. An analysis of such qualities, despite much of the academic history that it already possesses, will always help to enable others to emulate an entrepreneur's success. A regular assessment of these entrepreneurial qualities therefore, is never found unnecessary, as it is something like the benefits derived from curing meat or perfecting an already well-made *sambar* at home and, like wine, it gets better and better over time. Apart from the regular, self-analytical or autobiographical assessments of an entrepreneur's qualities, verifying the same, based on the attitudes of interest groups, is a known route to knowledge building. This paper chooses to highlight the attitudes of one such group in our society, namely the students' group. Therefore, it investigates the current attitudes of selected college going Indian students towards entrepreneurs and entrepreneurial activities, while hoping to understand better the extent of influence that certain key demographic factors have on these attitudes. The following research questions were thus looked into in this paper: What do the Indian youth think about entrepreneurs in general? What is the extent of influence that demographic variables have towards entrepreneurial qualities? Does the young Indian possess enough entrepreneurial potential? What are the types of entrepreneurial environments and the sociocultural moorings of the young collegian, which could help breed entrepreneurs in India?

Qualities of an Entrepreneur

'Qualities' mean the characteristics considered important for entrepreneurship as identified by McClelland (1961) in the forms of risk-taking behaviour, self-confidence, hard-work, goal setting behaviour, accountability and innovativeness. This study makes an assessment of the functions of an entrepreneur, more from the psychological and a sociological outlook, rather than from the economic viewpoint (Panda, 2000). Many other qualities loom into our minds when we try to characterize Indian entrepreneurs. Many of them possess a mix of positive and negative qualities, like being organized, helpful, decisive, assertive, ambitious, corrupt, social-minded, mature, or transformational in their attitudes, leadership and behaviour, while some are a disbanded lot and get noted for their exploitative practices and flattering chicanery. These entrepreneurs have negative qualities as they are always ready to fleece and, given the opportunity, brow-beat their customers to earn the fast buck. Also, they require tough laws to keep them under leash. Of course, there are also the socially conscious, believable and trust-worthy kind!

Many other theoretical expositions of entrepreneurial qualities and related issues exist in literature like the 'High Need for Achievement Level' (McClelland, 1961), creative and innovative responses of entrepreneurs to challenging environments (Rao and Pareek, 1978), among others like risk-taking and possessing various orientations such as goal or productivity, people, skill and managerial orientation and financial power.

Differences in contexts, societies, markets and business conditions require a creative combination of entrepreneurial qualities to best optimize a desirable outcome. These desirable outcomes could often be financial or egotistic satisfactions for the entrepreneur. These satisfactions could also be the result of emotional responses to simply survive the tough times and people. They may involve special skills—both tactical and strategic—to ensure success.

Indian Entrepreneurial Qualities

There is no denying the fact that Indian entrepreneurs are second to none in the world. However it is to be considered as to what is the ideal kind of entrepreneurship which is desirable for the particular socio-political and economic variety we have in India today? No known theory could match the kinds of variation and variety we have in the Indian markets, consumption patterns, languages, religion, castes, and so forth. There are contrasting realities which make the myth co-exist with the reality, like the big divide between the rich and the poor, the urban and the rural. Another such divide could be the presence of abject poverty and also the Rolls Royces and BMWs in the same neigbourhood, all of which pose a 'smart' challenge to the 'smart' entrepreneur in any nation. Who knows, entrepreneurs may bring about social equity too, in the long run!

The entrepreneurial qualities required for the average Indian environment can only be a creative outcome. Whether morality and business can move together is still a debatable issue for the scholars and literature shows different schools of thoughts! This thought, if positioned sensitively against the honest/hard-working entrepreneur, would reveal interesting insights into the moral and personal challenges faced by modern entrepreneurs. There are, of course, many such philosophies which have a bearing on the presence or absence of a characteristic or quality in an entrepreneur. The shaping of such philosophies will be decided by good governance at every level of development, be it in education or in resources utilizations, and so on. It will also have a positive ripple effect on the promotion of entrepreneurial tendencies among the youth in any society.

We need to regularly listen to the youth of a nation to provide the much needed clarity and insights on developing a requirement list for promoting entrepreneurs. India requires a mix of entrepreneurs who would identify and share their inspirational stories much more. This would surely encourage the younger generation to start new businesses and experience the pride of making useful contributions to a society. In the Indian entrepreneurship literature, educational levels, technical qualifications and formal work training do not seem to help the performance levels of Indian entrepreneurs (Tewari et al., 1990). Relevant experience seems to be the key to entrepreneurial success (Bhanushali, 1987). Some approaches in India may prescribe boldness, daring nature, pragmatism and high-need for achievement levels as prerequisites to entrepreneurship (Gaikwad and Tripathy, 1970). These approaches can be considered archaic, given the modern-day metric based, 24 × 7 hours/week, business models of the nouveau riche, particularly in the IT industry, epitomized especially by the BPOs and the call-centre operations which have, of late, set up large number of shops in India.

Also, entrepreneurial functions and related qualities need not always be production-oriented, as suggested by Hoselitz (1952) as his time had not seen the automation levels and six sigma operations of the 21st century corporations. However, the three types of business leadership, that is, merchant moneylender type, managerial type and entrepreneurial type, stated by him still hold good even today.

Mathew Manimala's (2002) seminal contribution related to personal traits of British and Indian entrepreneurs reveals some interesting personal factors like *allergy to ambiguity, optimism, complacency, entrepreneurial disinclination*, dislike for authority, self-made man orientation, risk-taking ability, concern for one's image and barriers of convenience. This is truly a pathbreaking contribution which opens up new areas of research and study related to entrepreneurial qualities. He cites the four italicized factors (in the earlier list) as rated highest by Indian entrepreneurs.

Kalyani and Chandralekha (2002) introduced the concept of the enterprise involvement index, where the development of women entrepreneurs and their enterprises depends upon the degree of involvement in various aspects of managing an enterprise. Again, different dimensions of entrepreneurial qualities are indicated here as motivation to be an entrepreneur, role in setting-up stages of enterprise, role in the management of the unit, role in major decision-making, time spent on unit related work, perceived satisfaction in life, and so forth.

Another dimension, probably not given enough attention to, is in understanding that the stress faced by entrepreneurs affects the whole value chain of business. Some years back, Pareek and Rao (1995) addressed this issue and showed how professional counseling would help entrepreneurs handle this professional hazard. Much work needs to be done on understanding the connection between the entrepreneur's health and his/her quality of contributions made to the business world.

A. Kanungo and Misra (1992) distinguished 'skills' from 'managerial competencies', the latter being the basic components of a manager's resourcefulness. Resourcefulness itself can be a critical quality of an entrepreneur in not only performing leadership roles but is required in order to cope with non-routine, unprogrammable and ill-structured tasks. Four competencies were identified, namely, basic competencies, and affective, intellectual, action-oriented and goal-oriented problem orientation.

A holistic representation of entrepreneurship is required by our societies. Integration and knowledge, technology and the creativity of the human mind could bring out the much-needed answers to solve much of man's pressing problems.

Methodology and Sample Description

A search for an appropriate list of variables to understand entrepreneurial qualities and student evaluations of the same led to a similar study initiated in Australia four years back, called the National Entrepreneurship Attitude Survey by the Commonwealth Department of Industry, Science and Resources, the Department of Education, Training and Youth Affairs. Making some modifications, the present study adopted the study questionnaire used in the Australian one. This was attempted as the survey instrument seemed to cover most of the qualities identified in the entrepreneurship literature and that the study report indicated satisfactory response ratios.

Two hundred questionnaires were distributed in the first week of October 2005, of which, about 154 questionnaires answered by undergraduate (UG) and postgraduate (PG) students were found to be complete and usable. This paper, however, focusses on the 128 samples, that of PG students. They represented Chennai-based arts and science colleges. Eight enumerators (senior M.Phil students, Loyola College) went in pairs to selected colleges in Chennai, with an official letter to the Principal/Head of the Department of the disciplines of Economics or Commerce, seeking permission to administer the questionnaire, while introducing the theme of study to them. As mentioned earlier, the survey instrument was suitably modified to suit Indian conditions and respondents. The pair-wise enumeration process ensured that the data collection process was carried out smoothly. There were 99 variables, mostly ordinal or nominal in nature. Only a few of them are presented in this paper. The statistical analysis was completed using statistical package for the social sciences (SPSS). The various tests employed to test for differences and association included *chi-square* and *tau-B*. These tests are ideally-suited for ordinal/ordinal or nominal/ordinal scale comparisons, as the popular analysis literature prescribes (Bryman and Cramer, 1999).

The chosen sample is restricted to PG students primarily because of their higher maturity levels and the expectation of gathering less biased responses from them. The seriousness in answering the questionnaire was also ensured as most of the questionnaires were administered under the recommendation/supervision of either the Head of the Department or a senior Professor in the college contacted.

Data Collection and Interpretation Approach

Apart from providing their personal profile data, respondents were asked to rate the following nine personal attributes of entrepreneurs (Table 7.1) in two ways:

(a) To evaluate entrepreneurs, by identifying a value from 1 to 10 on how important these characteristics are in helping entrepreneurs to be successful (*Evaluating Entrepreneurs*)

(b) To rate themselves out of 10 on each characteristic (Self-Rating).

Table 7.1 Personal Qualities Expected from Entrepreneurs and Self-rating

Qualities/Characteristics

1. Being good with people
2. Ruthlessness
3. Determination and persistence
4. Confidence
5. Honesty
6. Intelligence
7. Enthusiasm and energy
8. Accepting the possibility of loss in order to have a chance of succeeding
9. Creativity and the ability to be innovative

The objective was to assess the extent to which the respondents themselves possessed these attributes.

To help form a consistent frame of reference to the description of an entrepreneur, the following definition was included in the questionnaire:

An entrepreneur is a person who recognizes opportunities, has ideas and uses them to create or develop a business.

Interpretation of the Scores

Reverse Effect of Expectation Evaluations

The first set of evaluations is really the 'expectations' that the respondent has from entrepreneurs regarding the level of a quality or characteristic in question, which they need to possess in order to make them successful. The expectations scores are usually the expressions of the unreal, or 'expected' or the 'future' zone areas. They are attitudinal in nature. The mean ($\bar{x}$) values identified for each of the nine qualities to be possessed by the entrepreneurs actually refer to only the values they 'need to possess' rather than 'what they possess'. This means that the score values cannot be accepted on their face value, as they do not necessarily represent the real world. Expected values being the expressions of 'needs' are valuable indicators of where they can go to!

The scores provided by the student evaluators are on the ordinal scale of 1 to 10. The value used for interpretation will be the mean value. This mean score is expected to be either an overstated or an understated one, depending on the type of quality which is being evaluated. For example, a quality like honesty, being a time-tested value, can easily be accepted as a positive quality to be possessed by entrepreneurs. The mean value score analyzed will be an expected value and such expected values for positive qualities would usually be evaluated/rated/assigned higher values by the respondents. Such high value identification is natural as it is a positive value and is more desirable to possess.

Earlier, we stated that the positive qualities are rated higher simply because they are positive qualities. This means that they could be rated even higher. The same should be the case for negative qualities. When evaluations are made, they would need to be evaluated lower as they are not the desirable ones to possess. Keeping in mind these assumptions, the following propositions are made regarding the process of making evaluations.

Benefits of Reverse Effect Expectancy Scores

Expectancy scores could be a useful tool to assess the actual/current or real score which is never observed easily. There is also no proof or evidence that direct queries or similar data collection methodology will generate a foolproof and truthful evaluation about the phenomenon/person/thing assessed.

Evaluation score could be an ingenious method to assess the true level of evaluation or attitudinal assessment made about the phenomenon in question. If evaluation scores are expected to be more or less for positive and negative qualities respectively, then realistic assessment of the actual/current level of the presence of the quality or the attribute should be derived by downgrading the expected values based on certain principles and reasoning. It is probably too early for this explanation to explore the methodology of downgrading the reverse effect (RE) expectancy score.

The fact that expectancy scores are higher compared to the actual values (which should be lower or higher—depending on the positive or negative nature of the quality) can be termed as reverse effect phenomena, or expectation score. This paper does not venture further to discuss the modalities of how to correct this possible reverse effect on the expectation scales for now. It would suffice to conclude that in order to enable this analysis to contribute to a better and truthful understanding of the real world, the nine R-effected scores need to be interpreted with care and clarity.

This paper proposes certain assumptions related to how the RE phenomenon should be identified and interpreted keeping in mind the possible validation attempts which could be initiated in related research in the future.

The following are a series of steps which could be initiated in such an evaluation process:

1. First, a mental evaluation of the 'present' level of quality possessed by the entrepreneur about the quality in question, say 'honesty', is made. Such a mental evaluation will be an assessment of the level of 'honesty' that the evaluator believes the entrepreneurs seem to presently possess. This can be taken as the observed value, but which is not revealed by the evaluator.

2. The evaluator (in this study, the student) will now set an 'ideal-value' of the level of honesty, which he/she believes, an entrepreneur should possess. This can be either a higher or a lower value than the 'present' level of honesty, or the observed value, made earlier. The reason for this increase or decrease in value is not considered in this paper.

3. If the expected or 'ideal' level of honesty is *high*, it means that the evaluator expects a *higher* level of the attribute 'honesty' to be present in the entrepreneur/person/object evaluated. This is so because the evaluator believes that the attribute 'honesty' present in the entrepreneur/person/object evaluated possesses/contains *less* than the desirable level now. Also, as he prefers that the level of the attribute be *increased* in the entrepreneur/person/object evaluated, he recommends a *higher* level of the attribute to be present in the entrepreneur/person/object evaluated.

4. If the expected or 'ideal' level of honesty is *low*, it means that the evaluator expects a *lower* level of the attribute 'honesty' to be present in the entrepreneur/person/object evaluated. This is so because the evaluator believes that the attribute 'honesty' present in the entrepreneur/person/object evaluated possesses/contains *more* than the desirable level now. Also, as he prefers that the level of the attribute be *lowered* in the entrepreneur/person/object evaluated, he recommends a *lower* level of the attribute to be present in the entrepreneur/person/object evaluated.

This paper proposes to assess evaluations made on the expected qualities to be possessed by entrepreneurs in the following ways:

- Value of expectations that the respondents make on *positive qualities* will be higher than the current level or mental assessments of the presence of the attribute in the entrepreneur
- Value of expectations that the respondents make on *negative qualities* will be lower than the current level or mental assessments of the presence of the attribute in the entrepreneur

In other words, high scores (compared to the scores received for the list of qualities assessed) on a quality will be assumed to be an expression of the *need to have 'more' or an increase* of the attribute in the object or person evaluated or analyzed.

Similarly, low scores on a quality (compared to the scores received for all the list of qualities assessed) will be assumed to be an expression of the need to have *'less' or a 'reduction'* of the attribute in the object or person evaluated or analyzed.

Since the mean value will be the representative value of the evaluations made on an ordinal variable like 'honesty', in this study it will be considered as the expression of the real needs of the evaluator. The real need is the reverse of the evaluation value given by the respondent, which is often a lower value for a positive attribute and a higher value for a negative attribute.

The interpretation of these expected scores is not straightforward and hence requires careful assessment. It is more likely that the student community, while making an expectation like anybody who has an expectation from any thing/person, first makes an evaluation of the present state of affairs. For example, if a boss states that he expects his employee to do better, it is a clear expression of his unhappiness with the employee's present level of work. In other words, he expects his performance or any other quality/characteristic expected of him to be at a higher or a desirable level. Similarly, as the $\bar{x}$ score represents the evaluation scores for any one 'quality to be possessed' variable in the expectation list, it can be similarly interpreted, that is, the high mean value is an expression of a much lower level of the quality/characteristic to be possessed by the entrepreneur in the real world.

The reverse effect score assumption has to be validated by direct interviews with such respondents in future studies on similar lines and is one way that the 'reverse effect' proposition suggested in this paper can be validated. Also, longitudinal studies could be attempted in future to look for similarities in scoring over time periods. Along with that, repeat samples can be compared to look for similarity of scores and subsequent interpretation.

The following is a *quick summary* of the earlier discussion on how expectation scores need to be interpreted:

- High or low scores on a quality will be assumed to be an expression of the need for a reversal (reduction or increase) from the expected value to the current value level of the attribute
- High expectancy scores mean reversal of low current values
- Low expectancy scores mean reversal of high current values
- Low and high current values (observed) are error values and need correction
- Expectancy scores are expressions of need levels—seeking optimization

Interpretation of Self-rating Scores

The self-rating scales are interpreted in a more straightforward manner. The scores for these self-ratings can be assumed to be a surer answer as it is self-evaluative. Evaluation of another is expected to be done with a greater sense of trepidation and hence could be more sedate than the self-evaluations made. Though the scores are expected to be higher for self-rating, such increase could be more a reflection of the actual and personal experiences, and hence it is assumed that it can be accepted on its face value. This approach is followed in conventional research and therefore the interpretations are made accordingly.

Demographic Profile of Respondents

Each of these entrepreneurial qualities was compared with the following demographic variables (Table 7.2), whenever appropriate, to trace differences among the respondents. Most of them are either the 'category' or the 'dichotomous' type except for 'Age' which is the lone interval variable.

The pie diagram (Figure 7.1) shows that almost 40 per cent of the 128 PG students were males, the rest being female respondents.

Table 7.2   Demographic Profiling Variables Used in Study

Variables	
Code	Label
S1GEND	Gender
S2AGE	Age
S5LANG1	Mother tongue—(Tamil and others)
S6REL_BV	Religion (Hindu and others)
B2OWN	Will you start a business sometime soon?
B7SKILL1	Possessing skills to start business (recoded)
P1EDADBV	Father's education (school or university or no opinion)
P2DOCC_1	Father's occupation (recoded)
P3EMUMBV	Mother's education (school or university contrast)
P4MOCC_1	Mother's occupation (categories)
P5INCOME	Is your income less than or higher than Rs 10,000 p.m.?
W3C_UGPG	Course programme (UG or PG)

Figure 7.1   Respondents' Gender

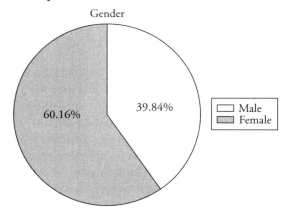

Some of the essential details of the sample are as follows:

- Ninty-five per cent of the respondents were below the age of 24 years. The age range was 11 years.
- The mother tongue of a majority of the student respondents (87 per cent) was Tamil.
- The respondents were predominantly Hindus (80 per cent).
- A majority (58 per cent) of the respondents felt that it was worth starting a business soon.

- About 48 per cent of the students feel that they possess the skills to start a business, though there is a sense of trepidation about skills possessed among the others. Thirty-four out of 128 respondents (about 27 per cent) did not respond to this query.
- An overwhelming majority (91 per cent) of the respondents agreed to the definition of entrepreneurship given in the survey instrument. About 47 per cent of the fathers of all respondents possess a university education. However, the 'no opinion' (31 per cent) responses also seem disturbingly high.
- The occupational status of the respondents' fathers is equally distributed between professional, self-employed and salaried classes. About 33 per cent did not respond to this question.
- A majority (63 per cent) of the mothers of the study respondents had only a minimum of school education, and about 33 per cent were university educated.
- Most mothers of the respondents are housewives. About 40 per cent did not respond to the question. Only 10 per cent of them are employed.

Results and Discussion

All the characteristics or qualities listed in Table 7.1 are probably necessary for an entrepreneur, as is evidenced in the literature too. Determination and persistence, confidence, honesty, intelligence, enthusiasm and energy are often given a special place as per the Australian Youth Survey. Honesty could be given more importance, as well as creativity, ruthlessness and just being 'good'. It should be interesting to see how our educated youth looks at the last three issues. More interestingly, how will the male and female respondents treat these entrepreneurial characteristics? We could expect many differences between them, given the conventional male dominated history of India.

In general, the students seem to rate the expectation qualities from entrepreneurs less than the values for themselves, as seen in Table 7.3.

This is obvious as man often has a higher image of himself when compared to expectations made, as the latter is about an 'away from self' or an 'away centred' evaluation of a phenomenon. The results indicated in the Table 7.3 (under the 'self' column) show that the five personal

Table 7.3   **Mean Values of Personal Qualities of Entrepreneurs and Self**

Entrepreneur qualities	Rating	
	Entrepreneurs	Self
Being good	7.37	8.18
Ruthlessness	6.00	6.30
Determination	7.20	7.74
Confidence	8.20	8.56
Honesty	7.57	8.10
Intelligence	7.67	8.00
Enthusiasm	7.94	8.40
Accepting a loss to succeed	7.62	7.69
Creativity	7.45	7.86

qualities: being good, confidence, enthusiasm, intelligence and honesty are ranked the top five in the list. It is interesting to note that 'determination' and persistence do not figure in the top five mentioned in the list. This is a major breakaway from the Australian survey results, where 'determination and persistence' was ranked No.1, followed by confidence, being good, enthusiasm and creativity.

Referring to Table 7.3 again, the Chennai students rated the quality of 'ruthlessness' in entrepreneurs the lowest, with a score of 6.0 on a possible 10.0, while rating 'being good', 7.37 (mean), and 7.45 for 'being creative'. As mentioned in the methodology section, if we interpret the expectations that students have on the personal qualities to be possessed by entrepreneurs as an expression of what entrepreneurs lack in real life, then the larger the $\bar{x}$ value on these qualities, the less degree of the quality in question is possessed by the entrepreneur today. Therefore, the high $\bar{x}$ values on 'confidence', 'being good', and so forth, are interpreted by this paper as qualities not possessed enough by Indian entrepreneurs. This interpretation is further explained in the following sub-section.

Personal Qualities to be Possessed by Entrepreneurs

Table 7.4 displays the descriptive statistics related to the estimation of personal qualities to be possessed by entrepreneurs by the respondent students.

The table provides the mean, standard deviation and variance for each of the nine qualities.

Table 7.4   **Personal Qualities to be Possessed by Entrepreneurs**

Variable		Descriptives		
Code	Label	Mean	SD	VAR
E24CONF	Confidence	8.20	1.95	3.79
E27ENTH	Enthusiasm and energy	7.94	1.92	3.68
E26INT	Intelligence	7.67	2.10	4.42
E28LOSS	Accepting the possibility of loss in order to have a chance of succeeding	7.62	1.85	3.41
E25HON	Honesty	7.57	2.39	5.73
E29INNO	Creativity and the ability to be innovative	7.45	2.34	5.49
E21GOOD	Being good with people	7.37	2.05	4.20
E23DET	Determination and persistence	7.20	2.14	4.59
E22TUF	Ruthlessness	6.00	2.30	5.27

The top three personal qualities to be possessed by entrepreneurs are confidence ($\bar{x}$ = 8.2), enthusiasm and energy ($\bar{x}$ = 7.94) and intelligence ($\bar{x}$ = 7.67). Interpreting mean values as per the special methodology suggested earlier, these three values should be meaning lower than what they are. These scores suggest that there is more room for improvement among the entrepreneurs today. These top three scores, 8.2, 7.94 and 7.67, when viewed conventionally, suggest that they represent a desirable state as they score more than 75 per cent proportion in the scale of 10. However, these qualities suggest that the high evaluations given for the qualities in the score of 10 do not reflect the truth about entrepreneurship in this country. These high expectation scores (that is, higher mean values) depict the desirable levels entrepreneurs could be in, which, according to our student evaluators at present, are actually not in.

In medicine, a true cure (a relief from all troublesome diseases) needs to be proved. Likewise, we need to look for arguments or evidence for this 'reversal coding' claim made for evaluations on expectations. In medicine, a therapeutic success is evidenced by a positive correlation between a 'disease-free state' (exhibited by positive symptoms) and 'clinical assessment'. In other words, patient's state (reduction of pain caused by cancer) should be evidenced as indicative of a total cure from the malaise (and not just a palliation). This is evident often from the physical verification of the affected organ and part. Therefore, a positive biopsy report is the only final proof of a cure apart from the observable symptoms. While the interpretation methodology introduced here for expectation variables needs further internal and external validation attempts, this paper seeks to take a first step in that direction by looking for real-life examples and suppositions to try and explain the 'reversal code' phenomena.

To help matters, this paper focusses on two of the results seen in Table 7.3, that is, the expected qualities which received the highest and the lowest mean values, namely for 'confidence' and 'ruthlessness'. This will be addressed separately in the next section.

However, the following is a summary of findings related to all other qualities expected of entrepreneurs. Figure 7.2 gives a summary of these mean scores for each of the qualities evaluated. The first bar indicates the lowest score 'ruthlessness' and the last and the longest bar indicates the highest mean value score for the quality of 'confidence'. Most of the discussions are based on the mean score values and the associative or difference quality that the results indicate.

Selective Results

Being good: 'To be an entrepreneur, one needs to be good'

Respondents rating the quality 'being good' seemed to show extreme differences between male and female students ($\chi^2 = 15.7$, p = .03). This means that the proportion of males and females with the attitude that entrepreneurs should 'be good' is not similar. In other words, there is a gender difference on this quality. When this trait was compared with 'B7SKILL1' (possessing skills to start business), there seemed to be considerable differences existing among male students ($\chi^2 = 18.43$, p = .05) on the issue.

Ruthlessness: Should entrepreneurs be ruthless? The general feeling of the youth is that they need not be so as the average recorded the lowest among the list of nine qualities expected of entrepreneurs. This seems to be a dramatic finding and is thus investigated in detail in the next section.

Determined: A comparative analysis of the responses of Tamil and non-Tamil students has shown significant difference on rating of being determined and persistent for business students, whose mother tongue was not Tamil seemed to attest that 'to be in business one needs to be

Figure 7.2 Qualities Expected of Entrepreneurs

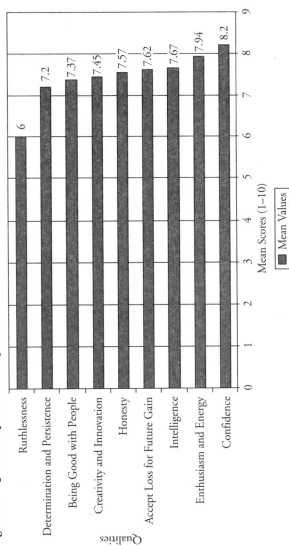

determined and persistent'. There are clear differences (<0.01) between students with Tamil and non-Tamil mother tongues. They seem more apparent among the male students who have a higher determination level average than the non-Tamil speaking students. This means that relatively, non-Tamil students had higher level of determination for business than the Tamil-speaking students.

Honesty: The expectation score of the level of 'honesty' from entrepreneurs was 7.57 on a scale of 10 and differences exist between genders, though more sedate (χ^2 = 12.24, p = 0.067).

A look at the descriptive statistics related to the nine personal qualities to be possessed by entrepreneurs reveal some other interesting insights. There seems to be high variance on the issues, 'creativity and innovation' (σ = 2.34), 'honesty' (σ = 2.3) and 'ruthlessness' (σ = 2.3). On a scale of 10, with the grand average of all the nine personal qualities being 7.44, these standard deviation (σ) levels show the fairly high level of differences on these issues.

Table 7.5   **Respondents' Rating on Personal Qualities**

Variable		Descriptives	
Code	*Label*	*Mean*	*SD*
E214CONF	Confidence	8.54	1.89
E217ENTH	Enthusiasm and Energy	8.41	1.64
E215HON	Honesty	8.16	2.02
E211GOOD	Being Good with People	8.05	1.72
E216INT	Intelligence	8.03	1.67
E219INNO	Creativity and the Ability to be Innovative	7.89	2.02
E213DET	Determination and Persistence	7.72	1.98
E218LOSS	Accept Loss for Future Gain	7.72	1.80
E212TUF	Ruthlessness	6.29	2.46

Self-rating on Personal Qualities

Table 7.5 (above) relates to the respondents' rating on the nine personal qualities. The top three qualities are seen as confidence ($\bar{x}$ = 8.54), being enthusiastic and energetic ($\bar{x}$ = 8.41) and being honest ($\bar{x}$ = 8.16). It is very interesting to note that 'ruthlessness', as a quality, received the last ranking ($\bar{x}$ = 6.3), similar to the earlier findings in the list of qualities expected of entrepreneurs.

For the value of 'honesty', most students felt that entrepreneurs should have higher levels and they have no differences among themselves on the self-rating scale on this issue. However, Hindu male students seem to have a higher rating for honesty compared to students belonging to other religions (8.58 and 6.25 in a scale of 10; χ^2 = 14.73, p = 0.04).

The least variance seems to be for the quality 'being good' (σ^2 = 2.68). This indicates a high level of unanimity among the respondents on this quality. However, male students with employed and unemployed mothers differ very significantly (33.53, p = 0.000), on the 'being good' quality. Similar variation was observed among male students with educated and less educated mothers (23.19, 0.01).

Significant Correlations

Female Students: A noteworthy positive association (r = 0.23, p = 0.03) is noted between the religious following of female students and their confidence levels. Though a weak 'r' value, this means that the more religious the student is, the more confident he/she could be. Other significant positive and negative associations exist among female students on the following personal qualities when contrasted with certain demographic variables.

1. Being enthusiastic versus religious belief (r = 0.25, p = 0.04)
2. Being confident versus religious belief (r = 0.23, 0.03)
3. Some negative correlations exist in the relationship between 'ability to accept losses now, for future gain' versus mother's educational background (r = –0.18, p = 0.05)

Male students exhibit the following negative correlation between:

4. Business intelligence levels versus the B2OWN, or the 'interest to own a business soon' (r = –0.025, p = 0.057)
5. Confidence levels versus the 'interest to own a business soon' (r = –0.30, p = 0.02)
6. Ability to accept losses for future gain versus father's occupation (r = –0.19, p = 0.05)
7. Ability to accept losses for future gain versus mother's education (r = –0.25, p = 0.04)

Investigating 'Confidence' and 'Ruthlessness' as Desirable Qualities of an Entrepreneur

Investigating 'Confidence' as an Evaluation Quality of an Entrepreneur

As explained earlier, this study assumes that the high scores on the qualities which are expected to be possessed by entrepreneurs would have the reverse effect. This means that the student evaluators have made an overestimation of the quality and going by the RE phenomenon application, the scores have to be interpreted at lower levels than what is indicated by the x̄ values and interpreted approximately. This section interprets the 'confidence' score which received the highest rating of 8.2 which, under the reverse effect, could be of any value less than 8.2. Keeping this in mind, the 'confidence' quality can be interpreted in the following way:

Entrepreneurs become confident if they work in a spirit of freedom and in environments which have less hurdles and corruption, so that they concentrate on the key task of running their businesses well. These confident entrepreneurs are expected to be socially committed and would not shy away from paying taxes. They would often be missionary in their business practices and dealings. Their products will naturally be world-class and they would not dream of doing harm to people, least of all to their customers. These confident players can never be the 'fly-by-night operator' kind of people. These entrepreneurs would ultimately end up managing great brands and that would be their success. Though entrepreneurs with supreme confidence never work for success alone, it comes naturally to them and probably that is the reason for their confidence.

The student's interpretation of giving the highest score to the expected level of entrepreneurial quality of 'confidence' can therefore be assumed here as indicative of the not-so-very high level of confidence they see in Indian entrepreneurs, at least in their experience and reality.

On the same line of argument, students feel that the other two qualities (which are part of the top three) that entrepreneurs lack are 'enthusiasm and energy', along with 'intelligence'. Although these are serious issues to be left undebated, yet space considerations force this paper to leave them to the reader's assessment and final judgment based on the facts presented here.

Investigating 'Confidence' as a Self-rating of Quality by Students

The personal quality of 'confidence' recorded the highest average both as an expected-quality from entrepreneurs and in the self-rating mode by respondents; hence it demands further investigation. The self-rating on the confidence variable was first compared with all the demographic variables listed in Table 7.1. Perceptions of the importance of the 'confidence' variable also appeared to be influenced by the occupational status of the respondent's parents. Those students whose mothers were employed saw confidence as least important compared to those whose mothers were either housewives or those who preferred not to mention their mothers' occupation (χ^2 = 25.24, p = 0.07). Similarly, participants who preferred to 'start a business sometime soon (variable code B2OWN), differed from those who did not plan to start one (χ^2 = 12.35, p = 0.055). 'Confidence' and 'ownership' variables were negatively correlated (r = –0.3, p = 0.02). Maybe this negative association could be traced to male students. Evidence shows that for the male students the B2OWN variable was negatively correlated with 'confidence' (r = –0.15, p = 0.08). Male students with different occupational status of mothers differed on the perception of the importance of self-confidence quality (c2 = 24.44, p = 0.02).

The following is a list of the other areas of differences existing on the self-rating on this issue, 'confidence' level/quality (variable code: E214CONF) among male students.

1. B2OWN: Will you start a business sometime soon?
2. B7SKILL1: Possessing Skills to start business (recoded)
3. S5LANG1: Mother tongue (Tamil and others)
4. S6REL_BV: Religion (Hindu and others)
5. P4MOCC_1: Mothers' occupation (categories)

Male non-Tamil students had poor confidence levels ($\bar{x}$ = 6.5) as compared to the Tamil ($\bar{x}$ = 8.73) students. This difference appears to be the most dramatic among the demographic variables tested (χ^2 = 28.72, p = 0.000). Differences also exist on other backgrounds of the respondents like 'skill levels to start business' (p = 0.06), 'mothers' occupation' (p = 0.02), and 'religion' (p = 0.07).

Investigating 'Ruthlessness'

An entrepreneur can be termed 'ruthless' if the concerns of the recipient member like the customer, employee, patient, or student, in their relationship with the entrepreneur, are not given enough consideration. The related qualities of ruthlessness, heartlessness, inhumane nature, exploitative tendency, among other similar natures could be similarly understood.

Consistent with the RE phenomenon interpretation on 'confidence', the low $\bar{x}$ level of 6.0 rating by students on this quality means that the respondents have given a higher rating than 6.0 in reality (as ruthlessness is a negative quality), which does not augur well or is a desirable level of this quality to be possessed by Indian entrepreneurs. However, the 6.0 point score means that the evaluators do not expect a higher level of ruthlessness quality to be possessed by entrepreneurs. This low evaluation score can therefore be interpreted to indicate that Indian entrepreneurs already possess high levels of ruthlessness. Do we see really confident and humane qualities among entrepreneurs in India, or in the world for that matter? Does Bill Gates come across any of us as possessing qualities which are other than 'cunning', 'tactical', 'strategic', 'quick', 'monopolist', among many other related terminologies, which are implicative of an exploitative tendency?

The challenge faced by the 'reverse effect' methodology claim is to look for validation. If not empirically, at least by face validation attempts like finding appropriate explanation or correlates in reality, which support the reverse effect proposition. Therefore, to support the claim that a low $\bar{x}$ score, for a quality like ruthlessness, actually represents the opposite or *ulta* (Hindi word) effect of the level of ruthlessness (that is, there is a high level of presence of ruthless entrepreneurs in the society), there is a need for a description of the ruthless nature observed in Indian society. If this description (made after careful and sincere observation) tallies with the effect of the claim (that the low mean value implies the presence of high level of ruthlessness in reality), then the claim made can be accepted.

Therefore, searching for evidencing material to support a claim made, based on the reversal effect (RE) of expectations, is a vital part of the validation process in testing an RE claim. To paraphrase it differently, the more the expected value ($\bar{x}$) from the objects/persons analyzed, it should mean that there is actually less of it present in the variable in question and vice versa. In this case, as the $\bar{x}$ of ruthlessness quality is the least, among the list of expected qualities as per the expectation of students, what it means is that they see more (*ulta* effect) of such a quality among the entrepreneurs in real life. This conclusion could be based on what they have seen and heard of in their life and they expect less of it as expressed by the lower mean value. This is a more desirable value for them. Maybe these students have seen more of the exploitative type of entrepreneurs in their lives. The following explanation will hope to validate this claim.

Let us try to reason out this argument in more detail. As the average age of the respondents is around 24 years, it is very likely that the student respondents have friends or relatives working in organizations. It is very likely that the messages they get from them on a daily basis are not as much about comfort zones and happy work environments rather more about employees or customers being misused or exploited.

Bringing the IT industry and the call-centre and BPO operations boom in India as a handy example into this train of thought, there are many an expression we hear of tough and long hours of work for the working class. Though well-paid, way past Indian standards, it is very likely that the youthfulness and energy of our young workers are unfortunately taken advantage of by our entrepreneurs. Therefore, the culture of oppression of a capitalist continues and we look at rigorous natures of work schedules, time usage, and so forth, which have comprehensively mechanized our work spots and the people in modern life. Although Taylorism is more than two centuries old, yet we see that the practices still continue and the propagators are entrepreneurs. Evidence of this is the coinage of the new term, '24 × 7' work hours, which is part of many of the new IT recruitment advertisements nowadays. This epitomizes the new work style *mantra* for the Indian businesses. These work styles are of course not restricted to the IT industry alone, but are the case in any buyer-seller relationship, where there is no balance of power or equity of the relationship in question.

These expressions need not be viewed as an anti-entrepreneurial stand of the author, rather as explanations to understand the 'reverse effect' of a simple $\bar{x}$ value when it comes to making real life expectations based on the negative or positive nature of an attribute and the appropriate interpretation of the quality/phenomenon being measured. In defence of the 'ruthlessness' quality, it can be interpreted positively as an expression of managerial competence. On the flip side, managers/entrepreneurs can also be negatively connoted as a bunch of efficient exploiters, which is the facet of the quality that these students have probably seen or heard in their lives.

The futuristic entrepreneur would surely prefer to be the less exploitative type, though not at the cost of efficiency of operation. A great entrepreneur would be a great operations manager, too. However, it is the overemphasis on efficiency for the sake of profit maximization which makes entrepreneurs tread the ground of 'exploitation' and move away from being the ideal 'preservation' or optimization zones of resources utilization. Great entrepreneurs can never be exploiters or ruthless. They optimize everything and that is what our students in this study make a plea for.

Income Differences and Entrepreneurial Qualities

Students with income less than and more than Rs 10,000 per month exhibited differences on their personal qualities of 'being good' ($\chi^2 = 15.7$, p = 0.03), 'intelligence' ($\chi^2 = 14.01$, p = .05), and 'creativity and innovation' ($\chi^2 = 16.95$, p = 0.05). They had extreme differences on the expectation of entrepreneurs to be intelligent ($\chi^2 = 17.43$, p = 0.03).

Conclusions

This study was initiated as an external validation exercise of the National Youth Entrepreneurship Attitude Survey undertaken in Australia in 2001. The survey instrument used in this study was an adoption of the telephone survey instrument in the Australian study and later stylized to suit Indian conditions. The purpose was to assess the minds of the average Indian students about entrepreneurial qualities and their belief systems about entrepreneurship as a vocation. One hundred and twenty-eight usable questionnaires representing the postgraduate students of commerce and economics in Chennai-based colleges provided enough data material for this study. The data generated was voluminous and the exercise of cutting through the volumes with an insightful empirical assessment of entrepreneurial qualities worked out well.

As most of the variables used were ordinal and nominal, the non-parametric analysis methods were the predominant analysis methods used. Descriptive analysis, primarily the mean, standard deviation and range, were used to make preliminary assessments. It was in one such analytical session that the insight that evaluations made by students about expected levels of qualities as attributes to be present in entrepreneurs was put through the idea screening sieve. This process generated simple axioms to apply the methodology. They were reported in the methodology section of this paper. Associative thoughts and much experience in similar assessments provided the right playground to dabble with the idea of expectation quantification made by the students' evaluations of qualities to be possessed by entrepreneurs, as in this paper. Could such evaluations be an expression of an objection to the reality or a reversed expression of the real and existing world was the key question addressed.

Further assessment and minor face validation interviews made with local entrepreneurs on this methodology and deeper thinking gave some confidence to propose this methodology as another way to assess evaluations. This paper realizes that this is merely a research methodology at the proposition level and not at all a proven technique. The paper realizes that further assessments and validations need to be attempted to either accept or reject this methodology. Nevertheless, a sincere attempt was made to extricate explanations and analogies to explain this methodology satisfactorily. Probably the 'reverse or *ulta* effect' of evaluations could provide assessments of the reality under evaluative conditions. The instrumentation and face validation exercise particularly in the pre-data collection stages also need to be adopted with care. Moreover, the evaluation set, if validated a bit in the past, would provide more confidence to apply it confidently.

Tests of difference were attempted using chi-square analysis for both the evaluation estimates of desirable qualities to be possessed by entrepreneurs and the self-rating sets of the same qualities made by respondents. The 18 variables representing qualities for both the entrepreneur and student respondents were individually compared with at least 10 demographic variables like gender, income, parental backgrounds, and so forth. Significant to moderately significant differences are reported voluminously in the paper. Some key findings were related to the differences found among the student population on the qualities 'being good', 'ruthlessness', 'being determined' and 'honesty' to be possessed by entrepreneurs. There are gender differences on 'being good', for example, while on the same item, there were differences between students who perceived themselves as skilled or unskilled to start a business. There is much to learn and assess from the various insights desired from the 'self-rating section' of personal qualities by the respondents. The top three ratings by students here were on the qualities of confidence, being good and being honest. As these are not the reverse affected scores, it can be concluded that the students possess good traits. In general, however, they feel that the qualities possessed by entrepreneurs are disappointing. This study reports the reason for this, which is that on the reverse-affected qualities analyzed, confidence, enthusiasm and intelligence are qualities which entrepreneurs do not possess enough. This may sound depressing but the finding in this study should make us think deeply, look at the reality of the problems in India and act fast.

Corrective action on the basis of these findings will help entrepreneurship become a popular tool to gain quick growth for an economy and help it be part of a more satisfying developmental model for society. Also, as the youth were the prime movers in this paper, with their ideas and thoughts influencing us now, the best way to recognize their competence and potential is to adopt corrective action to set right the mess which many of us in India have let ourselves be in. Although there is much talk of late about the faster growth rate of development and change in India, yet the growth could ride the graph quicker if the youth and the eligible workforce of India get the right climate to start businesses, not only as a survival response to a fast changing and competitive world, but as an expression of the many great possibilities that new and confident entrepreneurs could bring to our world.

Although this paper offers many good ideas for encouraging entrepreneurship in India, yet it suffers from certain limitations. Its chief limitation is the unvalidated methodology it has suggested in the form of the 'reverse effect' evaluation methodology. Though there are many good things that this methodology will achieve, like opening up more debates on the theme, the troublesome implication is that, if proven wrong, the conclusions drawn in this study may have to be reversed in the future. The paper, however, hopes that the proposed axioms and explanations offered will help establish this methodology as helpful tool for future research. Another limitation that this paper suffers from is underplaying the other key attitudes that the student community could have in terms of starting business, barriers to starting business, skills evaluation, and the role of influencers. Above all, given the other limitations like the never-ending time pressure under which this paper was prepared, it is likely that it suffers from verbosity and some errors in judgement and presentation, for which the author takes full responsibility.

References

Boeker, W. D. and C. F. Hofer. 1991. 'Theorizing about Entrepreneurship', *Entrepreneurship, Theory and Practice*, XVI-2.

Bhanushali, S. G. 1987. *Entrepreneurship Development*. New Delhi: Himalaya Publishing House.

Bryman Alan and Duncan Cramer. 1999. *Quantitative Data Analysis with SPSS Release 8 for Windows, A Guide for Social Scientists*. London: Routledge.

Covey, S. R. 1995. 'Ethics of Total Integrity'. *Executive Excellence*, 12(8): 3–4.

Department of Industry, Science and Resources and Education, Training and Youth Affairs, Australia. *National Youth Entrepreneurship Attitude Survey May 2001*. Canberra: Commonwealth of Australia (ISR 2001/072; ASBN 0 642 721947).

Gaikwad, V. R. and R. N. Tripathy. 1970. *Socio Economic Factors Influencing Industrial Entrepreneurs in Rural Areas*. Hyderabad: National Institute of Community Development.

Hoselitz, B. F. 1952. 'Entrepreneurship and Economic Growth', *The American Journal of Economics and Sociology*, XII(1): 97–101.

Kalyani, W. and K. Chandralekha. 2002. 'Association between Socio-economic-demographic Profile and Involvement of Women Entrepreneurs in Their Enterprise Management', *The Journal of Entrepreneurship*, 11(2): 219–248.

Kanungo, R. N. and S. Misra. 1992. 'Managerial Resourcefulness: A Re-conceptualization of Management Skills', *Human Relations*, 45(12): 1311–1331.

Manimala, J. Mathew. 2002. 'Founder Characteristics and Start-up Policies of Entrepreneurial Ventures: A Comparison between British and Indian Enterprises', *Journal of Entrepreneurship*, 11(2): 139–171.

McClelland, D. C. 1961. *The Achieving Society*. Princeton, New Jersey: Van Norstrand.

Panda, N. M. 2000. 'What Brings Entrepreneurial Success in a Developing Region', *The Journal of Entrepreneurship*, 9(2): 199–212.

Pareek, Udai and T. V. Rao. 1995 'Counselling and Helping Entrepreneurs', *The Journal of Entrepreneurship*, 4(1): 19–34.

Rao, T. V. and V. Pareek. 1978. *Developing Entrepreneurship: A Handbook*. New Delhi: Learning Systems.

Tewari, A. K., Joseph Philip and A. K. Pandey. 1990. *Small Scale Industry: Success and Failure*. New Delhi: Concept.

Examining the Relationship of Sociocultural Factors and Entrepreneurial Propensity among Professional Students

8

Kailash **B.L.** Srivastava

The major objective of this study was to explore the reason why some people choose the career of entrepreneurship, and the role of sociocultural factors in selecting such a career. The study measured entrepreneurial propensity and a number of sociocultural factors like religion, caste, perceived family support and education. The data was collected from 300 students from the Indian Institute of Technology (IIT) Kharagpur. The results showed that management students reported greater levels of entrepreneurial propensity on each of its dimensions. The entrepreneurial propensity was significantly related to sociocultural factors and it differed across some of these factors. Reasons for these differences are suggested and prospects for future research have been outlined.

Introduction

There has been resurgence in academic and popular literatures on entrepreneurship-related issues. Researchers have begun to critically address the processes surrounding venture creation, small business development, innovation, creativity and entrepreneurship. Of particular interest to practitioners have been the means through which entrepreneurship is cultivated. They further look into its historically uneven distribution throughout demographic segments of the society. Specifically, why some college-educated professionals choose entrepreneurial careers and others do not, is yet to be explored.

Economic growth calls for rapid emergence of a multitude of enterprises. This requires an environment that is conducive to the growth of existing enterprises and would help build up a wider base of population capable of successful entrepreneurial behaviour. Recently, the concept of entrepreneurial culture has received prominence and social scientists have observed that an entrepreneur is a product of the sociocultural milieu.

Researchers now emphasize the critical nature of entrepreneurial climate, with the recognition that a growing number of jobs in the next decade would be self-generated. In a similar vein, they have started exploring the type of social climate that is conducive to the creation of new ventures. However, one's proclivity for an entrepreneurial career is not only a function of the economic environment, but also of a personal one (Johnson, 1990) and cultural factors (Brodsky, 1993). In an attempt to identify the cultural and social factors that impact the likelihood of entrepreneurial career selection, the present study examined the nature of entrepreneurial propensity and the role of social and cultural factors among prospective entrepreneurs (that is, engineering and management graduates).

Theoretical Background

There are differing perspectives on entrepreneurship. Rumelt (1987) defined the term as the creation of new businesses with some element of novelty. Mintzberg (1973) viewed the entrepreneur as one who seeks to improve the organization through change initiation. Vesper (1983) provided the economists' perspective and said that an entrepreneur is one who coordinates resources to create profits. The economic importance of entrepreneurship is well established in the literature (Ireland and Van Auken, 1987; Krueger and Brazeal, 1994; Stumpf, 1992). Entrepreneurship has also been viewed as the identification of market opportunities and the recombination and allocation of resources to pursue them (Chamberlin, 1933; Kirzner, 1973; Schumpeter, 1934). Much of the present entrepreneurship literature rests on the assumption that the entrepreneur is a risk-taker (Balkin and Logan, 1988; Corman et al., 1988; Dunphy, 1990; Flamholtz, 1986; Johnson, 1990).

Many authors have discussed the role of non-economic factors in economic growth, including those developed in sociology and psychology (Lipset, 2000). In this context, Weber (1904) suggested that given the economic conditions for the emergence of a system of rational capital accumulation, whether or not such growth occurred in a systematic fashion would be determined by the values present. It is reasonable to expect an association between culture and the level of entrepreneurial activity. Weber (1958) argued that at the society level, differences in entrepreneurial activity can be explained by cultural and religious factors, specifically a society's acceptance of the Protestant work ethic. Building on Weber's thesis, McClelland (1961) theorized that socialization factors determine the need for achievement, which in turn generates an entrepreneurial propensity or predisposition within a society. Culture is a powerful force in shaping personality and behaviour patterns within a group or society, and to assume that entrepreneurial characteristics are universal would be unwarranted. Structural conditions make development possible, while cultural factors determine whether the possibility becomes an actuality (Lipset, 2000). This means that an appropriate sociocultural environment is a prerequisite for industrial or economic growth. The event of enterprise creation (entrepreneurship) can therefore be seen as a consequence of congruence between environmental conditions and the entrepreneurial behaviour of individuals, determined by their sociocultural background.

Literature Review

The earliest work in the field of entrepreneurship focussed on personal characteristics that distinguished entrepreneurs from non-entrepreneurs (Brockhaus, 1982; Naffziger et al., 1994). Many studies reported consistent relationships between individual factors, namely achievement, locus of control, motivation (McClelland, 1961) and entrepreneurship (Brockhaus, 1982; Gartner, 1985, 1988; Johnson, 1990). McClelland (1961, 1962) identified three behavioural traits associated with high need for achievement (nAch):

1. taking personal responsibility for finding solutions to problems,
2. setting moderate achievement goals and taking calculated risks to achieve them, and

3. desiring concrete feedback concerning performance. McClelland reported a number of studies linking high nAch with entrepreneurship (McClelland, 1965a, 1965b; McClelland and Winter, 1969), which reinforced his motivation entrepreneurship linkage (Klavans et al., 1985; Moore, 1986). Mclelland (1961), Berna (1960) and Fox (1969) reported a positive relationship between economic progress and culture.

They tried to explain the economic backwardness of India by linking it with the Indian culture. Some of these scholars argued that the spirit of enterprise was inhibited among the indigenous population of India by the religious philosophy of resignation embodied in the doctrine of *karma* and by the rigid social organization of the caste system and the joint family. For instance, it has been observed that the tradition-bound Indian society offered little freedom of choice of profession for its members as it was decided by caste (Tripathi, 1992, 1997; Weber, 1958). Consequently, the social base of entrepreneurial growth remained limited.

Researches were inconclusive regarding the role of sociocultural factors in supporting and promoting entrepreneurship, particularly in India. At the same time, empirical evidence regarding the role of and scope for structural interventions for influencing the sociocultural factors for the promotion of entrepreneurship is also inadequate.

There is a growing need in this country to create and maintain an appropriate environment that is conducive to the growth of existing enterprises and helps build up a wider base of population, capable of successful entrepreneurial behaviour. It would be meaningful to empirically examine the relationship between entrepreneurial propensity and sociocultural factors like caste, religion, perceived family support and education to identify the structural interventions that can be designed to make the influencing sociocultural attributes play a favourable role for the growth of entrepreneurship. It is reasonable to expect an association between culture and the level of entrepreneurial activity. Hisrich (1990) indicated that an entrepreneur demonstrates initiative and creative thinking, can organize social and economic mechanisms to turn resources and situations to practical account, and accepts risk and failure. Begley and Boyd (1987) found that the business founders scored significantly higher than non-founders in need for achievement, risk-taking propensity and tolerance of ambiguity. Brockhaus (1982) identified three attributes associated with entrepreneurial behaviour: need for achievement, locus of control, and a risk-taking propensity.

Religion, being an integral part of a cultural system, promotes social solidarity and reinforces social norms and values. Religion makes people share common beliefs and thus a common value system. India's spiritualism, philosophy of renunciation, fatalism and asceticism constitute insurmountable obstacles to material progress of the country (Singer, 1956). Tripathi also indicated that with the religious philosophy of resignation embodied in the doctrine of *karma* and the rigid social organization of the caste system, the Indian personality remained largely unentrepreneurial if not anti-entrepreneurial (Tripathi, 1992). Similarly, McClelland and Winter were of the opinion that the presence of a specific motivational structure, the desire to achieve purely for the sake of achievement—that is, the 'achievement motivation'—is of critical importance to successful entrepreneurship and they said that Indians lacked entrepreneurial values and motives (McClelland and Winter, 1969). But not all Hindu scriptures teach doctrines of self-denial or the cessation of desire in order to achieve personal salvation. Second, the secular doctrine abounds in works like Kautilya's Arthasastra, the Rig-Veda and Bhagavat Gita (Rao, 1986: 185–186).

Srinivas (1962) and others argued that the Indian population, by and large, is as materialistic in its daily life as its Western counterpart. Singer (1953) states that, 'The Indian world view encompasses both material and spiritual values.' He conducted an empirical study of Hindu industrialists in Chennai and said that they compartmentalize their religious lives and their business activities (Singer, 1972). Timberg (1978) and Saberwal (1976) also rejected Weber's thesis that religion, norms and values, behaviour and economic development are all interconnected. They were of the view that India's economic backwardness was due to certain structural conditions that were unsuitable for entrepreneurship and not because of social or cultural systems prevailing in the country.

Thus, the views of scholars regarding the influence of Indian religion on economic success are conflicting. However, the fact remains that the Indian economy remained stagnant for centuries. Historically, various explanations have been suggested to account for this, of which religion is one. A long period of foreign rule is another. Lack of modern educational facilities and other structural facilities for the growth of entrepreneurship is one of the consequences of foreign rule. Social and political institutions were also not conducive to economic development (Rao, 1986).

Among the social institutions that are held responsible for India's backwardness, the caste system is considered the most prominent one. All other social factors that inhibited development were only offshoots of, or closely related to, the caste system. Since caste is an important sociocultural attribute, information regarding caste of the respondents was therefore analyzed.

It can be argued that family is the cornerstone of society and forms the basic unit of social organization. It is the responsibility of the family as a social organization to internalize the society's culture and hence structure human personalities (Harlambos and Heald, 1980). The extent to which the moral and financial support of their families is valuable for them and possibility of their playing a significant role in enabling them to carry out their entrepreneurial activities is also examined.

Education is considered an important factor that influences the performance of an entrepreneur. It is believed that education received in schools and colleges inculcates the value of achievement and equality of opportunity and also enables people to acquire various types of technical skills. These values and skills have an important function in this advanced industrial society. Although formal education is not necessary for starting a new business, as is reflected in the success of many entrepreneurs who were high school dropouts, education does provide a good background (wherein technical and managerial skills are required) for a new venture creation.

This study was designed to explore the relationship of entrepreneurial propensity—a prospective entrepreneur's proclivity for choosing an entrepreneurial career, and culture and demographic factors among prospective entrepreneurs. It was believed that entrepreneurial propensity would be influenced by sociocultural factors. In addition to this, demographic variables like education, caste, family background and religion were also measured.

Research Propositions

The study was conducted in an exploratory framework to examine the relationship of sociocultural factors with entrepreneurial propensity. Some research questions were proposed to be examined. These propositions are given below.

1. Engineering and management students would differ in their level of entrepreneurial propensity and their intention to start a new business/enterprise.

2. Entrepreneurial propensity would be positively related to socio-cultural factors namely religion, perceived family support, caste and education.
3. Engineering and management students would differ in their perception of sociocultural factors.
4. Sociocultural factors would significantly predict entrepreneurial propensity.

Methodology

Sample

The sample used for this study was drawn from a data set containing over 300 responses to a survey of final-year engineering (160) and MBA students (140) of IIT Kharagpur. They belonged to different family backgrounds, religions, castes, and academic backgrounds.

Measures

Entrepreneurial propensity is a function of three factors, each associated with one of the three relationships (Parnell et al., 1995):

1. one's perceived level of entrepreneurial education, knowledge and competence concerning new venture operation.
2. one's beliefs concerning entrepreneurial opportunities in the economy (that is, financial rewards, employment, and so forth).
3. one's confidence in one's ability to access the available opportunities (that is, self-employment, risk, and so forth).

A 5-point scale was used.

The relationship between religion and entrepreneurial propensity (EP) of the respondents was examined by seeking information on their religious habits. It was measured on a 3-point scale with categories of high, medium and low. The information regarding caste was collected. Students were asked to identify whether they belong to the forward, the backward or the SC/ST category. The level of family support (financial and moral) received by the respondents (as perceived by them) was also measured. The final instrument consisting of these three factors addressing entrepreneurial intentions and sociocultural factors was administered to 300 students at IIT Kharagpur.

Results and Discussion

The first step in the data analysis stage was to validate the scale used to measure entrepreneurial propensity. The 11 EP scale items were factor-analyzed and three factors emerged explaining 66 per cent of variance. The factor analysis results are presented in Table 8.1. Factor loadings varied from 0.48 to 0.77. Coefficient alpha for the EP scale was 0.71; alphas for the three factors namely education (α = 0.67), self-confidence (α = 0.76) and opportunity (α = 0.73) were also computed separately, lending support to the internal consistency of the subscales considering the small number of items for each subscale.

Table 8.2 displays a correlation matrix for all the variables for which data was collected. As the table shows, there were a number of significant

Table 8.1   Factor Analysis Results of Entrepreneurial Propensity Scale

Items	Factor 1 (education)	Factor 2 (opportunity)	Factor 3 (self-confidence)
1.	0.75		
2.	0.48		
3.	0.73		
4.	0.72		
5.		0.56	
6.		0.64	
7.		0.77	
8.			
9.			0.70
10.			0.66
11.			0.71
Notes: Eigen Value-	3.34	3.29	2.97
% of Variance explained	37	20	9
Total Variance explained = 66%			

Table 8.2 Correlation Matrix among the Variables

	Education (knowledge and skill)	Opportunity	Self-confidence	Religion	Caste	Perceived family support	Type of education
Education	1.00						
Opportunity	0.36**	1.00					
Self-confidence	0.24**	0.20**	1.00				
Religion	0.10*	0.11*	0.34**	1.00			
Caste	0.07	0.06	0.09	0.17*	1.00		
Perceived family support	0.21**	0.19**	0.30**	0.16*	0.25**	1.00	
Type of education	0.28**	0.23**	0.32	0.14*	0.21**	0.31**	1.00

Notes: * Significant 0.05 level.
    ** Significant at 0.01 level.

relationships. Table 8.3 shows T-Tests showing the differences between students on dimensions of entrepreneurial propensity. Management students expressed greater intentions to open their own businesses both immediately after graduation (Option 1) and within five to 10 years following graduation. However, no differences were found in the intentions to open businesses 10 or more years following graduation (see Table 8.3). Management students reported greater levels of each of the three dimensions of entrepreneurial capacity—education, perceptions of entrepreneurial opportunity and self-confidence—and also on the overall measure. In addition, these students were more likely to plan to operate their own businesses both immediately after completing their study (within two years) and within10 years from graduation. However, there were no significant differences in the long-term plans for new venture creation among engineering and management students.

Table 8.3 **T-Tests Showing the Differences between Students on Dimensions of Entrepreneurial Propensity**

Variables	Management students (N = 140)		Engineering students (N = 160)		Significance	
	Mean	SD	Mean	SD	T- Value	Level
Education	3.67	1.29	3.01	1.90	5.17	.01
Opportunity	2.67	1.07	2.19	0.96	2.66	.008
Self-confidence	3.20	1.20	3.26	1. 19	0.82	.08
Option 1 (intention to start early)	4.12	1.02	3.68	1.28	3.47	.01
Option 2 (intention to start in long term)	3.19	1.23	3.30	1.27	0.83	.40

There can be some explanations for the differences found between the three samples. Management graduates from business schools look forward to a balance between careers in 'the corporation' and careers as entrepreneurs compared to engineering students who look for a job immediately after studies. Management graduates are better exposed to the opportunities that exist in the business. The differences in self-confidence may be attributed to the lack of a strong, independent business background, and the education system. Government ownership and partial ownership of key enterprises is common in India. Hard-working people visualize more success in private business ownerships. Hence, their preparation to enter the workforce is less intimidated about the prospects for failure. The differences in plans for new venture creation also existed. The results indicated that most engineering students are not as likely to pursue entrepreneurial careers within 10 years of graduation, but their long-term plans for business ownership were similar to those of the management students. Perhaps this reflects a lack of confidence and also a realization about the lack of opportunity and the direction in the beginning. Table 8.4a shows the respondents' religiosity and the extent of entrepreneurial propensity achieved by them. Almost 80 per cent respondents were found to have high religiosity or medium religiosity. Only a small minority of 20 per cent respondents was found to have low religiosity. All the respondents said they believe or have faith in God. Statistically, there was a significant relationship between religiosity and EP but almost all the respondents agreed that their religious functions, norms and practices helped them to develop confidence to overcome difficulties. Most of the respondents had high EP. It may be concluded that religion is definitely not a barrier to entrepreneurial success in India—rather it is a source of strength for entrepreneurs.

Table 8.4a   Religiosity Level

Religiosity	High		Moderate		Low	
	N	%*	N	%*	N	%*
Management students	**64**	**40**	**40**	**50**	**36**	**60**
High EP	52	81	32	80	21	58
Low EP	12	19	08	20	15	42
Engineering students	**95**	**60**	**40**	**50**	**25**	**40**
High EP	74	78	23	58	14	56
Low EP	21	22	17	42	11	44
Total	**159**	**53**	**80**	**27**	**60**	**20**

Note: * Percentage was rounded off.

The castes were grouped in three categories—forward caste, backward caste and SC/ST category. The caste composition is presented in Table 8.4b. As per Table 8.4b, in the forward caste category, 55 per cent were placed in the high EP category, whereas only 30 per cent and 15 per cent were in the average and lower EP category respectively. Out of the total SC/ST

Table 8.4b Caste Distribution

Caste	Forward		Backward		SC/ST	
	N	%*	N	%*	N	%*
Management students	**75**	**46**	**45**	**50**	**20**	**45**
High EP	55	73	37	82	14	70
Low EP	20	27	08	18	06	30
Engineering students	**90**	**55**	**45**	**50**	**25**	**55**
High EP	74	82	34	76	13	52
Low EP	16	18	11	24	07	48
Total	**165**	**55**	**90**	**30**	**45**	**15**

Note: * Percentage was rounded off.

respondents, majority belonged to the low EP category. There were a few respondents from the backward, scheduled and other caste groups but most of them were in the low EP category. Statistical results showed a significant relationship between caste and EP. There is some relationship between caste and the level of EP, but it has certain implications. The data suggests a majority of students were from high caste while low caste students were very few in number. It can be argued that high caste students could think of starting new ventures due to tacit support from their caste group members, even if they face failure at a certain stage. On the other hand, the low caste students thought that it would be difficult for them to get any such support. The findings of this study suggest that the EP level has not varied with caste. It means that students, who were exposed to a better educational environment, developed self-confidence to start a new venture irrespective of the caste they belonged to. Therefore, these findings do not conclusively support or reject the views of Weber and other researchers who consider the Indian caste system as a hindrance to entrepreneurship.

The moral and financial support received by students from their families plays a significant role in enabling them to carry out their entrepreneurial activities. In order to examine this proposition, the level of family support (financial and moral) to the respondents (as perceived by them) was measured and the relationship between the level of perceived family support and EP was explored. Table 8.5 presents the level of family support among students. It was found that the largest proportion of respondents, that is, 57 per cent of them, expected to get a high level of

Table 8.5   Perceived Family Support

Perceived family support	High		Moderate		Low	
	N	%*	N	%*	N	%*
Management students	90	53	35	40	15	30
High EP	72	80	23	66	9	60
Low EP	18	20	12	34	6	40
Engineering students	80	47	45	60	35	70
High EP	53	66	31	69	21	60
Low EP	27	34	14	31	14	40
Total	170	57	80	27	50	26

Note: * Percentage was rounded off.

family support if they started a new venture and 27 per cent of them said that they would get only moderate support from their families. Only 26 per cent students had low family support. It can be said that the majority of students expected to receive family support, morally as well as financially, to pursue their entrepreneurial activity. In the context of family support, it would be pertinent to point out that the majority of the students, who said that they would receive high support, were from nuclear families. Joint family system does not encourage entrepreneurship, which was supported by the findings of the other researchers who found that that it inhibited entrepreneurial activity (Tripathi, 1992). But Singer (1972) suggested that joint family units provide financial, physical and social security to make the entrepreneurial activity a success.

The education level for all the participants was very high as all of them were pursuing professional courses. It included 140 management students from the first and second year batches and 160 final year undergraduate engineering students from all disciplines. The results show a significant positive relationship between the educational level and the level of EP. All the respondents had a relatively higher level of education and were better exposed to the opportunities that existed in the environment, and this had also given them a higher level of self-confidence. In order to examine the impact of sociocultural factors, multiple regression analysis was performed. Entrepreneurial propensity was treated as dependent measures and sociocultural factors were treated as independent variables in this study (see Table 8.6). The result showed that these variables contributed 21 per cent variance for EP ($R^2 = 21$; $F_{(4, 296)} = 34.71$, $P > 0.01$).

Table 8.6   Multiple Regression Analysis Results Showing Sociocultural Factors as Criterion and EP as Predictors

Predictor variables	Criterion variable (Entrepreneurial propensity)						
	B	SEB	$\square$	Multiple R	R^2	$\underline{R}^2$	F
Religion	0.23	0.10	0.19**	0.38	0.22	0.21	34.71**
Caste	−0.33	0.06	−0.24**				
Perceived family support	0.37	0.07	0.22**				
Constant		1.84					

Note: ** P > 0.01 level of confidence.

Conclusions and Implications

The present study provided an insight into factors associated with students and their plans to pursue new venture creations. Variances of entrepreneurial propensity and direct plans for starting one's own business varied significantly among engineering and management students. Several avenues for future research have been identified. First, comparisons of samples from more institutions and colleges may provide more insight. Studies may also be conducted to identify how the EP levels vary among different regions/cultures. The findings of this study suggest that there is a definite relation between sociocultural attributes of the entrepreneurs and the level of EP. It was observed that caste did not influence the EP level, but it can influence the supply of entrepreneurs and the survival of the enterprise in difficult situations. The representation of the lower castes in the sample was very low. Therefore, these findings do not conclusively support or reject the views of Weber and other researchers who consider the Indian caste system as a hindrance to entrepreneurship.

Perceived family support and education level were two very important factors influencing the EP. Most of the students said that they were likely to receive greater family support in case they started a new business. An inference that can be drawn from the above findings is that one of the reasons for higher level of EP was greater family support for the high EP category compared to the low EP category. It also indicated that the joint family system of India had hindered the growth of entrepreneurship. With the changes that take place within the social and economic environment and disintegrated joint family system, more people are living in nuclear families. Economic compulsions are forcing them to be more innovative and creative and start a business which can bring financial independence. Highly educated respondents with professional qualification were found to be high on entrepreneurial propensity.

Religiosity had a significant correlation with EP as all the students were found to have faith in God. Indian religiosity is definitely not a barrier, rather a source of strength for the entrepreneurs.

The relationship between education and EP was positive. It means that education helps them to build confidence and also exposes them to new opportunities available in the environment. What needs to be explored is the way in which entrepreneurial training or course work influences the individual's career choice. It can be concluded that education influences the ability to introduce entrepreneurial innovations and to achieve entrepreneurial success. There is a need to develop an effective curriculum which incorporates theoretical content with practical exercises. This would help the students inculcate the ability to scan the environment to explore the available opportunities, develop self-confidence and a positive attitude to enable them to enter independent business careers.

Thus, it can be concluded that sociocultural influences are not a barrier for entrepreneurial activity. Rather, they affect the development of entrepreneurial quality. Hence, there is a need to build an environment where members from all castes and socioeconomic strata feel encouraged to choose entrepreneurship as their profession and contribute positively to the economic growth of the country.

Annexure: Measurement Scales

Entrepreneurial Propensity

1. If I decided to go into business for myself, I would not know where to start.
2. I am developing the skills necessary to successfully operate my own business.
3. Going into business for myself is too risky.
4. I am not sure how I would keep up with all aspects of running my own business.
5. Starting one's own business is a great opportunity for success.

6. I do not like working for someone else.
7. I believe I could operate a successful small business.
8. I would rather operate a small business than be a middle manager with a larger organization.
9. It is possible for small business owners to be successful in today's economy.
10. I have a lot of respect for successful small business owners.
11. With all of the regulation and red tape today, it is simply too difficult to run a profitable business.

Intention (options)

12. I plan to start my own business immediately or within two years after graduation.
13. I plan to operate my own business within 10 years after graduation.

Perceived Family Support

A set of three indicators was used to measure the perceived level of family support. Students were asked to give their choices on three questions.

1. How do you rate the level of support you are likely to receive from your family to start a new business carrying out your business?
   Very high/High/Low/Very low
   The students would get 0, 1, 2 and 3 points, respectively, for the four alter-native answers.

2. What would inspire to become an entrepreneur?

   (i) A success story
   (ii) Help from family, relatives and friends
   (iii) Previous related experience
   (iv) Technical training
   (v) Government support
   (vi) Other (specify)

   One point would be given if choice (ii) were answered.

3. I would like to become an entrepreneur because

   (i) I knew I would get full family support for this choice of career.
   (ii) I desired to be self-employed.
   (iii) There was prestige in being called an entrepreneur.

(iv) I had this idea that I would be able to make a lot of money in this profession.
(v) I did not have any other alternative.

One point would be given if choice (i) were answered.

The scale that was used consisted of three levels of family support. The total scores ranged from 0–5. Therefore, the respondents were assigned to the three levels as follows:

4–5: High
2–3: Medium
0–1: Low

Religiosity

A set of six indicators was used to measure religiosity. Information regarding the indicators was obtained from the respondents with the help of the following questions:

Q. Do you:
Have faith in God?	Yes/No
Have a place of worship in office?	Yes/No
Worship daily?	Yes/No
Celebrate all important festivals?	Yes/No
Visit the temple/public place of worship regularly?	Yes/No
Perform any other specific rituals?	Yes/No

The respondents were given one point for each affirmative answer. The scale that was used consisted of three levels of religiosity. The scores ranged from 0–6. Therefore, the respondents were assigned to the three levels as follows:

0–2: High
3–4: Medium
5–6: Low

Caste Categories

The various castes have been divided into three groups. They were (I) Higher/Forward caste (that is, Brahmins, Kayasthas, Kshatriyas and Vaishyas) (II) Backward caste (III) Scheduled caste or Scheduled tribe.

References

Balkin, D. B. and J. W. Logan. 1988. 'Reward Policies that Support Entrepreneurship', *Compensation and Benefits Review*, 20(1): 18–25.

Begley, T. M. and D. P. Boyd. 1987. 'Psychological Characteristics Associated with Performance in Entrepreneurial Firms and Smaller Businesses', *Journal of Business Venturing*, 2(2): 79–93.

Berna, J. G. 1960. *Industrial Entrepreneurship in Madras State.* Mumbai: Asia Publishing House.

Brockhaus, R. H. 1982. 'The Psychology of the Entrepreneur', in Kent, C., D. Sexton and R. W. Smilor (eds), *The Art and Science of Entrepreneurship*, pp. 3–23. Cambridge, MA: Ballinger.

Brodsky, M. A. 1993. 'Successful Female Corporate Managers and Entrepreneurs: Similarities and Differences', *Group and Organization Management*, 18(3): 366–378.

Chamberlin, E. H. 1933. *The Theory of Monopolistic Competition.* Cambridge: Harvard University Press.

Corman, J., B. Perles and P. Yancini. 1988. 'Motivational Factors Influencing High-Technology Entrepreneurship', *Journal of Small Business Management*, 26(1): 36–42.

Dunphy, S. M. 1990. 'Entrepreneur and Intrapreneur: Why One is Not the Other and the Other Does Not Exist', *Journal of Business and Entrepreneurship*, 2(1): 81–90.

Flamholtz, E. G. 1986. *How to Make the Transition from Entrepreneurship to a Professionally Managed Firm.* San Francisco: Jossey-Bass.

Fox, R. G. 1969. *From Zamindar to Ballot Box; Community Change in a North Indian Market Town.* Ithaca: Cornell University Press.

Gartner, W. B. 1985. 'A Conceptual Framework for Describing the Phenomenon of New Venture Creation', *Academy of Management Review*, 10(4): 696–706.

———. 1988. 'Who is an Entrepreneur is the Wrong Question', *American Journal of Small Business*, 12(4): 11–32.

Harlambos, M. and R. Heald. 1980. *Sociology: Theory and Practice.* New Delhi: Oxford University Press.

Hisrich, R. D. 1990. 'Entrepreneurship/Intrapreneurship', *American Psychologist*, 45(2): 209–222.

Ireland, R. D. and P. M. Van Auken. 1987. 'Entrepreneurship and Small Business Research: An Historical Typology and Directions for Future Research', *American Journal of Small Business*, 11(4): 9–20.

Johnson, B. R. 1990. 'Toward a Multidimensional Model of Entrepreneurship: The Case of Achievement Motivation and the Entrepreneur', *Entrepreneurship Theory and Practice*, 14(3): 39–54.

Kirzner, I. M. 1973. *Competition and Entrepreneurship.* Chicago: University of Chicago Press.

Klavans, R., M. Shanley and W. M. Evan. 1985. 'The Management of Internal Corporate Ventures: Entrepreneurship and Innovation', *Columbia Journal of World Business* 20(1): 21–27.

Krueger, N. F. Jr. and D. V. Brazeal. 1994. 'Entrepreneurial Potential and Potential Entrepreneurs', *Entrepreneurship Theory and Practice*, 18(3): 91–104.

Lipset, S. M. 2000. 'Values and Entrepreneurship in the Americas', in R. Swedberg (ed.), *Entrepreneurship, the Social Science View*, pp. 112–113. New Delhi: Oxford University Press.

McClelland, D. C. 1961. *The Achieving Society.* Princeton, NJ: D. Van Nostrand Company.

———. 1962. 'Business Drive and National Achievement', *Harvard Business Review*, 40(4): 99–112.

———. 1965a. 'Achievement and Entrepreneurship: A Longitudinal Study', *Journal of Personality and Social Psychology*, 1(4): 389–392.

———. 1965b. 'Achievement Motivation Can be Developed', *Harvard Business Review*, 43(6): 6–24.

McClelland, D. C. and D. G. Winter. 1969. *Motivating Economic Achievement.* New York: Free Press.

Mintzberg, H. 1973. *The Nature of Managerial Work.* New York: Harper and Row.

Moore, C. F. 1986. 'Understanding Entrepreneurial Behavior: A Definition and Model', in J.A. Pearce, II, and R.B. Robinson (eds), *Best Paper Proceedings: Academy of Management,* pp. 66–70. Forty-sixth Annual Meeting of the Academy of Management, Academy of Management: Chicago.

Naffziger, D. W., J. S. Hornsby and D. F. Kuratko. 1994. 'A Proposed Research Model of Entrepreneurial Motivation', *Entrepreneurship Theory and Practice*, 18(3): 29–42.

Parnell, J. A., W. R. Crandall and W. A. Carden. 1995. 'Entrepreneurial Propensity among College Students: A Preliminary Assessment', *Proceedings of the 1995 BusinessExpo/ Entrepreneurship Conference*, 4(1): 1–13.

Rao, V. L. 1986. *Industrial Entrepreneurship in India.* Allahabad: Chaugh Publications.

Rumelt, R. P. 1987. 'Theory, Strategy, and Entrepreneurship', in D.J. Teece (ed.), *The Competitive Challenge*, pp. 137–158. Cambridge, MA: Ballinger.

Saberwal, S. 1976. *Mobile Men; Limits to Social Change in Urban Punjab.* New Delhi: Vikas Publishing House.

Schumpeter, J. A. 1934. *The Theory of Economic Development.* New York: Oxford University Press.

Singer, H. W. 1953. 'Obstacles to Economic Development', *Social Research*, 20(1): 83.

Singer, M. 1956. 'Cultural Values in India's Economic Development', *The Annals of the American Academy of Political and Social Science,* 305: 81–91.

———. 1972. *When a Great Tradition Modernizes.* New York: Praeger Publications.

Srinivas, M. N. 1962. *Caste in Modern India and Other Essays.* New York: Asia Building House.

Stumpf, S. A. 1992. 'Career Goal: Entrepreneur?', *International Journal of Career Management*, 4(2): 26–32.

Timberg, T. A. 1978. *The Marwaris; From Traders to Industrialists.* New Delhi: Vikas Publishing House.

Tripathi, D. 1992. 'Indian Business Houses and Entrepreneurship: A Note on Research Trends', *Journal of Entrepreneurship*, 1(1): 75–97.

———. 1997. *Historical Roots of Industrial Entrepreneurship in India and Japan: A Comparative Interpretation.* New Delhi: Manohar Publications.

Vesper, K. H. 1983. *Entrepreneurship and National Policy.* Chicago: Heller Institute for Small Business.

Weber, M. 1904. (1930 English translation). *The Protestant Ethic and the Spirit of Capitalism.* New York: Scribner; London: Allen and Unwin.

———. 1958. *The Protestant Ethic and the Spirit of Capitalism.* New York: Charles Scribner's Sons.

Motivational Factors Influencing Industrial Entrepreneurship in Rajasthan

9

R. RAGHUNATHAN

Entrepreneurs provide stability and serve as an engine for economic growth. The industrial development of a country and its different regions depends significantly on the presence of an adequate number of entrepreneurs. Identifying the factors that influence an individual's choice to pursue independent business creation might, therefore, lead to insights that would have an impact on economic growth and development. A large number of leading industrialists in India have come from Rajasthan but the state is still industrially backward. A survey was carried out among industrial entrepreneurs of Rajasthan to find out the factors of motivation in people for starting their own businesses. The results of the survey convey that non-economic factors have been the most influential motive for starting a business in Rajasthan.

Introduction

Entrepreneurship through the development of large scale industries and small and medium-sized enterprises (SMEs) continues to be at the forefront of economic development. Entrepreneurship contributes to development in various ways, such as procuring scarce resources, employing those for production, innovating or imitating production processes or new production technology and expanding the horizons of market.

An entrepreneur is a catalyst for development; with him we prosper and without him we are poor (Tandon, 1975). Entrepreneurs are recognized with equal emphasis by academicians, anthropologists, political scientists, economists, sociologists, psychologists, historians and the government to be major determinants of economic growth. Entrepreneurs also help in creating innovative enterprises, which provide the foundation for building a nation's competitiveness. Entrepreneurship offers a solution to the growing employment problems and facilitates uniform distribution of wealth and balanced regional development. In the next 10 years, around 130 million people in India will be looking for their first jobs. It is the entrepreneurs who can create these new jobs and opportunities (Gupta, 2001).

The creation of new independent businesses accounts for nearly one-fourth to one-third of the variation in economic growth in many industrialized countries. To support and encourage entrepreneurs is the most important issue faced by any society. If these people are de-motivated or if we lose them, society will be the loser in the long run. Before recognizing and appreciating these entrepreneurs, one should know how to identify them and understand what motivates them (Cooper and Dunkelberg, 1987).

Determinants of entrepreneurship can be also studied according to the level of analysis. There are three levels: micro, meso and macro level of entrepreneurship. Micro level studies deal with studying individual entrepreneurs or businesses. Meso level deals with studying firms or sectors of the industry. Macro level deals with studying the national economy.

In a vast country like India where regions widely differ in the availability of resources and entrepreneurial capabilities, there is a great need for regional studies on industrial entrepreneurship. The marked differences among different regions with respect to economic history, political consciousness, sociocultural heritage, and so on, make a region-wise approach a necessity. Such an approach could help in identifying the potentialities and problems of certain regions and help in formulating suitable policies to develop them (Venkatraman, 1997).

The people of Rajasthan (*Marwari*) are highly industrious and known for their entrepreneurial and trading skills. They have established a number of successful industrial and business ventures in India and abroad. For more than 300 years, merchant traders have travelled from the villages in Rajasthan across northern and eastern India, as well as to Russia and

Central Asia. However, the status of industrial entrepreneurship within Rajasthan is very bleak. Hence, there is a requirement to study the reasons for motivation among the industrial entrepreneurs in Rajasthan.

Literature Review

Motivation refers to factors within an individual, other than knowledge, which energize, direct and sustain behaviour (Locke and Latham, 1990). Motivation can be extrinsic or intrinsic. Extrinsic motivation has a stronger relationship with material factors while in the case of intrinsic motivation, the individual basically tries to fulfil his aims in life. However, whatever the case may be, motivation has an influence on the actions of the entrepreneur.

Entrepreneurship motivation is described as the socio-psychological drive among people that leads to economic development of a country (Akhouri and Mishra, 1990). New businesses are not created by accident. The effort and time involved in starting a business would suggest that entrepreneurial actions are clearly intentional. Entrepreneurial behaviour, such as becoming self-employed or starting a business, is intentional and is thus predicted by intentions towards behaviour, not by attitudes, beliefs, personality or demographics. Intentions are assumed to capture the motivational factors that influence behaviour. They are immediate antecedents of actual behaviour (Krueger, Jr. and Carsrud, 1993).

Different schools of thought propose different motivations or reasons for starting a business. The economic view of entrepreneurship suggests that entrepreneurs are motivated by the objective of profit maximization. Psychologists contend that entrepreneurship is a matter of individuals and therefore consider issues, such as personality characteristics. Sociologists explain entrepreneurial motivation in terms of such factors as religious belief, ethnicity, class and caste identities. A combination of all these approaches would give a holistic picture of what motivates people. There are a number of motivational characteristics that have been found in the entrepreneurial research and these include innovativeness, independence, respect for work, economic considerations, affiliation, power, self-actualization and achievement (Sharma, 1979). Indian researchers have used motivation and personality traits interchangeably. Most of the studies on motivation in India are descriptive in nature.

The reasons for starting a business were examined in a pioneering study (Scheinberg and MacMillan, 1988) called the Society of Associated Researchers of International Entrepreneurship (SARIE) research. This research listed 38 reasons, which were classified into six broad categories for starting a business.

- Need for approval
- Need for independence
- Need for personal development
- Welfare considerations (in terms of contributing to the community)
- Perceived instrumentality of wealth, tax reduction
- Following role models.

Tables 9.1 and 9.2 provide information on various research studies carried out in finding out the reasons for starting business.

Table 9.1   Summary of Research Studies on the Reasons for Starting a Business

Reasons for starting business/ Factors studied or focussed	Research studies
Need for independence	Friberg, 1976; Schein, 1978; Hofstede, 1980; Smith and Miner; 1983: 51–71.
Innovation	McClelland, 1961; McClelland and Winter, 1969; Shane et al., 1991 (considered as 'learning'); Birley and Westhead, 1994; Sheinberg and MacMillan, 1988 (considered as 'need for personal development').
Need for material incentives (Financial Success)	Friberg, 1976; Knight, 1987; Scheinberg and MacMillan, 1988 (labelled as 'perceived instrumentality of wealth'); Birley and Westhead, 1994;
Desire to escape or avoid a negative situation	Collins and Moore, 1955; Cooper, 1971; Friberg, 1976; Hagen, 1962; Shapero, 1975
Need for social approval	Friberg, 1976; Maslow, 1943; McClelland, 1961; Bonjean, 1966; Vroom, 1967; Nelson, 1968.
Drive to fulfill personal values or norms (Self-realization)	Friberg, 1976; Gilbert, 1997
Desire to follow family traditions (Roles)	Hofstede, 1980; Shane et al., 1991
Tax considerations	Shane et al., 1991

Table 9.2   Categories of Entrepreneurship Reasons

Researchers	Innovation	Need for Independence	Recognition	Roles	Financial success
Schienberg and Macmillan (1988)	*Need for personal development* To develop an idea for product or business. To keep Learning. To be innovative and be in the forefront of new technology. Direct contribution to success of the company.	*Control of my own time* To have greater flexibility for private life. Freedom to adapt my own approach to work.	*Need for approval* Be respected by my friends. Achieve something and get recognition. Achieve higher position in society. Increase status of family. Have more influence in community.		
Shane et al. (1991)	*Learning* To develop an idea for product. To be innovative and be in the forefront of new technology.	*Independence* To control my own time. To have greater flexibility for private life. To have considerable freedom to adapt my own approach to work.	*Recognition* To achieve a higher position for myself in the society. To have more influence in community. To be respected by my friends.	*Roles* To continue a family tradition. To have more influence in community. To follow the example of a person I admire.	Perceived instrumentality of wealth. Desire to have high earnings. Need more money to survive.

Study	Need for personal development	Need for Independence	Need for approval	Follow role models	Perceived instrumentality of wealth
	To continue learning.		To achieve something and get recognition. To increase status and prestige of my family.		Give self and family security. Access to indirect benefits.
Birley and Westhead (1994)	To be innovative and be in the forefront of new technology. To develop an idea for product. To continue learning.	To have considerable freedom to adapt my own approach to work. To have greater flexibility for private life. To control my own time.	To achieve a higher position for myself in society. To be respected by friends. To increase the status and prestige of my family. To achieve something and get recognition for it. Desire to have higher earnings. To have more influence in my community.	To follow the example of a person I admire.	To give myself, spouse and children security. To contribute to the welfare of my relatives.

Source: Carter et al., 2003.

Another study by Kolvereid (1996) explored the reasons given for self-employment versus organizational employment. He proposed that there were 11 types of reasons for choosing between self-employment and organizational employment: security, economic opportunity, authority, autonomy, social environment, work load, challenge, self-realization, participation in the whole process, avoiding responsibility, and career choice. He found that individuals who were self-employed were more likely to choose economic opportunity, authority, autonomy, challenge, self-realization and participation in the whole process, compared to those choosing organizational employment.

Methodology

This study is based on primary data collected through a structured mailed questionnaire (see Annexure) from a sample of industrial units in Rajasthan. The sample was chosen to be typically representative of the population in terms of the characteristics under study. Therefore, the results obtained could be generalized.

The target population was business enterprises, that is, all those firms which were registered and involved in manufacturing. Three major sources were used to identify the contact address of the sample. The list of enterprises in Rajasthan available at the online database of the Bureau of Investment Promotion, Government of Rajasthan, List of medium and large-scale industries available at the District Industrial Center, Commissionarite of Industries, Government of Rajasthan, and various directories, such as Directory of Manufacturers, Rajasthan Business Pages, Rajasthan Industries' Directory, Rajasthan Chamber of Commerce and Industry, Directory–2002 (Udaipur Chamber of Commerce and Industry) and Kothari's Industrial Directory 1996–97.

With the above sampling frame, 617 firms were selected randomly and the questionnaires were sent in four stages. The details are given in Table 9.3. For the purpose of analysis, the data collected were coded.

Results and Discussion

Out of 617 questionnaires sent, 38 questionnaires were returned by the Postal and Telegraph department citing reasons like non-existence of

Table 9.3   Details of Questionnaire Despatch

Stages	Questionnaire despatch date	No. of questionnaires sent	Remainder despatch date
Stage I	24 September, 2003	357	31 October, 2003
Stage II	16 February, 2004	93	26 March, 2004
Stage III	22 June, 2004	92	2 July, 2004
Stage IV	13 August, 2004	75	24 September, 2004
Total		617	

the company, closure of business, non-existence of address, and so forth. Of the remaining 579 respondents to whom the questionnaire was despatched, 60 replies were received. The filled questionnaires provided all the requisite data for the study. Hence, none of the filled questionnaire was omitted due to incompleteness, illegible handwriting or any other reasons.

Based on the literature survey, the reasons for starting a new business can be broadly classified into six categories: business opportunity, business reasons, government, profit, personal characteristics and social objectives. In the following paragraphs each one of these element is discussed in detail.

Business Opportunity

Entrepreneurs are able to spot unique opportunities (Milton, 1989). They are able to identify new opportunities, needs or problem solutions (Corman et al., 1988). Entrepreneurs have the ability to turn the common business opportunities into unique and unexpected prospects. People start business to tap these opportunities.

Business Reasons

These are the reasons that occur because of the entrepreneurs' existing business. The business can take the form of forward integration, backward integration, expansion, diversification, promoting business in other geographical regions, availability of inputs, joint venture, monopoly business and lack of competition.

Government

This refers to the government promotional policies, incentives and infra-structure facilities. This factor acts as an external encouragement to start a company.

Personal Characteristics

It is actually individuals who start businesses. Their personal character-istics influence their intentions to start a business. These personal char-acteristics can be:

Independence

This characteristic is an individual's desire for freedom, control and flexi-bility in the use of his time. He has a need for autonomy and desire for personal control (Carter et al., 2003) and he seeks to be his own boss (Amit et al., 1996; Knight, 1987).

Recognition

An individual's intention to have status, approval and recognition from one's family, friends and from those in the community, thus making a name, standing out in the crowd.

Roles

An individual's desire to follow family traditions or emulate the example of others.

Self-realization

Pursuing self-directed goals, realizing their own ideas about how the organization should evolve, utilizing their full range of talents.

Innovation

An individual's intention to accomplish something new. Introducing original ideas about products or services, pursuing something new or different; desire to build something of one's own.

Stability

Security or stability for the family and others and for both the current and future generations. The objective is to have a better future prospect and a secure life.

Profit

An individual's intention to earn more money, become wealthy, meet financial needs and goals and also to provide benefits to the shareholders leads him to start a new business.

Social Objectives

Social objectives that become a reason for entrepreneurs to start a new business are to provide employment, contribute to the community, region or country in terms of general economic development, act as a source of revenue, earning foreign exchange, and so forth.

The reasons for starting a business have remained the same, irrespective of whether such data has been collected through close-ended or open-ended questions (Shaver et al., 2001). In the present study, the respondents were asked an open-ended question '*What was the promoter's motivation for starting this firm?*'. The responses provided were coded and sorted into the six categories as mentioned earlier. In response to this question, a few respondents provided more than a single reason. Figure 9.1 provides details of the number of distinct answers (reasons) given by the respondents. Most respondents provided a distinct answer to the question. Around 32 per cent of the respondents gave more than two distinct answers to the question.

Figure 9.1   Distinct Answers Provided

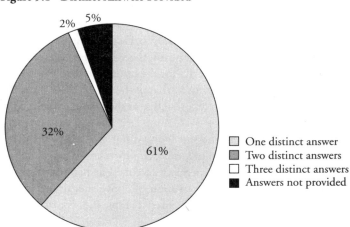

Table 9.4 depicts the reasons for starting the venture. Entrepreneurs in Rajasthan have started businesses primarily because of their personal characteristics. The predominant motives were independence, autonomy, accomplishment, achievement and self-actualization. This was followed by business reasons, specifically with regard to the availability of raw material and the expansion and diversification policies of the existing firms. Only 12 per cent of the entrepreneurs started their business in Rajasthan because of the easy availability of business opportunities. This clearly indicates that there is a lack of easy availability of business opportunity in the state of Rajasthan. Around 11 per cent of the entrepreneurs started businesses because of their social commitments and involvement.

Table 9.4   Reasons for Starting a Business

Reasons	Frequency	Percentage
Business Opportunity	10	12.35
Business Reasons	17	20.99
Government	6	7.41
Profit	5	6.17
Personal Characteristics	31	38.27
Social Objective	9	11.11
Not Available	3	3.70
Total No. of Responses	81*	100

Note: *The total number of responses (81) is more than the total number of respondents (60) because of multiple answers provided by the respondents.

Contrary to the general belief that individuals start businesses with the prime aim of making money, only 6.17 per cent of the entrepreneurs stated that they started their businesses with this objective in mind. Money was not a significant motive for the initiation of new businesses in Rajasthan. This finding conforms to that of the GEM 2003 India Report (Manimala, 2003: 12), which reported that at the national level, economic motives were secondary.

The study also tried to find out if any difference exists in the motivation across age, education, joint family, employment of parents, financial standing and prior business experience factors. Further analysis has been carried out for knowing the motivation of above-mentioned categories of respondents. The results are presented in Table 9.5. It can be observed

Table 9.5 Reasons for Starting a Business—Specific Factors

(in percentage)

Reasons	Age				Education qualification				
	18–24	25–34	35–44	Above 44	Primary	Secondary	Higher secondary	Graduate	Post graduate
Business Opportunity	1.23	4.94	11.11	6.17	0	1.23	0	9.88	12.35
Business Reasons	0	7.41	3.7	6.17	0	1.23	1.23	12.35	2.47
Government	0	1.23	1.23	4.94	0	1.23	0	2.47	3.7
Profit	0	1.23	1.23	3.7	0	0	0	4.94	1.23
Personal Characteristics	1.23	12.35	7.41	8.64	1.23	2.47	0	14.81	11.11
Social Objective	0	1.23	4.94	4.94	0	0	0	8.64	2.47
Not Available	2.47	0	1.23	1.23	1.23	0	1.23	1.23	1.23

Reasons	Joint family		Parents self-employed		Financial standing			Prior business experience	
	Yes	No	Yes	No	Above Avg.	Avg.	Poor	Yes	No
Business Opportunity	19.75	3.7	20.99	2.47	14.81	8.64	0	22.67	2.67
Business Reasons	17.28	0	14.81	2.47	9.88	7.41	0	14.67	2.67
Government	6.17	1.23	4.94	2.47	4.94	2.47	0	2.67	2.67
Profit	3.7	2.47	4.94	1.23	3.7	2.47	0	5.33	1.33
Personal Characteristics	20.99	8.64	18.52	11.11	12.35	16.05	0	14.67	14.67
Social Objective	9.88	1.23	11.11	0	3.7	7.41	0	9.33	2.67
Not Available	3.7	1.23	3.7	1.23	1.23	2.47	1.23	2.67	1.33

from this table that personal characteristics have been the most quoted reason for starting a business by all except *respondents belonging to the categories of postgraduates, those in the age group of 35 to 44, those with prior business experience, and whose parents are self-employed.*

Conclusion

Contrary to the belief that money motivates people to choose entrepreneurship as a career option, personal characteristics followed by business reasons were the most important influencing factors in starting up a business in Rajasthan. Initiatives by the government and other institutions involved in promoting entrepreneurship should focus on developing and triggering the personal characteristics of the individuals such that it makes them choose entrepreneurship as a career option. There is also an urgent need for inculcating these attributes in individuals through educational training programmes at the school and college levels. This can also be done through special programmes like the motivation camps that are organized by the Department of Science and Technology (DST) to promote entrepreneurship in Rajasthan. The government should also take the initiative to recognize and accredit the contribution of entrepreneurs to the society by providing rewards and titles to them. Profiles of successful entrepreneurs should be set before young adults for motivating them to start their own business. Well-established entrepreneurs should also be involved as mentors for providing guidance to aspiring entrepreneurs.

Annexure

R. Raghunathan

Management Group
Faculty Division-I
BITS
Pilani-333031
September 24, 2003

Research Questionnaire

Dear Sir,

Please allow me to introduce myself as a student working towards his Ph.D at Birla Institute of Technology and Science, Pilani. The topic of my thesis is 'Evolution and Growth of Industrial Entrepreneurship in Rajasthan'. The objective of the study is to identify the various motivations that propel an entrepreneur to start a venture and the problems commonly faced by them. The study will also attempt to project the future of industrial entrepreneurship in Rajasthan.

I am happy to inform you that your organization finds a place in my shortlist of samples. As I enclose a brief questionnaire for you to fill in, I want you to know that your responses and thoughts will be a part of the most valuable inputs to my study.

I wish to assure you that the information provided by you will be used only for academic purpose. I request you to kindly fill in the questionnaire with utmost sincerity and then mail the same to me latest by 25 October 2003.

I thank you for your kind assistance.

Yours truly,

R. Raghunathan

Encl.: As above

Evolution and Growth of Industrial Entrepreneurship in Rajasthan

Please Respond in as Much Detail as Possible

1. Name of the firm: _____

2. Year of establishment: _____

3. Who started this company?

   Yourself ☐   Your relative ☐

   Others (Please specify the name of the promoter): _____

4. Promoter's age of the time of promoting

   18–24 ☐   25–34 ☐   35–44 ☐   45–59 ☐

5. Educational Attainment

   No formal education   ☐   Higher Secondary   ☐

   Primary School   ☐   Graduate   ☐

   Secondary School   ☐   Post Graduate   ☐

6. Was the promoter born in Rajasthan?

   Yes ☐   No ☐

   If No, please mention the place of birth _____

7. Did the promoter belong to a joint family?

   Yes ☐   No ☐

8. Were the promoter's parents self-employed?

   Yes ☐   No ☐

9. What was the financial standing of the promoter's family at the time of promoting this firm?

   Above average ☐   Average ☐   Poor ☐

10. What was the promoter's motivation for starting this firm? _____

11. Before establishing this firm, did the promoter have any other business?

    Yes ☐   No ☐

    If Yes, what was the business and when was that established? _____

    If No, what were the nature and number of years of his experience, if any?

    _____

12. What problems/obstacles did the promoter face in course of establishing this firm? _____

13. Do you plan to start a new firm in the next three years?

    Yes ☐   No ☐

    If Yes, what is the reason for doing so? _____

    And what is the kind of business that you propose to start? _____

    And when do you propose to start this new business? _____

Thank You

References

Akhouri, M. M. P. and S. P. Mishra. 1990. 'Entrepreneurship Education: A Conceptual Base, Approach and Methodology', *Indian Management, XXIX–11* (November–December): 48–59.

Amit, R., K. R. MacCrimmon and J. Oesch. 1996. 'The Decision to Start a New Venture: Values, Beliefs, and Alternatives', paper presented at Babson Entrepreneurial Research Conference, Babson College, Wellesly, MA.

Birley, S. and P. Westhead. 1994. 'A Taxonomy of Business Start-up Reasons and Their Impact on Firm Growth and Size', *Journal of Business Venturing*, 9(1): 7–31.

Bonjean, C. M. 1966. 'Mass, Class and the Industrial Community: A Comparative Analysis of Managers, Businessmen, and Workers', *American Journal of Sociology*, 72(2): 149–162.

Carter, N. M., W. B. Gartner, K. G. Shaver and E. J. Gatewood. 2003. 'The Career Reasons of Nascent Entrepreneurs', *Journal of Business Venturing*, 18(1): 13–39.

Collins, D. F. and D. G. Moore. 1955. *The Enterprising Man*. New York: Double Day.

Cooper, A. 1971. *The Founding of Technologically Based Firms*. Milwakee, WI: Center for Venture Management.

Cooper, A. C. and W. C. Dunkelberg. 1987. 'Entrepreneurial Research: Old Questions, New Answers and Methodological Issues', *American Journal of Small Business*, 11(3): 11–23.

Corman, Joel, Benjamin Perles, and Paula Vancini. 1988. 'Motivational Factors Influencing High-technology Entrepreneurship', *Journal of Small Business Management*, 26(1): 36–42.

Friberg, M. 1976. *Is the Salary the Only Incentive for Work?* New York: Free Press.

Gilbert, M. R. 1997. 'Identity, Space and Politics: A Critique of the Poverty Debates', in Jones, J. P., H. J. Nast and S. M. Roberts (eds), *Thresholds in Feminist Geography: Difference, Methodology and Presentation*, pp. 29–45. Lanham, MD: Rowman and Littlefield.

Gupta, Rajat. 2001. 'Creating Indian Entrepreneurship'. Available online at http://www.mckinsey.com/aboutus/mckinseynews/pressarchive (downloaded on 15 October, 2001).

Hagen, E. E. 1972. *On the Theory of Social Change: How Economic Growth Begins.* Homewood, IL: Dorsey Press.

Hofstede, C. 1980. *Culture's Consequences: International Differences in Work Related Values.* Beverly Hills, CA: Sage Publications.

Knight, R. M. 1987. 'Can Business School Produce Entrepreneurs?', in *Frontiers of Entrepreneurship Research*, pp. 603–604. Wellesley, MA: Babson College.

Kolvereid, L. 1996. 'Organizational Employment Versus Self-employment: Reasons for Career Choice Intentions', *Entrepreneurship Theory and Practice*, 20(3): 23–31.

Krueger, N. F. Jr. and A. L. Carsrud. 1993. 'Entrepreneurial Intentions: Applying the Theory of Planed Behavior', *Entrepreneurship and Regional Development*, 5(4): 315–330.

Locke, E. A. and G. P. Latham. 1990. *A Theory of Goal Setting and Task Performance.* Englewood Cliffs, NJ: Prentice-Hall.

Manimala, Mathew J. 2003. 'Global Entrepreneurship Monitor, India Report 2002', in Paul D. Reynolds, William D. Bygrave, Erkko Autio (eds), *Global Entrepreneurship Monitor, Executive Report, 2003.* Kansas City, MO: Kauffman Center for Entrepreneurial Leadership.

Maslow, A. H. 1943. 'A Theory of Human Motivation', *Psychology Review*, (4; July): 370–396.

McClelland, D. C. 1961. *The Achieving Society.* New York: Free Press.

McClelland, D. C. and D. G. Winter. 1969. *Motivating Economic Achievement.* New York: Free Press.

Milton. 1989. 'The Complete Entrepreneur', *Entrepreneurship Theory and Practice*, 13(3): 9–19.

Nelson, J. I. 1968. 'Participation and Integration: The Case of the Small Businessman', *American Sociology Review*, 33(3): 427–438.

Schein, E. H. 1978. *Career Dynamics: Matching Individual and Organizational Needs.* Readings, MA: Addison-Wesley.

Scheinberg, S. and I. C. MacMillan. 1988. 'An 11-Country Study of Motivations to Start a Business', in B. A. Kirchoff, W. A. Long, W. E. McMullan, K. H. Vesper and W. E. Wetzel (eds.), *Frontiers of Entrepreneurship Research,* pp. 669–687. Wellesley, MA: Babson College.

Shane, S., L. Kolvereid and P. Westhead. 1991. 'An Exploratory Examination of the Reasons Leading to New Firm Formation Across Country and Gender', *Journal of Business Venturing*, 6(6): 431–446.

Shapero, A. 1975. 'The Displaced Uncomfortable Entrepreneur', *Psychology Today*, 9 (November): 83–88.

Sharma, S. V. S. 1979. *Small Entrepreneurial Development in Small Asian Countries: A Comparative Study.* New Delhi: Light and Life.

Shaver, Kelly G., William B. Gartner, Elizabeth Crosby, Karolina Bakalarova and Elizabeth J. Gatewood. (2001). 'Attributions about Entrepreneurship: A Framework and Process for Analyzing Reasons for Starting a Business', *Entrepreneurship Theory and Practice*, 26(2): 5–32.

Smith, N. R. and J. B. Miner. 1983. 'Type of Entrepreneur, Type of Firm, and Managerial Innovation: Implications for Organizational Life Cycle Theory', in *Frontiers of Entrepreneurship Research*. Wellesley, MA: Babson College.

Tandon, B. C. 1975. *Environment and Entrepreneur.* Allahabad: Chugh Publications.

Venkatraman, S. 1997. 'The Distinctive Domain of Entrepreneurship Research', in J. Katz (ed.), *Advances in Entrepreneurship, Firm Emergence and Growth*, 3, pp. 119–138. New York: JAI Press.

Vroom, V. H. 1967. *Work and Motivation.* New York: Wiley.

Psychosocial Perceptional Differences

An Empirical Exploratory Study on Indian Food Processing Women Entrepreneurs

10

R. GANESAN, R.P. PRADHAN AND
R.C. MAHESHWARI

Perception as a whole is a complex inter-linked phenomenon cum action emerging from the action/intuition of the self and the environment in justification with certain substantiating factors or parameters in common. It derives the constructive and destructive approaches by an individual towards performing an action or reciprocating to an activity or causation at any given point in time. Over the years, across the globe, women entrepreneurship has become a subject matter of interest for economists, sociologists, psychologists, anthropologists, policy makers, planners, researchers and facilitators. This field still has scope to explore many untouched aspects and develop a comprehensive framework for systematic study. Ever since the wake of women entrepreneurship, it has been seen that their lacunae, dilemmas and derelicts in venturing into any start-up process lag behind numerically in the statistical picture, particularly with reference to women entrepreneurs/actors in the Indian context. This is despite constituting benefactors in terms of policies and programmes which are still acting as direct promulgators and emancipators. We place our argument here in terms of the change required in the perception of those women to emerge as entrepreneurs. Women need the example of successful enterprising women to change their perception in terms of the social system and socio-background deviations. The present study attempts to find the social and background differences on perceptional psychosocial variables. These are staunch factors for women that enable them to enter, sustain and foresee their prospects in their enterprises through their entrepreneurial abilities. In the present study, date was collected on administering an intensive interview schedule with 32 women entrepreneurs/ actors who were running food processing enterprises/start-ups. The results were analyzed using the 'T' test analysis. Significant mean differences were found with socio-background variables on psychosocial variable and discussed accordingly.

Introduction

The primary objective of this paper is to analyze and understand the gamut of women entrepreneurship in India which is at a growing stage. However, given the liberalization and globalization processes all around, it is no more advisable to look at women entrepreneurship in India in isolation. It is in this context that the present paper—apart from focussing on the Indian scenario—has attempted a comparative review of the economic participation rates of women at international levels.

International Women Entrepreneurship Perspective

Internationally, women entrepreneurs represent a major share in the economic development. This is the main reason for women entrepreneurs to be considered to be the key players in any developing country, particularly in terms of their contribution to economic sustenance and development (Baker et al., 1997). Today, women are starting businesses at a rate twice as that of men (Allen, 1999). Research conducted by the National Foundation for Women Business Owners (NFWBO, 1998) internationally in Latin America and other regions, found that women business owners have many things in common regardless of nationality. They share common personal characteristics and are similar in many ways in the lines of business they pursue. They encounter similar issues and challenges while starting up and growing their enterprises. Also, an analysis of the relationship between economic activity in general, incorporation of the managerial skills, entrepreneurial activity and economic growth throughout Latin America and the Carribean shows that the support for entrepreneurial development efforts has a significant impact on the growth and prosperity in the region. Women-owned businesses employ more than 15 million workers in the United States and the sales generated amount to approximately US$ 1.4 trillion (Nelton, 1996). However, the current scenario is likely to be much more impressive in terms of their participation in economic avenues.

In 1995, the United Nations compiled the most comprehensive international summary of quantitative information on the economic activity of women in Latin America and categorized this under three indicators which ensured excess rate of women participation in economic activity: share of administrative or managerial salaried workers, share of employers and own-account workers, and business ownership and consistency. The rate of business ownership by women ranges from 25 per cent to 35 per cent in Latin America and the Caribbean with a low rate of participation at 10 per cent in Suriname and a high rate of 48 per cent in the Netherlands Antilles. A major transition has occurred during 1970–90, wherein women employers in Latin America and the Caribbean increased to more than double—from 22 per cent to 48 per cent. Also, it revealed only a lack of access to capital and technology. It is surprising to note that entrepreneurial characteristics and attributes are not indicated as parameters in westernized countries.

Research on women entrepreneurship, their contribution and socio-background were woefully inadequate—more so with reference to developing countries like India (Singh, 1993). A study conducted by Anwar (1992) in Bangladesh tried to project the characteristics of the activities managed by women entrepreneurs. He observed that the constraints of social norms prevailing there have prevented women entrepreneurs to manage their business independently. Those norms have restricted their mobility and thereby affected interaction with others, particularly for obtaining accurate information for business operation. Besides these, there is also a gap in availing of the training opportunities for skill formation.

In comparison with developed and developing countries, women entrepreneurship is not only significant in general for economic development but also for gaining social status in particular in the cases of Latin America and other regions. In lieu of this statement, Reynolds et al. (1999) in their findings in the research report in Global Entrepreneurship Monitor indicated that most of the countries studied showed that the biggest and most rapid gain in firm start-ups has been achieved by increasing the participation of women in the entrepreneurial process, and women entrepreneurship is critical to a long-term economic prosperity. A study by Julie and Seiler (2001) compiled a detailed paper on women entrepreneurship in Latin America which indicated that in Mexico, larger businesses owned by women having 26–99 employees are more likely to have their homepages on the World Wide Web. This indicates their awareness of media and e-business for the emancipation of their enterprises towards sustenance and promotion. An online business website has been established by the Women's Business Centre in the United States which currently funds 71 centres. The Women Business Ownership Act of 1988 (Public Law 100–533) in the United States established the National Women's Business Council. Similarly, South Korea replicated this process in 1998 for promoting women's economic participation. According to Jalbert (2000), most of the available literature on women's business ownership concentrate on entrepreneurial development in industrialized countries at the national level and within the less developed formal sector. The economic participation and growth has been considered as the major shift in women entrepreneurship irrespective of food processing or any other enterprising activity. This has been the major reason for the focus on perspectives at international women entrepreneurship irrespective of entrepreneurial domain. Keeping this in view, the study attempted to find the mean socio-background differences on psychosocial perceptional variables.

Psychosocial Dimensions

Psychosocial aspects have the depiction of both the self and the environment—the former 'self' which is the prime area of concentration to clear the unwanted clouds and nurture entrepreneurial vision. Entrepreneurial vision, associated with positive happenings and events, gears enterprising acumen amongst women as a whole. Besides the social learning theory (Rotter, 1966; Rotter et al., 1972) and the achievement motivation theory (McClelland, 1961, 1962; Winter, 1969), other similar personality theories were also important for entrepreneurial growth and these theories had supported many contemporary researches on entrepreneurship, determining the entrepreneurial capabilities of entrepreneurs in terms of need, motivation, achievement and perception, and, in turn, had given dimensions and inclinations to entrepreneurship development in practicing it.

Women entrepreneurship was not foreseen much on the psychosocial angles especially in developing countries like India. Rather, it was seen in terms of target achievement ideology where the real training mechanism does not truly inculcate the perceptional personality dimensions of women entrepreneurs. This might be one strong reason which prevents women to enter into an entrepreneurship for long. Of course, the patriarchal social system, norms and taboos might have dominated them over years in a country like India. For long, women have been unable to get involved in an economic activity. Surprisingly, in India, women entrepreneurship started to sprout in the late 1980s—initially at a slow pace and then gradually gaining momentum. However, they are still stagnant with their percentage of contribution in enterprises. This is not very encouraging. Also, the number of successful women entrepreneurs is numerically less in comparison to the hefty population of the country. The question arises as to why the situation has remained the same for so long despite all the governmental policies, plan of actions, financial schemes, training mechanisms, facilitating organizations, interfacing institutions, academic institutions and universities that pursue gender studies, concentrating on women entrepreneurship and empowerment. In comparison to men, Indian women who are equally talented and potentially capable have still not been perceived as the significant agents of entrepreneurship and contributors to the economic growth of the country. Investigation about the flaws associated with such a view or perception became the main aim of researchers in order to put forward the policy implications. This made the researcher very inquisitive about the probable factors that were associated with it: whether the flaw lay in the mechanism, governmental policies, financial schemes/institutions in support of women, commissions specified for the upbringing of women economically and socially, or training methodologies adopted across the nation. The earlier works have resented more so with aspects rather the perception by itself as an action or drive for them to go for an activity. This lacuna has been found in the earlier studies too, because of perception as an entry barrier to any action. Interestingly, negative perceptions were surmounting women workforces at all corners in such andro-centric system which are quite natural too and can be explained only in terms of motivation and personality theories.

The theories on motivation and personalities in the Indian context, on a larger scale, that could tap the real potential of women workforces as potential entrepreneurs, have not been properly or fully adopted to bring a participatory climate. In other words, the nascent entrepreneurs were not moulded with perceptional training, which is the need of the hour and the yardstick in the facilitation process. Mere technicalities, education, costing, budgeting, accounting, calculating breakevens and the management will be of no use or, more precisely, an overall failure if the righteous perceptions are not within reach of nascent women entrepreneurs with an inclination for entrepreneurship. This, in turn, hampers their enterprising and income generating minds altogether. It is crucial to note the reason why women's entry into enterprising activity has been considerably meagre in comparison to the men's and why the closures and clashes were more in the case of income generating units, group enterprises out of self-help groups, more precisely with women engaged with food processing enterprises.

Need and Relevance of the Study

Tiny enterprises were considered to be the best suited for Indian women— especially food processing enterprises which had their genesis long back wherein women were involved in traditional food processing to meet the requirements of the family. Now it has grown to a commercial plank for their expedition. Statistically speaking, although the growth potential of the food processing enterprise was high (Saigal, 2001) in the last decade, the research on women entrepreneurs in food processing enterprises had not been carried out effectively in any of the entrepreneurial research studies in India. Literature on the demographic profile of women entrepreneurs and factors or problems affecting the enterprises owned by women were woefully limited. Researches pertaining to the food processing sector were not considerably high and, moreover, the food processing entrepreneurs were mostly found in the unorganized sectors. So the wholesome status was not visible. The gateways to enter a business enterprise could vary on the basis of background parameters and the psychosocial profile, which were highly indispensable for a woman entrepreneur's emergence and success. However, paucity of research in the area left no tangible and integrative picture of the issue which was to be addressed carefully. Therefore, focussing on this could throw a new light on the attitudes and behaviour of women entrepreneurs in establishing, managing and sustaining their enterprises. Moreover, to pursue any-thing beyond the limits of social role could be more demanding, as at some point in time, social comparison with their male counterparts could affect women's perceptions and hence performance.

To rejuvenate the economic development, small women entrepre-neurs in the food processing enterprises were taken for the present study. More precisely, this would help to identify the grassroot facts and pro-blems of women entrepreneurs so that the methodologies and facilitative measures in any training programme can be developed accordingly. The study has taken psychosocial variables (perceptions of ladder of success at present, perceptions of entrepreneurial expectations about the future, perceptions about self-achievements and perceptions of success) as de-pendent variables and background variables (such as age, education, social category, previous self-occupation, years of experience, family income, mem-berships in association, entrepreneurship and technical training, place of enterprise, father's present occupation and husband's education) as inde-pendent variables. Thus, the present study attempts to bring forth a threshold on different perceptional variables and their significant differ-ences in accordance with the governing socio-background variables which enable such perceptions and substantiate them to perform an enterprising activity.

Objective

The objective of the study is to find out the significant mean differences on psychosocial perceptional variables using socio-backgrounds.

Method of Study

Assumption

Indian women entrepreneurs are generally caught up in the dual re-sponsibility of running a family and entering the enterprising world, where both the responsibilities are highly demanding and need proper organ-ization of time allocation, management and psychological frame of mind. Hence, the age of entry into the enterprising world becomes crucial for a successful venture. Similarly, social categorization and stratification have been important in playing a vital role since time immemorial, not only in India but also in other parts of the globe. Literacy, better socio-psycho-educational family environment, occupational structure and the financial conditions of the family, status of women, and so forth, result in a significant difference between them and the people belonging to other backward castes and classes in each area of functioning in India. The level of education of the entrepreneurs plays a major role in helping them to understand and to cope with the problems that they confront in the daily management of their enterprises. In addition to the place of enterprise, their fathers' previous occupation and husbands' education dominate, persuade, and permit them to opt for their enterprising activity, respectively.

Hypotheses

The prime hypothesis is that psychosocial perceptions would differ significantly by different socio-background variables.

Hypothesis I

Perceived ladder of success at present would differ significantly in different socio-background variables.

Hypothesis II

Perception of entrepreneurial expectations about the future would differ significantly by different socio-background variables.

Hypothesis III

Perceptions about self-achievements would differ significantly in different socio-background variables.

Hypothesis IV

Perceptions of success would differ significantly by different socio-background variables.

Sampling

Selection of the Area

Keeping the nature of the present study, two non-governmental organizations (MOOWES and AWAKE), having common objectives in women empowerment through entrepreneurship training and marketing, were selected and the entire list of the registered women entrepreneurs, exclusively in the food processing enterprises, was obtained.

Profile of the Study Area
Marketing Organization of Women Entrepreneurs (MOOWES)

Marketing Organization of Women Entrepreneurs (MOOWES) was founded in Chennai in 1990 with 12 members. The activities of this organization included: first, sharing their views and the difficulties while running their enterprises by forming networks amongst the women entrepreneurs; second, assisting women in the field of marketing by face-to-face contacts with the customers and thereby gaining confidence within the women entrepreneurs; and last, conducting periodic training programmes for women on various aspects required for running a business successfully and developing entrepreneurial skills.

Association for Women Entrepreneurs of Karnataka (AWAKE)

Association for Women Entrepreneurs (AWAKE) of Karnataka was founded in December 1983 comprising 500 members in Bangalore with an aim to empower women economically through entrepreneurship development. Activities of this organization primarily included counselling, entrepreneurship awareness programmes (EAP), entrepreneurship development programme (EDP), trainers' training programme (TTP), development agency/non-governmental organizational sensitization programmes, and follow-up programmes.

Procedure and Technique

The investigators got the response from 32 women entrepreneurs out of total 78. The women entrepreneurs in food processing enterprises were mostly involved in the preparation of jams, jellies, pickles, *papads* and squashes. For the present study, the bakeries were studied to be located in two metropolitan cities, namely Chennai (N = 16) and Bangalore (N = 16), their numbers being equally divided numerically. Data was collected through an interview schedule administered to the selected sample in two phases, that is, Chennai and Bangalore entrepreneurs. The total span of data collection was almost six months in both the cities inclusive of identifying the women entrepreneurs in food processing enterprises, approaching them, convincing them for the interviews, selecting the sample among them and personally interviewing and extending interview schedule. Purposive random sampling technique has been adopted for the study.

Variables and Tools

In the present study, there are two categories of variables: socio-background and psychosocial.

Socio-background Variables

The socio-background variables included were age (A), education (E), social category (C), previous occupation (O), year(s) of experience in running the enterprise (Y), family income (FI), membership in associations (MA), entrepreneurship and technical training (ETT), place of enterprise (P), father's present occupation (FPRO) and husband's education (HE), and their sample distribution are represented in Table 10.1.

Table 10.1 Sample Distribution across Different Socio-background Variables

Age group	Respondents (f)	Percentage
30–44	18	56.25
45–59	14	43.75
Education	Respondents (f)	Percentage
Graduates	23	71.87
Non Graduates	9	28.13
Social Category	Respondents (f)	Percentage
General	24	75.00
Backward Class	8	25.00
Previous Occupation	Respondents (f)	Percentage
Working Women	22	68.75
Housewives	10	31.25
Years of Experience	Respondents (f)	Percentage
1–4 years	16	50.00
5 years and above	16	50.00
Family Income	Respondents (f)	Percentage
Up to INR 4500	22	68.75
INR 4501–10000	10	31.25

(Table 10.1 continued)

(*Table 10.1 continued*)

Age group	Respondents (f)	Percentage
Membership in Associations	Respondents (f)	Percentage
Yes	23	71.87
No	9	28.13
Entrepreneurship and Technical Training	Respondents (f)	Percentage
Yes	24	75.00
No	8	25.00
Place of Enterprise	Respondents (f)	Percentage
Chennai	16	50.00
Bangalore	16	50.00
Father's Present Occupation	Respondents (f)	Percentage
No occupation	24	75.00
Business	8	25.00
Husband's Education	Respondents (f)	Percentage
Graduates	23	71.87
Postgraduates	9	28.13

Notes: N=32, Respondents (f)—Respondent Frequency/Number of Respondents.

Psychosocial Variables

Psychosocial variables included perceived ladder of success at present (LASP), perceptions of entrepreneurial expectations of the future (EE), perceptions of self-achievements (POA), and perceptions of success (POS). The present study clubbed these four variables into psychosocial variables, and these variables were related to women entrepreneurship due to its self ↔ environment nature, and the sample distribution amongst these variables is indicated in Table 10.2.

Perceived Ladder of Success at Present (LASP): Perceived ladder of success at present (LASP) comprises 10 steps in which the entrepreneur rated herself in steps that are currently operating with respect to her functioning of enterprise and enterprising skills. (Step 1–Step 10).

Perceptions of Self-Achievements (POA): The perceptions of the self-achievements of women entrepreneurs comprised six self-devised questions about their accomplishment perceptions with appropriate responses and administered for the present study scores on a 4-point scale (range 6–24).

Table 10.2 Sample Distribution across Different Psychosocial and Psycho-entrepreneurial Variables

Psychosocial variables		
*Ladder of success at present**	*Respondents (f)*	*Percentage*
Step 2	1	3.13
Step 4	4	12.50
Step 5	18	56.25
Step 6	6	18.75
Entrepreneurial Expectations about the future	Respondents (f)	Percentage
Very Bright	–	0.00
Bright	8	25.00
Moderate	20	62.50
Uncertain	4	12.50
Perceptions of Self-achievements	Respondents (f)	Percentage
6–12 (Low)	–	0.00
13–19 (Medium)	30	93.75
19 and above (High)	2	6.25
Perception of Success	Respondents (f)	Percentage
6–12 (Low)	1	3.13
13–19 (Medium)	31	96.87
19 and above (High)	–	0.00

Notes: N = 32, Respondents (f)—Respondent Frequency/Number of Respondents, *Steps were taken according to the response for stratification.

Perceptions of Success (POS): The perceptions of success of women entrepreneurs comprised six self-devised questions, self-rating on their functioning of their enterprises, about their success perceptions with appropriate responses and administered for the present study scores on a 4-point scale (range 6–24).

Perceptions of Entrepreneurial Expectations of the Future (EE): A self-scale of 10 to 100 per cent to assess entrepreneurs themselves about the success rate of their enterprise since its inception.

Statistical Analysis

The mean differences were found using the 't' tests in order to compare groups with different socio-background variables on psychosocial variables. The psychosocial variables taken for the present study included perceived ladder of success at present, perception of entrepreneurial expectations of the future, perception about self-achievements, perception of success and entrepreneurship awareness and technical know-how skills respectively, which were scored. Socio-background variables included age, education, social category, self-previous occupation, years of experience in running the enterprise, previous self-occupation, family income, membership in associations, entrepreneurship and technical training, place of enterprise, father's present occupation and husband's education were coded and taken for the 't' analysis as comparable groups. Mean differences by these socio-background variables on psychosocial variables, such as perceived ladder of success at present, entrepreneurial expectations about future, perceptions of self-achievements and perceptions of success were drawn out using the Statistical Package for Social Sciences (SPSS10.0) in the present study.

Results

The results of the 't' test analyses using different perceptional psychosocial variables with socio-background variables were represented accordingly.

Perceived Ladder of Success at Present

Table 10.3 revealed the 't' values on the ladder of success at present by using different background variables and showed that the significant mean differences were found between women in two social categories with and without entrepreneurship and technical training.

Women entrepreneurs who belonged to the backward class perceived their ladder of success at present at a significantly higher level (M = 5.75) than women entrepreneurs in the general category (M = 4.96); thus 't' was found significant ('t' = 2.07, p < 0.05). Similarly, at the 95 per cent level ('t' = 2.07, p < 0.05) the finding on 't' between women who had and the ones who did not have entrepreneurship and technical training was also significant. This implied that women entrepreneurs without entrepreneurship training perceived a higher ladder of success at present (M = 5.75) than women entrepreneurs with entrepreneurship and technical training (M = 4.96). Thus, women in backward category and those who did not undergo any training had a higher level of perceived ladder of success at present than their counterparts in the general category and those with entrepreneurship and technical training.

Table 10.3 The 'T' Test on Perceived Ladder of Success at Present (LASP)

Background variable		Mean	S.D.	't' Value
(A)	30–44 years	5.00	0.26	1.02
	45–59 years	5.36	0.23	(NS)
(E)	Graduate	5.13	0.24	0.23
	Non Graduate	5.22	0.15	(NS)
(C)	General Category	4.96	0.95	2.07
	Backward Category	5.75	0.88	(p < 0.05)
(O)	Salaried	5.05	1.04	0.94
	Housewife	5.40	0.84	(NS)
(Y)	≤ 5	4.94	0.31	1.26
	> 5	5.37	0.15	(NS)
(FI)	INR ≤ 4,500	4.95	0.99	0.69
	INR 4,501–10,000	5.60	0.84	(NS)
(MA)	Yes	4.96	0.17	0.025
	No	5.67	0.41	(NS)
(ETT)	Yes	4.96	0.99	2.07
	No	5.75	0.71	(p < 0.05)
(P)	Chennai	4.06	0.99	0.86
	Bangalore	3.75	1.06	(NS)
(FPRO)	Nil	5.13	0.71	0.31
	Business	5.25	1.58	(NS)
(HE)	Graduate	5.30	0.87	1.37
	Postgraduate	4.78	1.20	(NS)

Notes: NS—Not Significant; p—level of significance
Socio-Background Variables (SBV): A—Age, E—Education, C—Social Category, O—Self-previous Occupation, Y—Year of Experience, FI—Family Income, MA—Memberships in Association, ETT—Entrepreneurship and Technical Training, P—Place of Enterprise, FPRO—Father's Previous Occupation, HE—Husband's Education, Psychosocial Variable (PV)—LASP—Perceived Ladder of Success at Present.

Perceived Entrepreneurial Expectations about the Future

It was revealed from Table 10.4 that significant mean differences were found among groups of women with different monthly family income: those who had membership in associations and those who did not have any membership in associations, those who had undergone entrepreneurship and technical training and those without training, different places of

Table 10.4 The 'T' Test on Perceived Entrepreneurial Expectations about the Future

Background variable		Mean	S.D.	't' Value
(A)	30–44 years	2.28	0.57	1.65
	45–59 years	1.93	0.62	(NS)
(E)	Graduate	2.04	0.64	1.22
	Non-graduate	2.33	0.50	(NS)
(C)	General Category	2.17	0.56	0.68
	Backward Category	2.00	0.75	(NS)
(O)	Salaried	2.18	0.50	0.78
	Housewife	2.00	0.82	(NS)
(Y)	≤ 5	2.06	0.68	0.57
	> 5	2.18	0.54	(NS)
(FI)	INR ≤ 4,500	2.32	0.47	2.98
	INR 4,501–10,000	1.70	0.67	(p < 0.01)
(MA)	Yes	2.30	0.47	2.98
	No	1.67	0.71	(p < 0.01)
(ETT)	Yes	2.29	0.55	3.01
	No	1.63	0.52	(p < 0.01)
(P)	Chennai	1.75	0.45	4.39
	Bangalore	2.50	0.52	(p < 0.01)
(FPRO)	Nil	2.25	0.53	2.12
	Business	1.75	0.71	(p < 0.05)
(HE)	Graduate	2.04	0.64	1.22
	Postgraduate	2.33	0.50	(NS)

Notes: NS—Not Significant; p—level of significance
ocio-Background Variables (SBV): A—Age, E—Education, C—Social Cat-egory, O—Self-Previous Occupation, Y—Year of Experience, FI—Family Income, MA—Memberships in Association, ETT-Entrepreneurship and Tech-nical Training, P—Place of Enterprise, FPRO—Father's Previous Occupation, HE—Husband's Education; Psychosocial Variable (PV); EE—Entrepreneurial Expectations.

enterprise and women whose fathers had business as their present occupation and those who did not have any occupation on entrepreneurial expectations.

The entrepreneurial expectation of women entrepreneurs about their future differed significantly among two groups with different family incomes. This meant that those with family income less than INR 4,500 had significantly higher ('t' = 2.98, p < 0.01) entrepreneurial expectations (M = 2.32) than those with family income of more than INR 4,500

(M = 1.70). Thus, women presently with low monthly income had higher expectations about their future in entrepreneurial activities.

Entrepreneurial expectations also differed significantly ('t' = 2.98, p < 0.01) among those women who had membership in some professional association and those who did not have any membership. However, women entrepreneurs with membership in associations (M = 2.30) had higher entrepreneurial expectations than those who did not have any memberships in associations (M = 1.67). This indicated that awareness about the upcoming and ongoing events—both technological advancements and marketing standards, of the product through activities of the associations—helped the women with membership to increase their future expectations.

In the same line as the earlier finding, it was found out that those women entrepreneurs who had entrepreneurship and technical training (M = 2.29) differed significantly ('t' = 3.01, p < 0.01) from those who did not have entrepreneurship and technical training (M = 1.63) on entrepreneurial expectations, thus indicating that the former group has higher entrepreneurial expectations. Entrepreneurial expectations also significantly varied among two places of enterprises. It was found out that women entrepreneurs from Bangalore (M = 2.50) had significantly higher entrepreneurial expectations ('t' = 4.39, p < 0.01) than their counterparts from Chennai (M = 1.75). It was found from Table 10.5 that women entrepreneurs whose fathers did not have any occupation (M = 2.25) exhibited significantly higher ('t' = 2.12, p < 0.01) entrepreneurial expectations than those with fathers who pursued business as their present occupation (M = 1.75).

Perceptions about Self-achievements

Results on the 't' test on perception of self-achievement (Table 10.5) revealed that out of all the background variables, significant mean differences were found only by place of enterprise. It was revealed that women from two metro cities, that is, Chennai and Bangalore, differed significantly in terms of their perception of self-achievements. The findings indicated that women belonging to Chennai had more perceptions of self-achievements (M = 17.25) than women entrepreneurs belonging to Bangalore (M = 15.44; 't' = 3.12, p < 0.01) which indicated that women belonging to Chennai have more achievements, which enhanced

Table 10.5   The 'T' Test on Perception of Self-achievements

Background variable		Mean	S.D.	't' Value
(A)	30–44 years	15.83	1.72	1.83
	45–59 years	17.00	1.88	(NS)
(E)	Graduate	16.30	1.96	1.87
	Non-graduate	16.44	1.67	(NS)
(C)	General Category	16.38	1.79	0.16
	Backward Category	16.25	2.19	(NS)
(O)	Salaried	16.36	1.89	0.09
	Housewife	16.30	1.89	(NS)
(Y)	≤ 5	16.06	1.81	0.85
	> 5	16.63	1.93	(NS)
(FI)	INR ≤ 4,500	16.00	1.51	1.59
	INR 4,501–10,000	17.10	2.38	(NS)
(MA)	Yes	16.17	1.67	0.82
	No	16.78	2.33	(NS)
(ETT)	Yes	16.33	1.81	0.05
	No	16.38	2.13	(NS)
(P)	Chennai	17.25	1.88	3.12
	Bangalore	15.44	1.36	$(p < 0.01)$
(FPRO)	Nil	16.25	1.67	0.49
	Business	16.63	2.45	(NS)
(HE)	Graduate	15.61	0.99	1.09
	Postgraduate	15.11	1.54	(NS)

Notes: NS—Not Significant; P—level of significance
Socio-Background Variables (SBV): A—Age, E—Education, C—Social Category, O—Self-Previous Occupation, Y—Year of Experience, FI—Family Income, MA—Memberships in Association, ETT—Entrepreneurship and Technical Training, P—Place of Enterprise, FPRO—Father's Previous Occupation, HE—Husband's Education; Psychosocial Variable (PV), POA—Perceptions of Self-achievements.

their perceptions of self-achievements. However, no other background variable had significant differences with respect to perceptions of self-achievements.

Perception of Success

Results of the 't' test on the perception of success (Table 10.6) revealed that significant mean differences were found only in the case of years of experience of women entrepreneurs in running their enterprises, implying that no other background variable had made significant differences with

Table 10.6   The 'T' Test on Perception of Success

Background variable		Mean	S.D.	't' Value
(A)	30–44 years	15.33	1.28	0.74
	45–59 years	15.64	1.01	(NS)
(E)	Graduate	15.39	1.31	0.60
	Non Graduate	15.67	0.71	(NS)
(C)	General Category	15.25	1.03	1.92
	Backward Category	16.13	1.35	(NS)
(O)	Salaried	15.41	1.22	0.42
	Housewife	15.60	1.08	(NS)
(Y)	≤ 5	15.06	1.18	2.08
	> 5	15.88	1.02	(p < 0.05)
(FI)	INR ≤ 4,500	15.41	1.22	0.42
	INR 4,501–10,000	15.60	1.08	(NS)
(MA)	Yes	15.43	1.16	0.26
	No	15.56	1.24	(NS)
(ETT)	Yes	15.38	1.17	0.78
	No	15.75	1.17	(NS)
(P)	Chennai	15.50	0.97	0.15
	Bangalore	15.44	1.36	(NS)
(FPRO)	Nil	15.58	1.02	0.96
	Business	15.13	1.55	(NS)
(HE)	Graduate	15.61	0.99	1.09
	Postgraduate	15.11	1.54	(NS)

Notes: NS—Not Significant; P—level of significance
Socio-Background Variables (SBV): A—Age, E—Education, C—Social Category, O—Self-Previous Occupation, Y—Year of Experience, FI—Family Income, MA—Memberships in Association, ETT—Entrepreneurship and Technical Training, P—Place of Enterprise, FPRO—Father's Previous Occupation, HE—Husband's Education; Psychosocial Variable (PV); POS—Perception of Success.

respect to perceptions of success. From Table 10.7, it was revealed that women from two experience groups differed significantly, that is, less than or equal to five years of experience and more than five years of experience, differed significantly with the perception of success. This indicated that women entrepreneurs with more than five years of experience had more perception of success (M = 15.88) than women entrepreneurs with less than or equal to five years of experience (M = 15.06; 't' = 2.08, p < 0.05). It clearly indicated that women entrepreneurs with more experience in running their enterprises obviously tend towards success and their perception of success is high. However, no other background variable has made significant differences with respect to perceptions of success.

Table 10.7   Hypotheses Distribution on Psychosocial Variables with Socio-background Variables

	Hypothesis		
Variable	Rejected***	Accepted	't' Value
LASP	A, E, O, Y, FI, MA, P,	C	2.07*
	FPRO, HE	ETT	2.07*
EE	A, E, C, O, MA, HE	FI	2.98**
		MA	2.98**
		ETT	3.01**
		P	4.39**
		FPRO	2.12*
POA	A, E, C, O, Y, FI, MA, ETT,	P	3.12**
	FPRO, HE		
POS	A, E, C, O, FI, MA, ETT, P,	Y	2.08*
	FPRO, HE		

Notes: * Significant at 0.05 level; ** Significant at 0.01 level; *** NS—Not Significant.

A—Age, E—Education, C—Social Category, O—Self-previous Occupation, Y—Year of Experience, FI—Family Income, MA—Memberships in Association, ETT—Entrepreneurship and Technical Training, P—Place of Enterprise, FPRO—Father's Previous Occupation, HE—Husband's Education, PV—Psychosocial Variables, LASP—Perceived Present Ladder of Success, EE—Entrepreneurial Expectations, POA—Perceptions of Self-achievements, POS—Perceptions of Success.

Discussion

There would be significant mean differences by age, education, social category, previous occupation, years of experience, family income, membership in associations, entrepreneurship and technical training, place of enterprise, husband's education and father's present occupation on vari-ous psychosocial variables, such as (a) present ladder of success, (b) entrepreneurial expectations of the future, (c) perception of self-achievements, and (d) perceptions of success. The results were discussed in lieu of the hypotheses.

Hypothesis I

There would be significant mean differences between groups of women with different socio-background (such as age, education, social category, previous occupation, year of experience, family income, membership in associations, entrepreneurship and technical training, place of enterprise, husband's education and father's present occupation) on perception towards perceived ladder of success at present and perception of success.

The present study revealed that women entrepreneurs belonging to backward category perceived themselves on the higher steps in the present ladder of success. This finding could be interpreted by using the individualistic theory of Adler (1917). The theory proposed that normal surroundings tend to compound the inferiority feelings in people belonging to the backward segment of the society, thus making them try hard to develop and strengthen their compensatory mechanisms to achieve superiority (exhibited in placing higher steps in ladder of success). As such, the women belonging to the backward category were not economically stable due to the prevalence of under employment despite employment policies, which could induce an inferiority complex in them. The instinct to overcome that resulted in inaccurate and inflated perception of placing themselves higher in the ladder of success. Women rated themselves high in the perceived ladder in the case of backward category (see Table 10.3), which is an indirect inference on the achievement motivation perception through which they perceive themselves to be an achiever futuristically and differed significantly.

Women entrepreneurs without entrepreneurship and technical training perceived higher growth in their ladder of success. This could be due to the reason that women without entrepreneurship and technical training were unaware of the technicalities and complexities involved in running their enterprises. Hence, the evaluation of the enterprise made by them might not have been based on the actual rating of their enterprise. Second, whatever success they were getting might be perceived by them in a different way, leading to inflated perceptions, which resulted in placing themselves in the higher ladder of success. Third, their self-satisfaction with whatever they were getting might also have fostered their perception.

Thus, the earlier-mentioned hypothesis on perceived ladder of success at present was partially accepted only for social category, entrepreneurial and technical training and years of experience.

Hypothesis II

There would be significant mean differences among different groups of women on the basis of selected socio-background variables (age, education, social category, previous occupation, years of experience, family income, membership in associations, entrepreneurship and technical training, place of enterprise, husband's education and father's present occupation) on perception towards entrepreneurial expectations about the future.

Another interesting and unexpected finding was that the women who belonged to the lower income group ($\leq$ INR 4,500) showed (see Table 10.4) more entrepreneurial expectations as compared to women belonging to the higher income group (> INR 4,501 and above). This could be due to the fact that women belonging to the lower income group in the present study tried to achieve and become economically secure—hence, placed themselves high in their entrepreneurial expectations. Due to economic insecurity and underemployment, women in the backward category were motivated to become entrepreneurs, which resulted in higher entrepreneurial expectations.

Women entrepreneurs who had memberships in associations had higher entrepreneurial expectations than women without membership in associations. This finding could be attributed to the factor that women holding memberships in associations associate themselves in forums, discussions and gather information on current trends, technology advancements and policy initiatives towards women entrepreneurship development. They also gained the motivational drive by comparing themselves with the experienced women entrepreneurs. This formal sharing of knowledge enhanced their knowledge towards innovative and appropriate technologies, time management, and so forth, which perhaps nourished their entrepreneurial skills. This affected their entrepreneurial expectations in a positive way. Similarly, entrepreneurs with technical training had higher entrepreneurial expectations than women who did not have these. Due to the training, they learnt the technicalities involved according to requirements of their enterprise and got equipped with entrepreneurship skills—hence increased the entrepreneurial expectations.

An interesting finding was that the entrepreneurial expectation of women entrepreneurs varied with the place of establishment of their enterprise. It was found that women belonging to Bangalore had high entrepreneurial expectations than women who had established their enterprises at Chennai. This could be attributed to the different sociocultural and the economic conditions prevailing in the two metropolitan cities. It was found that women whose fathers were not occupied exhibited more entrepreneurial expectations than women whose fathers currently pursued an occupation. This could be attributed to two factors. First, women entrepreneurs perceived that to run a family in metropolitan living conditions and maintain their lifestyle was not possible with single income. Hence they decided to support their families while performing an income generating activity (running their enterprises). Second, respondents had seen that their fathers, who did have any income or were currently retired from the government profession, could not meet all the requirements with a meagre income for sustaining themselves, and this had triggered their expectations that their enterprise should perform better so that they could gain enough output (profit). Thus, this hypothesis on entrepreneurial expectations was accepted only in the case of family income, memberships in associations, entrepreneurial and technical training, place of enterprise and father's present occupation.

Hypothesis III

There would be significant mean differences on perceptions of self-achievements among groups of women with different background (age, education, social category, previous occupation, years of experience, family income, membership in associations, entrepreneurship and technical training, place of enterprise, husband's education and father's present occupation).

Findings revealed that women entrepreneurs hailing from Chennai had a higher perception of achievements (see Table 10.5) than women hailing from Bangalore. This could be attributed to the fact that women hailing from Chennai were aware of the enterprising scenario much more than women entrepreneurs from Bangalore. Women entrepreneurs from Bangalore had high market competition for their products in comparison to those from Chennai. Hence, women entrepreneurs in Chennai perceived their achievements much more than those in Bangalore. Thus, the hypothesis stating that there would be significant mean differences between different groups of women on perceptions about self-achievements was accepted only in the case of the place of enterprise.

Hypothesis IV

There would be significant mean differences on perceptions of success between groups of women with different backgrounds (age, education, social category, previous occupation, years of experience, family income, membership in associations, entrepreneurship and technical training, place of enterprise, husband's education and father's present occupation).

It was found that women entrepreneurs with more experience (>5 years) had high perceptions of success (see Table 10.6) than women with less experience (<5 years), as expected. This could be due to the fact that women being experienced in running their enterprises keep updating their entrepreneurial skills to manage better. On the other hand, the less experienced ones were in the process of establishing their enterprises and encountered problems in stabilizing their start-ups to stabilize, which resulted in low perceptions about success. Thus, the hypothesis stating that there would be significant mean differences between different groups of women on the perception of success was accepted only in the case of considering the years of experience in running their enterprises.

Significance summary of socio-background variables on psychosocial variables and their corresponding 't' values were indicated in Table 10.7 and commonalities were inferred on selective socio-background variables which were significantly different from the psychosocial variables taken for the present study. First, perceived ladder of success at present and perceptions on entrepreneurial expectations of the future differed significantly ($p < 0.05$; $p < 0.01$) with entrepreneurship and technical training. Second, perceptions on entrepreneurial expectations of the future and perceptions about self-achievements differed significantly ($p < 0.01$) with the place of enterprise.

However, the other socio-background variables, such as age, education, self-previous occupation and husband's education have no influence on the psychosocial variables. However, in a study of 48 female entrepreneurs, Sexton and Kent (1981) reported that in the case of 56 per cent of samples there was a direct relation between present occupation (small entrepreneurs) and the previous job.

Conclusion, Limitations, Suggestions and Implications

Certain conclusions were drawn out of the present study on perception in terms of psychosocial variables and their significance with selective socio-background variables. The present study envisaged the perceptional psychosocial factors associated with the women entrepreneurs running food processing enterprises. Perceptional psychosocial attribution training has to be imparted to the nascent women workforces to become potential and vibrant entrepreneurs. Sustenance in the entrepreneurial domain is very significant and it enhances more so with perception in the case of women entrepreneurs who view it with regard to their peer groups. Perceptions about self-achievements and perceptions of success were compared significantly with the place of enterprise and, the number of years of experience in running their enterprise is an interesting finding in the present study, which also throws light on the inter-linkages of rural women into enterprising activities.

Achievement motivation perception is indirectly inferred with the perceived ladder of success at present in which women hailing from backward category had a perception of placing themselves in higher steps. This throws a ray of hope on the social upliftment of women hailing from backward categories—a common aspect in developing countries. Memberships in associations and places of enterprise also play a crucial role in improving their entrepreneurial awareness, and helps to update themselves with current trends in order to view their future expectations against their present advancements.

Entrepreneurial talent exists in every society and in all sections of the society. In developed countries, a favourable socioeconomic environment helps in exploiting latent entrepreneurial talent. However, in less developed countries, particularly in certain backward areas, an unfavorable socioeconomic environment hinders the emergence of entrepreneurial talents (Saini and Bhatia, 1996) which has a truer sense in the wake of women entrepreneurship development. It is reported in a study by Singh et al. (1986) that in metros and other urban areas, women entrepreneurs were from business and non-business backgrounds and were engaged in both traditional and non-traditional fields against the common belief that they only chose products with a feminine nature. Hence in the context of women entrepreneurship, appropriate need-based interventions and conventions are to be developed to avoid derelicts.

Another important aspect is that skill (entrepreneurial or technical) can be acquired and accumulated at any point of time, where gender does not play any role and thus, women entrepreneurs have scope for advancement in this competitive era. This is because women are mostly side-lined in an enterprising endeavour. Also, a study reported by Anwar (1992) tried to project the characteristics of the activities managed by women entrepreneurs. It indicated that the constraints of the prevalent social norms there have prevented the women entrepreneurs to manage their business independently, and those norms have restricted their mobility and thereby affected interaction with others, particularly for obtaining accurate information for business operation. Besides this, there is also a gap in availing of the training opportunities for skill formation.

The processes of entrepreneurship development and growth enhancement rely on periodical entrepreneurial mechanisms and interventions that trigger and gear up the innovation process, thereby creating vibrant entrepreneurial instances for an innovative entrepreneur. This is essential and highly indispensable, especially in the case of women entrepreneurs in general and food processing in particular. The reason is that technological advancements that keep changing with time have undue and stiff competition at global levels and an effect on day-to-day functioning at local levels.

It is noteworthy that age, education, self-occupation and husband's education were expected to differ from perceptions due to their socioeconomic and sociocultural nature, more precisely for an economic woman or a woman entrepreneur in India. Surprisingly, they have not shown any positive significance with psychosocial variables opted for the present study, which also attributed that women were independent without being backed by male counterparts—a common phenomenon in developing countries like India which have a patriarchal social system. However, this study has a few limitations in its own way. The present study is limited to food processing enterprises in two metros, namely, Bangalore and Chennai. Keeping the time frame in mind, the sample size was restricted to 32 women who agreed to participate in the interview. The perceptional psychosocial variables and their corresponding differences on socio-backgrounds were studied and economic variables (profit, rate of returns, sales turnover per year, breakeven target, market pricing) were not included in the present study. Future researchers could extend the same work to a larger sample according to their localities and situation which further spell out the socio-background differences on other non-significant psychosocial variables in this present study. Researchers in future may attempt examining cross-comparison between males and females on perception of same measures as the economic factor will have its impact.

This may throw newer light on the dimensions of entrepreneurship research. For instance, one can compare positive perceptional orientation versus more profit, perceptions of success versus sales turnover per year, perceptions about self-achievements versus higher rate of returns, perceptions about entrepreneurial expectations about the future versus breakeven target. However, a similar study extended with suitable modifications about rural women entrepreneurs engaged in food processing enterprises will give new vistas on entrepreneurship research.

To conclude, entrepreneurship education is a must for the uplift-ment of women on an economic plank for a country like India. Separate financial institutions like women entrepreneurship development banks could be instituted at the national level which not only act as statutory nodal agencies but also as propellers and gateways for propelling positive perceptions on women and facilitating choice options, respectively. Any institutional curriculum with homogeneous populace of women must ensure entrepreneurship education from the high school level. Successful women entrepreneurs can be often tapped for the implementation of entrepreneurship developmental programmes devised for women. Finally, women's participation in economic activity will be the channel for sustaining the economy of India at large.

References

Adler, A. 1917. 'A Study of Organ Inferiority and its Physical Compensation, Nervous and Mental Disorder', *Monograph*, (24): 1–15.

Allen, K. 1999. *Launching New Ventures: An Entrepreneurial Approach*, Boston: Houghton Mifflin Co.

Anwar, F. S. 1992. 'Management of Rural Women Entrepreneurship in Bangladesh: A Case of Bangladesh', *Journal of Business Administration*, 18(3 and 4): 156–165.

Baker, T., H. E. Aldrich and N. Liou. 1997. 'Invisible Entrepreneurs: The Neglect of Women Business Owners by Mass Media and Scholarly Journals in USA', *Entrepreneurship and Regional Development—An International Journal*, 3(9): 22–238.

Jalbert, S. E. 2000. 'Women Entrepreneurs in the Global Economy'. Paper presented at the Center for International Private Enterprise (CIPE) internet-based (virtual) Conference for Women Entrepreneurs, on *Women: The Emerging Economic Force*, held at Washington D.C. June 14–16, 2002.

Julie, R. W. and D. Seiler. 2001. 'Women's Entrepreneurship in Latin America: An Exploration of Current Knowledge', *Technical Paper Series*, Washington D.C: Sustainable Development Department, Inter-American Development Bank.

McClelland, D. C. 1961. *The Achieving Society*. Princeton: Van Nostrand.

———. 1962. 'Business Drive and National Achievement', *Harvard Business Review*, 40(4): 99–112.

National Foundation for Women Business Owners (NFWBO). 1998. *Issues Affecting Women Business Owners in Argentina and other Latin-and-Iber-American Countries*. Executive report of results from a survey conducted at the VIIIth Congreso Iberamericano de Mujeres Empresarias. Mar Del Plata, Argentina.

National Women's Business Council, Interagency Committee on Women's Business Enterprise. 2000. *United States Case Study: Successful Public and Private Sector Initiatives Fostering the Growth of Women's Business Ownership*. Presented at the 2000 OECD Conference on Women Entrepreneurs in Small and Medium Enterprises. Paris. 29–30 November 2000.

Nelton, S. 1996. 'Women-owned Firms Grow in Number and Importance', *Nation's Business*, 7 April. Available online on *http://findarticles.com/p/articles/mi_m1154/is_n4_v84/ai_18149381*

Reynolds, P., M. Hay and S. M. Camp. 1999. *Global Entrepreneurship Monitor, Executive Report*. Kansas City: Kauffman Centre for Entrepreneurial Leadership.

Rotter, J. B. 1966. 'Generalized Expectancies for Internal Versus External Locus of Control of Reinforcement', *Psychological Monographs*, 80(1): 1–28.

Rotter, J. B., E. J. Chance and E. J. Phares. 1972. *Application of a Social Learning Theory of Personality*. New York; Holt, Rinehart and Winston.

Saigal, O. 2001. 'Food Processing Industry: Current Scene and Prospects', *Yojana*, (January): 33–34.

Saini, J. S. and B. S. Bhatia. 1996. 'Impact of Entrepreneurship Development Programmes', *The Journal of Entrepreneurship*, 5(1) (Jan–June): 65.

Sexton, D. L. and C. A. Kent. 1981. 'Female Executives and Entrepreneurs: A Preliminary Comparison', in K. Vesper (ed.), *Frontiers of Entrepreneurship Research*, pp. 40–55. Wellesley, MA: Babson University Press.

Singh, K. P. 1993. 'Women Entrepreneurs: Their Profile and Motivation', *The Journal of Entrepreneurship*, 2(1): 47–57.

Singh, N. P., P. Shegal, M. Tithani and R. Sengupta. 1986. *Successful Women Entrepreneurs—Their Identity, Expectations and Problems*. New Delhi: National Institute for Entrepreneurship and Small Business Development.

United Nations. 1995. *The World's Women, 1995: Trends and Statistics*. New York: United Nations.

Winter, D. W. 1969. *Motivating Economic Achievement*. New York: Free Press.

A Study of Life-situation Antecedence, Personality and Motivational Patterns of Small Scale Women Entrepreneurs

11

T.J. KAMALANABHAN AND V. VIJAYA

This research study focusses on the psychological aspects of the entrepreneurial intention of small scale women entrepreneurs in the manufacturing, trading and service sectors. The variables studied were life situation antecedence, personality, entrepreneurial motivation and business-related variables. The tools used for the study were life situation antecedence scale, personality questionnaire and entrepreneurial motivation scale. Three hundred women entrepreneurs from the manufacturing, trading and service sectors and 200 non-entrepreneurs from supervisory and clerical cadres from India participated in this study. Univariate and multivariate analyses were done to process the data. The results reveal that life situation antecedence, personality and business-related variables contribute significantly to the entrepreneurial intention of the small scale women entrepreneurs. The women entrepreneurs have been found to possess lower psychological support, poorer work conditions and lesser competence compared to the women non-entrepreneurs in life situation antecedence. Certain life situation antecedence variables, personality variables and motivational factors were found to explain differences in the entrepreneurial intention of women entrepreneurs in the manufacturing, trading and service sectors.

It has been recognized that women have an important role to play in synthesizing social progress with economic growth of developing countries. With the socio-psycho-cultural and economic changes taking place in India, women are slowly entering the field of entrepreneurship. It is increasingly recognized that women have potential entrepreneurial talents that could be easily harnessed towards achieving success. In India, women entrepreneurship is slowly gaining credibility as an important activity in contributing to the national economy, helping to foster economic independence of women by letting them hold the reins of their destiny, thus leading to empowerment. Small and medium-sized entrepreneurs play a very important role in social and economic development (UNIFEM, 1995). Running a business is never easy, especially for women in a society like India where definitions are not always consistent with the notions of women playing important economic roles involving risk-taking, initiating, planning and coordinating market-oriented activities. Capability, credibility and confidence are the terms used while evaluating women entrepreneurs and also for aspects that pose problems for them (Cannon et al., 1988).

A number of research observations have been made by Indian researchers and these throw light on the psychological implications of women entrepreneurs in India.

Mohuiddin (1987) discussed that:

> Women entrepreneurs as an opportunity of productive work for women is not merely a means of higher income, but as a means of self respect to the development of their personality and to a sense of participation in the common purposes of the society. Women entrepreneurs in India represent a small group who have broken away from the beaten track and are exploring new vistas of economic participation and achievement satisfaction. They have long stories of trials and hardships; their task has been full of challenges. They have even encountered public prejudice and criticism. Family opposition and social constraints have to be overcome before establishing themselves as independent entrepreneurs. The most serious barrier to women entrepreneurs undoubtedly continues to be the persistence of the belief held by both men and women, that entrepreneurship is a male domain. The resistance, apathy, shyness, inhibition, conservatism, poor response are all governed and generated by cultural traditions, value systems and social sanctions.

Iyer (1991) points out that the women's own personality traits, such as shyness, lack of articulation, inability to communicate and attitude towards money matters inhibit and limit their growth as entrepreneurs.

One striking fact that can be noted from all these observations is that the women who take up entrepreneurship, in spite of the reported difficulties and psychological barriers, are the ones who have the courage to transcend the limited boundaries that the culture generally prescribes for them. Women also run a lot of risks in the process of venturing into business. The question now arises: 'If there is so much of a price to pay in the process and with a number of other career options available to them, why are they taking up entrepreneurship?' This query is one of the motivating factors in venturing into this research study.

Literature Review

Based on the school of psychoanalysis, the psychodynamic interpretation by Ket de Vries (1977, 1996), entrepreneurship emerges from a burdensome psychological inheritance centred around the problems of self-esteem, insecurity and lack of confidence and with repressed aggressive wishes towards people in control. From a family background of hardships, the entrepreneur thus becomes a deviant, drifting from job to job, unable to fit into any organization and, in the process, develops a rebellious, non-conformist stance. Distrust and suspicion of everyone in a position of authority forces the entrepreneur to search for non-structured situations where he can assert his control and independence. Consequently, to design one's own organization becomes the only alternative. This complete clinical emphasis in explaining the evolution of the entrepreneurial person has some criticisms, one of which holds that this interpretation may not be generalized for every entrepreneur (Chell, 1985).

Kanitkar and Contractor (1992) asserted that a search for identity during the mid-life crisis, an anchor of business by people weary of life on the move, the monotony of a routine job, the urge to achieve something in life, such as an education or skill procurement, were significant factors for women. Work experience and encouragement from husbands were also important. The authors asserted that in the predominantly masculine business world, women form a minority and have very little secure position. As they are often denied access to positions of power and authority, women naturally look to other sources of employment and create their own opportunities. This could be motivating women to set up independent ventures. The inspiration for entrepreneurs to create business has also been found to be the desire to gain control over one's destiny, to reach one's full potential, to benefit financially and also to contribute to society and be recognized for one's effort (Zimmerer and Scarborough, 1996).

Sonnenfeld and Kotter (1982) presented a model that describes the process of the development of a career. The key entities are the individual's life space with progressing times from childhood to adulthood. The important attributes in this model that interact are the individual's personality, adult developmental history, the individual's current perspective, the childhood family environment, the adult family history, the current family situation, the educational environment, work history and the current work situation that explain the dynamics of career choice. Bowen and Hisrich (1986) have stressed the importance of this model in trying to predict the possible determinants of the female entrepreneur's career development. Fann (1986) observed that a woman entering business is influenced by the external environment, life experience, individual needs and transitional events. As no clear personality pattern emerged, it is stated that patterns of child rearing, maternal deprivation, experiences of social marginality and other factors may, in some cases, lead to a high need for achievement, which, under certain conditions, express themselves as entrepreneurial activity of some kind.

The implications of life experience in women entrepreneurship have been vividly described by Joanne Wilkens (1987). She has researched the precipitating and predisposing factors that inspire women into business. Focussing on their experiences, she has stated that stressful experiences like widowhood, divorce, and so forth, are important. Change in the marital status, moving to a new city, the career change of the husband, and readiness to resume work after the child/children are born or have entered school are some of the most important transition points. The women entrepreneurs of today were found to maintain a surprisingly independent course. Even in their childhood they saw the world as full of fascinating promises and possibilities and were able to bypass such restrictions and take up activities that challenged their abilities. These women ignored gender-related restrictions, pushed beyond stereotypes and successfully followed their paths. In general, these women remembered their fathers as surprisingly distant, absent or 'weak'. Early in life, they learned to function independently and without any close male support. Business ownership was a means to avoid the damaging pattern they experienced in their youth, either by abandonment and disappointment offered by the father or the dependency and frustration exhibited by the mother. A few businesswomen were found to experience frustration in the job situation, like lack of recognition in the male-dominated world that does not reward independence or initiative in women but perpetuates distorted images of femininity. Existing models by Shapero and Sokol (1982) treat the individual decision process largely in 'blackbox' terms, providing little insight on how family history or social forces shape the individual decision process. They stated that these models served as models of individual choice that actually disregarded the individual. Observing India, it has also been stressed that the promotion of entrepreneurship, specially of intermediate technology, cannot leave out the cultural, ethnic and religious factors. Studies and experiences recounted by entrepreneurs themselves show that the image of an entrepreneur incorporates three factors related to the individual person—upbringing, childhood experience and work experience.

Scherer et al. (1990) reported that social learning differences have a strong impact on shaping preference for an entrepreneurial career. While explaining the possible reasons for reluctance of women to take up entrepreneurship, they propose that women have lower self-efficacy and career entry expectations for entrepreneurship because of lack of experiences, either personal or vicarious, related to successful accomplishment of entrepreneurial tasks. Observations on the experience of women entrepreneurship in India give an insight into the fact that this career choice, while being taken and after having taken, is not very easy for a woman (Iyer, 1991). In spite of these reasons, women are doing it. More often than not, a great decline in prestige, status and income is a common phenomenon in the initial phase of entrepreneurship. The period preceding recognition of one's entrepreneurial abilities can be a time of extreme hardship during which considerable psychosocial sacrifices have to be endured (Bishth and Sharma, 1991). Sunder (1996) in his study found that personality characteristics also influence the decision to become an entrepreneur. The study attempts to distinguish entrepreneurs from entrepreneurial aspirants and non-entrepreneurs on a number of personality variables.

Women have also been found to take up entrepreneurship when they experience some stress factors which act as precipitators. Iyer (1991) observed that a significant number of women become entrepreneurs owing to economic compulsions arising out of the death of spouse, desertion, divorce or separation. She also states that as far as society is concerned, the bias against women is strong because of the cultural and traditional mores that are the primary determinants of the inferior status and role of the female. It was observed by scholars that the struggle for recognition had characterized the lives of women entrepreneurs before the business start-up. The independence, control and strong sense of doing things on their own were the major satisfactions or rewards that these women gained by taking up business. Owning a business helped them to regain the lost self-esteem and to develop greater self-confidence. It is important to note that these women have had the spirit of 'resilience' or of 'hardiness' in reacting positively and intensely to sublimate their energy and potential in a constructive manner. They also noted that entrepreneurs as a group did feel different from others while growing up (Collins and Moore, 1970). Ket De Vries (1977) observed that the degree of social participation of entrepreneurs also varied.

Some personality variables may operate as 'personal resources' during stressful periods (Sarason et al., 1978). In a study, Pearlin and Schooler (1978), found that a coping strategy involving a tendency to selectively ignore the worst aspects of a stressful circumstance and to focus instead on some positive aspect of the situation was effective in dealing with stressors in the economic sphere. These can be some explanations for the behaviour of the women entrepreneurs who might have had difficult life situation antecedence.

Gundry and Welsch (2001), in their study, attempted to identify the strategic paths chosen by entrepreneurs and the relation of those paths with the growth orientation of the firm. 832 women business owners from all industrial classifications responded to the survey. The study also measured the perceived importance entrepreneurs attached to strategic success factors.

The life situation antecedence of women entrepreneurs is found to be characterized by lower psychological support, poorer work conditions and lesser competence. Could the women entrepreneurs interpret it that under these difficult conditions, taking up entrepreneurship by them could be an act of the ego defence mechanism of sublimation? By channelizing behaviour in socially approved channels that also gain social recognition in the process, they have taken up entrepreneurship as a means to meet this end. Due to the stress experienced in their lives, women entrepreneurs may be using their personality skills to operate on the environment in order to gain control and social recognition by taking up entrepreneurship. Gathering from these, women's entrepreneurship may be seen as an act of resilience and sublimation by women who are subjected to stress in life. Aggarwal (1997) observed that the entrepreneur is one who penetrates the space between established boundaries and seizes opportunities that are otherwise overlooked by others. This ability to penetrate established conventions and to think of the unthinkable gives the entrepreneur a decisive advantage. The woman entrepreneur seems to be acting this way. A conceptualization of the typical entrepreneur is someone who refuses to acknowledge failure or defeat and who regards all business problems as learning experiences or even disguised opportunities rather than obstacles. Timmons (1990) seems to give further credence to this interpretation. From these research observations, the importance of sociocultural factors, psychological predispositions of a person including his personality, preferences, cognitive evaluations, and so forth, can be understood. Consequently, this study also focusses on the psychological variables of personality and motivation, and the environmental variables of life situation antecedence in contributing to the entrepreneurial initiation decision. This study is based on the Sonnenfield and Kotter (1982) career development model.

Hypotheses

1. There is no contribution of personality, life situation antecedence and demographic status towards the entrepreneurial intention in women.
2. There are no differences between women entrepreneurs in the manufacturing, trading and service sectors in personality, life situation antecedence, entrepreneurial motivation, demographic status and the status of certain business-related variables.

Methodology

The research tools used for the study were questionnaires. The 16 personality factor scale has been used. This scale has already been used to study personality of entrepreneurs with dependable reliability (Sunder, 1996). The life situation antecedence scale and the entrepreneurial motivation scale have been developed specifically for this purpose. Validity and reliability of these tools were ascertained by testing on appropriate samples. The samples for the initial study consisted of 40 normal adults, 20 males and 20 females aged over 40 years, specifically for the life situation antecedence scale. The other sample consisted of 195 potential women entrepreneurs attending an entrepreneurship development programme. The sample selection of potential women entrepreneurs was justifiably based on the assumption that the intention of potential entrepreneurs to start a business was comparable to that of entrepreneurs. The reason for choosing non-entrepreneurs is because they are included for the main study. The factor loading for the life situation antecedence scale ranged from 0.21 to 0.89. The five factors that evolved were psychological support, benefit from environment, previous work condition, financial status and competence. The total cumulative variance explained by the five factors is 68 per cent. For the entrepreneurial motivation scale, the minimum factor loading observed was 0.37 and the maximum loading was seen to be 0.76. The five factors that evolved were entrepreneurial core motivation, work core motivation, social core motivation, individual core motivation and economic core motivation. The total cumulative variance explained by the five factors is 46 per cent.

The design was an exploratory analytical study. Purposive sampling, which is the most advised, other than stratified sampling, or variable probability sampling was used (Hofer and Bygrave, 1992) to collect the data. It was an ex-post-facto design. The respondents for the study were women entrepreneurs from the three sectors of business activities. In the manufacturing sector, the businesses ranged from manufacture of food products, textiles, handicrafts, leather accessories, hardware appliances, chemicals, to industrial components, and so forth. In the trading sector, the enterprises were supermarkets, garment shops, shops dealing with electrical appliances, books, grocery, food products, stationary, florist, and so forth. In the service sector, women entrepreneurs were engaged in screen-printing, computer servicing, beauty parlours, financial agencies, travel agencies, marketing research, printing and publishing, telephone booths, and so forth. Data was collected from 300 women entrepreneurs and 200 women non-entrepreneurs from South India. The women non-entrepreneurs consisted of employed women in the executive cadre and clerical cadre in banks and public sector organizations. For this sample, the convenience sampling procedure focussing on the proximity was adopted.

Results and Discussions

The multivariate test was done to find out the significant contribution of these variables to entrepreneurship in association with each other. The logistic regression was used. The main hypothesis, the tests and the interpretation of the findings are presented. As the groups to be analyzed indicated dichotomy, in this case, the presence or absence of entrepreneurial activity, the logistic regression was decided to be the ideal analysis to understand the multivariate contribution to women entrepreneurship. The logistic regression is lately being thought of as a more appropriate method than discriminant analysis. In logistic regression, any mixture of categorical and numerical data can be used (as done in this analysis). The regressors need not follow a multivariate normal distribution and the correlations among regressors and the standard deviations of regressors need not be equal across each category of the dependent variable (Darlington, 1990). Logistic regression is based on calculating the probability of occurrence/non-occurrence (success/failure) of the dependent variable with the unit changes in the independent variables. The resultant output gives the significance of the contribution of each variable that enters the equation. First, the chi-square test was done to understand the significance of the contribution of variables. The model chi-square tests (Table 11.1) are done in logistic regression which tests the null hypothesis that the coefficients for all the terms in the current model, except the constant, are 0.

Table 11.1 Results of the Chi-square Test Showing the Significance of the Contribution of Variables in Logistic Regression

−2 log likelihood	352.387
Goodness of Fit	401.374
Model λ^2	148.072**
Improvement λ^2	148.072**

Notes: ** p > 0.01 It is to be noted that in the output
  B = Estimated coefficient Wald statistic ~ = Ratio of B I SE B
  R = Partial correlation Exp (B) = Change in odds ratio. for every unit change in y, where
  Odds = Probability of occurrence (y) I Prohability of non-occurrence (y) and
  Odds Ratio = odds when x = 1

It can be seen that the chi-square value of 148.072 is extremely significant. This indicates that the logistic regression model based on the contribution of the independent variables is significantly different from the model assumed in which only the constant is present and rest of the coefficients of the independent variables are 0. From the results of the logistic regression in the table, it can be seen that the significant predictors in life situation antecedence are psychological support, benefit from environment, previous work condition and competence. Among them, psychological support, previous work condition and competence are negative contributors while benefiting from environment is positive. The significant personality traits are timidity versus social boldness, emotional stability versus instability, tough mindedness versus tender mindedness, trust versus suspiciousness, self-assuredness versus apprehensiveness, conservatism versus liberalism and group dependency versus self-sufficiency. Entrepreneurs are found to be more timid, more emotionally unstable. The three demographic variables: education, education of spouse and childhood geographical background also are emerging significant with a positive contribution. The strength of the contribution of the significant variables can be gathered from R, the partial correlation.

From Table 11.2, it can be seen that the correct classification percentage of the non-entrepreneurs group is 66 per cent and of the entrepreneurs group is 82.3 per cent. So, the overall correct classification is found to be 75.8 per cent which ensures a fairly good prediction of group membership based on the significant contribution of the variable.

Table 11.2 Classification and Prediction of Group Membership of the Women Entrepreneur and Non-entrepreneur Groups Based on Logistic Regression

		Predicted		Correct %
		NE	E	
Non-entrepreneurs NE	200	132 66%	68 34%	66%
Entrepreneurs E	300	53 17.7%	247 82.3%	82.3%
Overall correct classification percentage 75.8%				

The validation of the prediction of the logistic regression equation was done using a hold-out sample with 56 non-entrepreneurs and 68 entrepreneurs selected on a random basis (see Table 11.3). While validating on the hold-out sample, the classification percentage has been reduced by about 10 per cent, from 75.8 per cent to 66.9 per cent. However, the classification percentage based on the validation is also quite satisfactory.

Table 11.3 Classification and Prediction of Group Membership Results for Validation of Results Based on Logistic Regression Variables

		Predicted		Correct %
		NE	E	
Non-entrepreneurs	56	38	18	
NE		67.9%	30.1%	67.9%
Entrepreneurs	68	23	45	
E		33.8%	66.2%	66.2%
Overall correct classification percentage 66.9%				

From the results of the multivariate analysis (Table 11.4), it can be seen that there are significant differences in the status of certain life situation antecedent variables, personality variables and demographic variables between women entrepreneurs and non-entrepreneurs. Hence, Hypothesis 1 is not accepted. There is a significant contribution of life situation variables, the personality and environmental demographics to the entrepreneurial decision. From the life situation antecedence, it is seen that the entrepreneurs are found to have had lower psychological support, poorer previous work condition and lesser competence, but better benefit from environment. Research literature supports the fact that the decision to take up entrepreneurship can be instigated by a feeling of internal inadequacy because of a poor psychological environment (Silver, 1992). Job dissatisfaction due to role stress, discrimination at the work place, monotony of work, and so forth, also have been found to be negative motivators (Sharma, 1979). Casale (1986) had also reported negative pushes, such as trouble getting ideas advanced, lack of reward, lack of organizational fit and lack of advancement as being some of the main reasons for starting new ventures. That economic motivation is important in entrepreneurship cannot be refuted. Also,

Table 11.4 Results of the Logistic Regression Analysis Showing the Significant Multivariate Contribution to Women Entrepreneurship through Discrimination of Women Entrepreneurs and Women Non-entrepreneurs

Variable	B	SE B	Wald statistic	R	EXP (B)
Life Situation Antecedents					
Psychological Support	−0.1284	0.0402	10.2001**	−0.1104	0.8795
Benefit from Environment	0.1457	0.0512	8.0958***	0.0952	1.1568
Previous Work Condition	−0.1970	0.0795	6.1455***	−0.0785	0.8212
Competence	−0.1554	0.0825	3.5440*	−0.0479	0.8561
Personality Traits					
Emotional Stability vs Instability	0.2510	0.0921	7.4322**	0.0898	1.2853
Timidity vs Social Boldness	−0.3324	0.0869	14.6330**	−0.1370	0.7172
Tough Mindedness vs Tender Mindedness	0.1425	0.0826	2.9775*	0.0381	1.1532
Trust vs Suspiciousness	0.1907	0.0872	4.7788*	0.0643	1.2101
Self-assuredness vs Apprehensiveness	0.1500	0.0885	2.8731*	0.0360	1.8607
Conservatism vs Liberalism	0.2898	0.0906	10.2273**	0.1106	1.3362
Group Dependency vs Self-sufficiency	0.3171	0.0874	13.1477**	0.1287	1.3731
Demographics					
Childhood Geographical Background	0.4210	0.1479	8.1061**	0.0953	1.6564
Education	0.2588	0.1299	3.9656*	0.0540	1.7720
Education of Spouse	0.5351	0.1260	18.0230**	0.1543	1.5856

Notes: ** Significance at P > 0.01 level.
    * Significance at P > 0.05 level.

financial stress as a life situation antecedent could have precipitated the need of women entrepreneurs to use entrepreneurship as a stable means to financial security, in spite of certain risks involved. Regarding the benefit from environment, some studies do support the fact that entrepreneurs come from personally and occupationally enriched environments. The high-technology, high-growth founder has been profiled as an independent individual who comes from a family where entrepreneurship was practiced, is well-educated, is in the mid-thirties and has the experience of starting up both small and large firms (Feeser and Dugan, 1989). Other studies stress the fact that in order to make up for whatever they did not achieve, coupled with a feeling of inadequacy, they take up entrepreneurship as a means to overcome these shortcomings (Silver, 1992).

In understanding their personality, the results reveal that entrepreneurs are emotionally more unstable, more suspicious, more timid and more apprehensive than non-entrepreneurs. They are also found to be more tender-minded, more liberal and more self-sufficient than non-entrepreneurs, as found by Caird (1988). The finding that the personality of women entrepreneurs is significantly different in some respects from women non-entrepreneurs has been able to substantiate some specific clinical observations on the personality of entrepreneurs (Ket De Vries, 1977). All these findings on the personality and life situation antecedence give some evidence of earlier findings that explain the shaping of the entrepreneur's psyche (Collins and Moore, 1964).

Since entrepreneurship has been explained to be a multivariable phenomenon, the findings of the study seem to support that fact. As observed earlier in research literature, certain life situation antecedents characterized by a poor psychological environment might be creating a personality characterized by less emotional stability, more suspiciousness, more apprehensiveness and more timidity (Ket De Vries, 1996), with an inclination towards liberalism and self-sufficiency. When these factors are coupled together with less job satisfaction and lesser competence, the individual seems to be motivated to take up entrepreneurship. Education of self as well as that of the spouse are also significant contributors and seem to be important when the woman decides to take up business as a career. Caputo and Dolinsky (1998) observed that the husband's business knowledge and experience is greatly beneficial to women being self-employed. The presence of young children and the husband's provision of child care also contributes to women's self-employment. However, marital status has not been found to have an impact on occupational choice. The other variable found in this study, an urban background, also seems to raise the probability of awareness about entrepreneurial opportunities and consequently the decision to take up entrepreneurship.

We can thus conclude that life situation antecedence, personality and demographic factors play a significant role in contributing to the entrepreneurial intention in small scale women entrepreneurs. The findings seem to support some observations on the clinical implications of the entrepreneurial personality.

To compare the three groups of women entrepreneurs in the manufacturing, trading and service sectors, and understand the multivariate contribution to membership in the three groups, the Multivariate Analysis of Variables (MANOVA) was first used to see if there were any significant differences between the three groups. As the tests showed high significance, multiple discriminant analysis was used next to classify group membership in the manufacturing, trading and service sectors, based on the contribution of variables.

The discriminant analysis is usually used only for continuous data. However, it was used in this comparison which also included the demographic and business-related variables which were categorical data. In situations where the independent variables are a mixture of continuous and dichotomous variables, most evidence suggests that the linear discriminant function often performs reasonably well (Gilbert, 1968).

The results of the three types of tests: Pillai's, Hotelling's and the Wilks' Lambda, reveal very high significance between the groups based on the contribution of the variables (see Table 11.5). The 'F' value of 5.5203 revealed is very significant. Based on this confirmation, the discriminant analysis was conducted to further understand the contribution of the variables.

Table 11.5 **Results of the MANOVA Test to Ascertain Significant Differences between the Manufacturing, Trading and Service Women Entrepreneurs**

Test	Value	'F'	Significance
Pillai's	0.38186	5.52903	0.000
Hotelling's	0.61777	5.52903	0.000
Wilks' Lambda	0.61814	5.52903	0.000

Table 11.6 shows the results of the discriminant analysis to study the three entrepreneurial groups showing the significance of the discriminant functions.

Table 11.6 Results of the Discriminant Analysis to Study the Three Entrepreneurial Groups Showing the Significance of the Discriminant Functions

Fn.	Eigen value	Variance	Canonical r	Wilks' λ	χ^2	df	Significance
1	1.2402	67.02	0.7441	0.2771	366.321	48	0.000
2	0.6103	32.98	0.6156	1.6209	136.025	23	0.000

We can observe that the two functions that have evolved are emerging to be very significant. The first function is found to contribute to 67 per cent of the variance and the second function contributes to about 33 per cent of the variance. The canonical correlations of 0.74 and 0.61, respectively, indicate a moderately strong relationship.

Table 11.7 gives information on the validation of the classification and group using the hold-out sample chosen at random. The correct classification is found to be 66 per cent which is slightly lower. However, this percentage is to be valid enough to explain group discrimination. It can be concluded that a number of variables contribute to the entrepreneurial ventures; the manufacturing entrepreneurs seem to have had lower psychological support, better benefit from environment and a better financial status than of the other entrepreneurs. Regarding the life situation antecedents, work condition and competence, there are no differences among the groups. In personality, difference is evident in nine factors. In motivation, there are significant differences in four dimensions of entrepreneurial motivation. Demographic variables and business-related variables also seem to contribute to the differences in business venturing.

Table 11.7 Results of the Validation of Classification and Group Membership Prediction in the Manufacturing, Trading and Service Sectors of Women Entrepreneurship

		Predicted			Correct %
		M	T	S	
Manufacturing	32	22	0	10	68.8%
		68.8%	0%	31.2%	
Trading	46	3	38	2	82.6%
		13%	82.6%	4.4%	
Service	48	4	24	30	51.7%
		6.9%	41.4%	51.7%	
Overall correct classification percent age 66.18%					

Regarding these observations, it could be reasoned out that many women, not just entrepreneurs, undergo a lot of strain in life and that under such circumstances, they can well choose some other career also. Even among entrepreneurs, a good number are not just pushed because of negative factors, but have considerable supportive and encouraging sources in life to be motivated into entrepreneurship. Despite this observation, the interpretations made can be valid to substantiate the earlier observations on the psychological implications of the shaping of the entrepreneur's psyche. As they aspire for entrepreneurship, it surely indicates that this vocation gives women entrepreneurs a sense of control and independence, and is a socially marvelled channel to express one's individuality. Watkins and Watkins (1986) have stated that business start-up for women may be an alternative to dependence on men in conventional marital relations. The undertaking of entrepreneurship by women may be explained as an act of 'sublimation' under an unsatisfactory condition for the 'ego' and consequently in the process of coping, entrepreneurship may be explained as a mode of operation by the women on the environment to gain control and to cope with certain psychological inadequacies.

Thus, the findings on the life situation antecedent status and personality differences between women entrepreneurs and non-entrepreneurs seem to lead to two different kinds of interpretations. One, that there are personality strengths of resilience in women who sublimate their inner potential in times of stress by taking up entrepreneurship. The other is that the woman entrepreneur's personality has some clinical psychological implications as observed in the earlier research. Consequently, taking up entrepreneurship is a form of gaining control to cope with internal inadequacies. Both these interpretations have important implications in terms of handling the counselling sessions for women entrepreneurs prior to and during the entrepreneurial process. Based on the findings on the psychology of women entrepreneurs, if a woman has personality traits of emotional instability, suspicion, timidity and more apprehensiveness, and is also found to be more tender-minded, more radical and more self-sufficient, and in antecedence has experienced lower psychological support, an unsatisfying work condition and lesser perceived competence, but has had a better benefit from the environment, in terms of education as well as education of spouse and if she has a strong intention to earn money, is it possible that she will take up entrepreneurship as a profession?

Since entrepreneurship has been explained to be a multivariate phenomenon, other factors in the environment like awareness of entrepreneurial opportunities in the environment, availability of credit sources, encouragement by the government, exposure to the entrepreneurship development programmes, and so forth, will certainly increase the probability of such women taking up entrepreneurship. The woman under such circumstances will try to optimize her potential by focussing on entrepreneurship.

Among the three entrepreneurial groups, in addition to life situation antecedence, personality and demographic variables, the type of entrepreneurial motivation and the status of certain business-related variables are found to contribute to the decision of the type of business venture: manufacturing, trading or service. Among the manufacturing, trading and service entrepreneurs, significant differences in personality are revealed. The entrepreneurial motivation scale has been able to ascertain differences in the motivational patterns. Some of the significant findings are that the manufacturing entrepreneurs have a lower social core motivation, the trading entrepreneurs have a higher economic core motivation, and the service and trading entrepreneurs have a higher work core motivation. Assessment through the life situation antecedence scale revealed that the manufacturing entrepreneurs have lower psychological support but better benefit from environment and better financial status compared to the other sectors. The manufacturing entrepreneurs have more family involvement in business. The same has been found by Ramamurthy (1990) regarding involvement of family wherein the husbands were also involved in business.

These facts can have major implications for understanding the psychology of the woman entrepreneur in deciding on the type of venture and also during the entrepreneurial process. These findings give credence to the fact that each type of entrepreneurship is a distinctly different endeavour and requires a certain type of psychological disposition of personality and motivation in combination with a certain kind of life situation antecedence. This observation will be helpful in identifying aptitudes for different types of business undertakings and also in providing differential counselling sessions to women, prior to and during the entrepreneurial process.

The degree of relationship, the correlations between the discriminating variables and the canonical discriminant functions, and the contribution of the variables towards the discriminant functions can be seen from Table 11.8. The four dimensions of life situation antecedence, two variables of personality, four factors of the entrepreneurial motivation, two variables of demographics and one business-related variable and source of finance significantly contribute to the first function. Seven variables of personality, one demographic variable and two business-related variables contribute to the second function.

Table 11.8 The Unstandardized Canonical Discriminant Function Coefficients to Discriminate the Manufacturing, Trading and Service Women Entrepreneurs

Variables	Function 1	Function 2
Life situation antecedents		
Psychological support	0.0498769	−0.0257698
Benefit from environment	0.0856747	0.0930691
Financial Status	0.1127876	0.0616779
Competence	0.0888983	−0.1447757
Personality Traits		
Reservation vs Outgoingness	−0.1334793	0.3947383
Emotional stability vs Instability	−0.2171264	−0.4235011
Submissiveness vs Dominance	0.2651233	−0.0442937
Seriousness vs Liveliness	0.0377840	0.1615167
Low super ego strength vs High super ego strength	−0.0779186	0.0816584
Tough-mindedness vs Tender-mindedness	0.1152276	0.2369512
Conservatism vs Liberalism	−0.0206073	0.2523877
Group dependency vs Self sufficiency	0.2223073	0.1805382
Relaxation vs Tension	−0.0758452	0.1641375
Motivation		
Entrepreneurial core	−0.0229954	0.1750955
Work core	0.1208508	0.0780211
Social core	−0.2808423	−0.1935672
Economic core	−0.1279139	0.0626329
Demographics		
Childhood geographical background	0.3932606	−0.0885585
Education	−0.1575881	−0.4592409
Education of spouse	0.7540902	−0.2328948
Business-related variables		
Source of finance	0.7383654-	0.6283665
Type of ownership	0.0957935	0.5974528
Family involvement in business	0.4932964	0.5586478
Constant	−0.5575247	−7.2248028

From the results of the multivariate analysis, it can be seen that there are significant differences in the status of certain life situation antecedent variables, personality variables and demographic variables, between women entrepreneurs and non-entrepreneurs. They contribute significantly to the entrepreneurial decision. From the life situation antecedence, it is seen that entrepreneurs are found to have had lower psychological support, poorer previous work condition and lesser competence, but better benefit from environment. Research literature supports the fact that the decision to take up entrepreneurship can be instigated by a feeling of internal inadequacy because of a poor psychological environment (Silver, 1992). Job dissatisfaction due to role stress, discrimination at the work place, monotony of work, and so forth, also have been found to be negative motivators (Sharma and Rebello, 1998). These findings seem to support certain observations made by researchers who stress that entrepreneurs hail from difficult family backgrounds (Wilken, 1979). Entrepreneurs are known to be very skilled in their capacity to utilize the resources optimally (Stevenson and Gumpert, 1985). This study also shows that entrepreneurs have been able to make use of the opportunities in their lives gaining a better benefit from environment. The implications of this study are valid to substantiate the earlier observations on the psychological implications of the shaping of the entrepreneur's psyche. The fact of women undertaking entrepreneurship may be explained as an act of 'sublimation' under an unsatisfactory condition for the 'ego' and consequently in the process of coping, entrepreneurship may be explained as a mode of operation by the women on the environment to gain control and to cope with certain psychological inadequacies. This observation seems to be very relevant in the Indian context, where women entrepreneurs seem to sublimate their potential, in spite of barriers imposed by the culture in the form of familial and social pressures. Thus, the findings on the life situation antecedent status and on personality differences between women entrepreneurs and non-entrepreneurs seem to lead to two different kinds of interpretation (see Table 11.9). One, that there are personality strengths of resilience in women who sublimate their inner potentials in times of stress by taking up entrepreneurship. The other is that the woman entrepreneur's personality has some clinical psychological implications as observed in earlier research. Consequently, taking up entrepreneurship is a form of gaining control to cope with internal inadequacies. Both

these interpretations have important implications in terms of handling
the counselling sessions for women entrepreneurs prior to, and during the
entrepreneurial process.

Table 11.9 Discriminant Function Loading—Structured Correlations
between Discriminating Variables and Canonical
Discriminant Functions

Variables	Function 1	Function 2
Life situation antecedents		
Psychological Support	0.37571*	−0.03297
Benefit from Environment	0.38363*	0.03693
Financial Status	0.20780*	−0.03642
Competence	0.10753*	−0.08660
Personality Traits		
Reservation vs Outgoingness	−0.14449	0.34718*
Emotional Stability vs Instability	−0.21580*	0.14213
Submissiveness vs Dominance	0.17578*	0.14362
Seriousness vs Liveliness	−0.1868	0.34704*
Low Super Ego Strength vs High Super Ego Strength	−0.19438	0.26400*
Tough-mindedness vs Tender-mindedness	−0.00003	0.48188*
Conservatism vs Liberalism	0.01514	0.36658*
Group Dependency vs Self-sufficiency	−0.00621	0.26340*
Relaxation vs Tension	0.03800	0.14508*
Motivation		
Entrepreneurial Core	−0.19516*	0.19062
Work Core	−0.10690*	0.08578
Social Core	−0.34632*	−0.05480
Economic Core	−0.24655*	0.13830
Demographics		
Childhood Geographical Background	0.20213*	−0.10089
Education	0.09426	−0.14778*
Education of Spouse	0.27694*	−0.05978
Business-related variables		
Source of Finance	0.21958*	−0.18127
Type of Ownership	0.03612	0.16772*
Family Involvement in Business	0.09559	0.13263*

Note: *Significance at p > 0.05 level.

Conclusions

The results reveal that entrepreneurs are emotionally unstable, more suspicious, more timid and more apprehensive than non-entrepreneurs. Entrepreneurs are also found to be tender-minded, more radical and more self-sufficient than non-entrepreneurs. The finding that the personality of women entrepreneurs is significantly different from women non-entrepreneurs has been able to substantiate some specific clinical observations on the personality of entrepreneurs that entrepreneurship is an attempt by them to cope with certain psychological inadequacies. From the life situation antecedence, it is seen that entrepreneurs are found to have had lower psychological support, poorer previous work condition and lesser competence. With the fact that women undertaking entrepreneurship may be explained as an act of 'sublimation' under an unsatisfactory condition for the 'ego', entrepreneurship can be explained as a way of functioning by women in the environment, to gain control and to cope with certain psychological inadequacies.

Among the manufacturing, trading and service entrepreneurs, significant differences were seen in the life situation antecedence, personality, entrepreneurial motivation, demographics and business-related characteristics. The assessment through the life situation antecedence scale has revealed that the manufacturing entrepreneurs have lower psychological support but better benefit from environment and better financial status compared to the other sectors. Manufacturing entrepreneurs have personality traits of reservation, emotional stability, dominance, radicalism, self-sufficiency, low super ego and tough-mindedness. Trading entrepreneurs have personality traits of outgoingness, emotional instability, submissiveness, liveliness, conscientiousness, tender-mindedness, radicalism and self-sufficiency. Service entrepreneurs have personality traits of reservation, emotional stability, submissiveness, seriousness, low super ego, tough-mindedness, conservatism and group-dependency. Manufacturing entrepreneurs have a lower social core motivation, the trading entrepreneurs have a higher economic core motivation, and the service and trading entrepreneurs have a higher work core motivation.

The finding on the status of demographics shows that there are more entrepreneurs from the urban setting, with higher education and a well-educated spouse. Regarding the status of the business-related variables, a higher percentage of trading entrepreneurs inherited business and internal sources of finance. Compared to the other two sectors, fewer service entrepreneurs are engaged in sole proprietorship. Family involvement is significantly higher in the manufacturing sector of business. These findings give credence to the fact that each type of entrepreneurship is a distinctly different endeavour. Entrepreneurship requires a certain type of psychological disposition of personality and motivation and a certain kind of life situation antecedence. This observation will be helpful in identifying aptitudes for different types of business undertakings and also in providing differential counselling sessions to women, prior to and during the entrepreneurial process.

References

Aggarwal, R. 1997. 'Innovativeness in Entrepreneurship: Major Issues in the New Era of Globalization', *Abhigyan*, 15(4): 65–72.

Bishth, S. N. and Pamila K. Sharma. 1991. *Entrepreneurship, Expectations, and Experience.* New Delhi: Himalaya Publishing House.

Bowen, D. D. and R. D. Hisrich. 1986. 'The Female Entrepreneur: A Career Development Perspective', *Academy of Management Review*, 11(2): 393–407.

Caird, S. 1988. *A Review of Methods of Measuring Enterprising Attributes.* Durham: Durham University Business School.

Cannon, T., S. Carter, R. Peter, B. Lesley and M. Rosemary. 1988. *Female Enterpreneurship: A Report by Scottish Enterprise Foundation.* Stirling: University of Stirling. Available on request at: *http://www.emeraldinsight.com/Insight/manulDocumentRequest.do?hdAction= ref_document_request&r_contentId=0&r_atitle=&r_jtitle=Female%20Entrepreneurship &r_issn=&r_year=1988&r_volume=&r_issue=&r_startpage=&r_endpage=&r_publish er=Scottish%20Enterprise%20Foundation*

Caputo, K. Richard and Arthur L. Dolinsky. 1998. 'Women's choice to Pursue Self-Employment: The Role of Financial and Human Capital of Household Numbers', *Journal of Small Business Management*, 36(3): 36–43.

Casale, A. M. 1986. *Tracking Tomorrow's Trends.* Kansas City: McNeel and Parker Sons.

Chell. E. 1985. 'The Entrepreneurial Personality: A Few Ghosts Laid To Rest', *International Small Business Journal*, 3(3): 43–54.

Collins, G. R. and D. G. Moore. 1970. *The Organization Makers: A Behavioral Study of Entrepreneurs. New York:* Appleton.

Collins, O. and D. G. Moore. 1964. *The Enterprising Man.* East Lansing: Michigan State University Press.

Darlington, R. B. 1990. *Regression and Linear Models.* United States: McGraw Hill.

Fann, G. L. 1986. 'Women Entrepreneurs: Entering the Economic Main Stream', *Dissertation Abstracts International*, 47, (1579-A).

Feeser, H. R. and K. W. Dugan. 1989. 'Entrepreneurial Motivation: A Comparison of High and Low Growth High Tech Founders', in R. H. Brockhaus Sr., N. C. Churchill, J. A. Katz, B. A Kirchhoff, K. H. Vesper and W. E. Wetzel Jr. (eds), *Frontiers of Entrepreneurship Research*, pp. 13–27. Wellesley, MA: Babson College, Center for Entrepreneurial Studies.

Gilbert, E. S. 1968. 'On Discrimination Using Qualitative Variables', *Journal of the American Statistical Association*, 63(December): 1399–1412.

Gundry, L. K. and H. P. Welsch. 2001. 'The Ambitious Entrepreneur: High Growth Strategies of Women Owned Enterprises', *Journal of Business Venturing*, 16(5): 453–470.

Hofer, W. C. and D. W. Bygrave. 1992. 'Researching Entrepreneurship. Entrepreneurship Theory and Practice', *Entrepreneurship Theory and Practice*, 16(3): 91–100.

Iyer, Lalitha. 1991. *Women Entrepreneurs: Challenges and Strategies*. New Delhi: Friedrich Ebert Stiftung.

Joanne, Wilkens. 1987. *Her Own Business: Success Secrets of Entrepreneurial Women*. USA: McGraw Hill.

Kanitkar, A. and Nalinee Contractor. 1992. *In Search of Identity—The Women Entrepreneurs of India*. Ahmedabad: Entrepreneurship Development Institute of India.

Ket De Vries, M. F. R. 1977. 'The Entrepreneurial Personality: A Person at the Crossroads', *The Journal of Management Studies*, 14(1): 34–57.

———. 1996. 'The Anatomy of the Entrepreneur: Clinical Observations', *Human Relations*, 49(7): 853–883.

Mohuiddin, A. 1987. 'Entrepreneurship in Rural Women: A Study', *Kurukshetra*, 35: 19–25.

Pearlin, L. I. and C. Schooler. 1978. 'The Sstructures of Coping', *Journal of Health and Social Behavior*, 19(1): 2–21.

Ramamurthy, Savithri. 1990. *Women Entrepreneurs in Delhi, Their Motivation, Management Practices and Problems*. Doctoral thesis. University of Delhi, New Delhi.

Sarason, I. G., J. H. Johnson and J. M. Siegel. 1978. 'Assessing the Impact of Life Change: Development of the Life Experience Survey', *Journal of Consulting and Clinical Psychology*, 46(5): 932–946.

Scherer, R. F., J. D. Brodinski, and F. Wiebe. 1990. 'Entrepreneur Career Selection and Gender Socialization Approach', *Journal of Small Business Management*, 28(2): 37–43.

Shapero, A. and L. Sokol. 1982. 'The Social Dimensions of Entrepreneurship', in C. A. Kent, D. L. Sexton and K. H. Vesper (eds), *Encyclopaedia of Entrepreneurship*. Englewood Chiffs, NJ: Prentice Hall.

Sharma, S. D. and Peter Rebello. 1998. *Business Environment and Public Policy*. New Delhi: Anmol Publication.

Sharma, S. V. S. 1979. *Small Entrepreneurial Development in Some Asian Countries: A Comparative Study*. New Delhi: Life and Light Publishers.

Silver, A. D. 1992. *The Entrepreneurial Life: How to Go forIit and Get It*. New York: John Wiley and Sons.

Sonnenfeld, J. and Kotter J.P. 1982. 'The Maturation of Career Theory', *Human Relations*, 35(1): 19–46.

Stevenson, Howard and David E. Gumpert. 1985. 'The Heart of Entrepreneurship', *Harvard Business Review*, (March–April): 33–42.

Sunder, D. L. 1996. *A Study of the Entrepreneurial Personality*, Unpublished doctoral dissertation, Indian Institute of Technology, Chennai, India.

Timmons, J. 1990. *Entrepreneurship in the 1990s.* Homewood: Irwin.

UNIFEM. 1995. *Women, Environment and Development: Agenda 21—An Easy Reference to Specific Recommendation on Women.* New York: UNIFEM.

Watkins, J. M and D. S. Watkins. 1986. 'The Female Entrepreneur: Her Background and Determinants of Business Choice—Some British Data' in Curran, J., J. Stanworth and D. Walkins (eds), *The Survival of the Small Firm: Vol 1, The Economics of Survival and Entrepreneurship.* Aldershot: Grower.

Wilken, P. H. 1979. *Entrepreneurship: A Comparative and Historical Study.* NJ: Ablex Publishing Corporation.

Zimmerer, T. W. and N. M. Scarborough. 1996. *Entrepreneurship and New Venture Formation.* NJ: Prentice-Hall.

Women Entrepreneurship
A Case of Microenterprises

12

N. Manimekalai and
A. Mohammed Abdullah

Entrepreneurship is an important factor determining the economic growth of a nation. Originally, theories of entrepreneurship were centred around male entrepreneurs and limited to only a few communities which claimed themselves to be business communities. However, it was felt that in order to climb the ladder of development, it is necessary to create new entrepreneurs and accordingly, institutional efforts were made to inculcate the spirit of entrepreneurship among new communities.

As a significant factor contributing to economic development, the entrepreneurial potential must be tapped properly to improve the industrial base in any economy. Industrially developed countries could reach the status of being developed only because of a sufficient entrepreneurial base created. In theory, since the industrial revolution entrepreneurship had been associated with only males, the models of entrepreneurship have also been largely focussed on the males. In developing countries, till a decade or two ago, entrepreneurship was not even thought of. It is only after the United Nations declared 1976–1985 as the Decade of Women Empowerment that there has been a shift in the policies and change in the perspective of treating women as mere beneficiaries to agents of development. In the beginning of identifying the new class of entrepreneurs, the focus was primarily on men who could start their own business in small and micro scales and no focussed attention was given to women. Moreover, women were not recognized as agents of development and change till the eighties. Only after the declaration of the Decade of Women Empowerment 1976–1985 by the UN that treating women as beneficiaries under welfare schemes could be changed and accordingly women entrepreneurs had also been encouraged to become owners of enterprises. Thankfully the microcredit revolution in the nineties had really improved the entrepreneurial base among the women at the grass-root level, though it was on a micro scale both in the rural and urban areas. The women microentrepreneurs normally tend to be found in the microenterprises in the informal sector, whose contribution has hardly been accounted in the national income. However, the contributions of these women cannot be ignored.

Global Scenario of Women Entrepreneurship

It is observed that the rate at which the women-owned enterprises grow has been faster than the men-owned enterprises. Probably the women entrepreneurs have just started emerging whereas the men have already reached saturation and that is the reason why the women-owned enterprises are growing at a faster rate.

The GEM study by Nan Langowitz (2004) on women's entrepreneurship emphasizes the critical role women have in new venture creation and provides insights to inform policies focussed on increasing and extending the scope and reach of their entrepreneurial activities. These findings support our goal of understanding, featuring and supporting the entrepreneurial efforts of women worldwide. According to the GEM 2004 Report on Women and Entrepreneurship, regardless of per capita income, a strong positive and significant correlation exists between knowing other entrepreneurs and a woman's involvement with starting a new business. 'Our results suggest that employed women who know other entrepreneurs are the most likely to start a new business,' said Babson Professor Maria Minniti, one of the authors of the report. 'These women tend to be older and better educated in high-income countries than in low- and middle-income countries. We also found that a woman's perceptions of environmental opportunities as well as confidence in her own capabilities are powerful predictors of her entrepreneurial behaviour,' she said. It was suggested that much female entrepreneurship in low income countries is motivated by necessity thus starting a new business represents an effective and flexible way for women to emancipate themselves and provide for their families. Areas of importance for policy makers should include literacy and financial assistance.

Related Studies

Several studies have been carried out on various dimensions of entrepreneurs around the globe and different countries, depending upon the social and economic backgrounds, exhibited different types of entrepreneurship among women. Berg (1997), Chandra (1997), Manimekalai and Rajeswari (2000), Shah (1996), Singh (1992) and Singh et al. (1986) in their studies underlined the diverse characteristics of women entrepreneurs. It is underlined in almost all the studies that women from diverse backgrounds—both business and non-business—engage in both traditional and modern entrepreneurial activities. Contrary to the general belief, it was shown in studies that women are engaged in manufacturing and trading sectors in both feminine and non-feminine activities; women entrepreneurs do not face any financial problems and they are with both formal and non-formal training. They did not face any conflict in family and are much concerned with expansion, diversification and modernization.

Bird (1989) held that women entrepreneurs were concentrated in the retail and service sectors, and concluded that such individual differences appeared to influence the entrepreneurs' choice of the kind, size and success of the business venture. Vineze and Dubashi (1987) found that the concept of women in their young and middle age from middle class families becoming entrepreneurs is a recent phenomenon. Similarly, Hisrich and Brush (1986) underlined that female entrepreneurs tend to start business in their late thirties. Surti and Sarupriya (1983) investigated the psychological factors affecting women entrepreneurs and found that unmarried women experienced less stress and fewer dependents than married women, and similarly those from joint families tended to experience less stress than those from nuclear families, probably because they share their problems with other family members.

Relevance of Male Models of Entrepreneurship to Female Entrepreneurs

Symons (1990) underlined that the male model of entrepreneurial development is not entirely applicable to the women's working lives. The heirs who enjoy being independent have been thrown into management at an early age. Also, the challenges, risks and sacrifices that women entrepreneurs assume are similar to those faced by men but women face additional hurdles. Hence, it may be underlined that the women do get encouraged by the same factors that motivate men to become entrepreneurs. At the same time, the obstacles and hurdles that they face differ considerably as they bear the double burden of managing both—household and business. Very often, cultural reasons put down their initiative wherein the family members themselves discourage the initiative of women becoming entrepreneurs as they associate women only with household activities. However, studies have proved that once the women prove themselves as successful entrepreneurs, they are able to win the confidence of the family members and are later supported by all those who discouraged them including husband, in-laws, and so forth.

Both the pull and push factors are responsible for women to become entrepreneurs. Berns (1986) held that in India, women entrepreneurs emerge mostly because of the 'push factors' which emphasize the responsibility thrust on them. In Western societies, women in services tend to become entrepreneurs because of job discrimination in promotion, sexual harassment, and so forth.

Asath (1987), Buttner and Rosen (1988), Bird (1989) and Gladys L. Symons (1990) have all underlined that women who are dissatisfied with their bosses assume entrepreneurial roles and start enterprises on their own either as heirs or founders. Le, Anh. T. (2000) and Carter and Allen (1997) found that having the capital to grow and expand business operation through commercial businesses, loans and private sources in addition to a personal bank relationship, and a focus on profit and growth contribute significantly to the size of women-owned business. It was inferred that the availability of financial resources is a major influence on the entrepreneur's business intention and choice of lifestyle.

There are many studies to be found on microcredit and women micro-entrepreneurs. Buvinic (1986), Reichmann (1992) and Berger (1985) have observed that the credit projects, in addition to stabilizing income or generating additional income, contribute to improving the women's self-esteem and status within their households and when allowances are made for indirect training benefits and multiplier effects of the investment in small enterprises, microcredit projects yield a high return.

Kilby and D'Znula (1985), Everett and Savara (1984) and Manimekalai (1999) criticized the credit schemes for being too costly and failing to create employment. The increased incomes of women are used to make interest payments rather than for business reinvestment to provide long-lasting benefits, indicating that such credit may be of greater importance for stabilizing income than for increasing income and employment.

Studies on the impact of training in creating women entrepreneurs, including those by Patel (1988), Shah and Bhuptani (1989), Kirve and Kanitkar (1993), Poojary (1996) and Manimekalai (1993), agree that women entrepreneurs, after training with Entrepreneurship Development Program (EDP), could start business in the fields of engineering, electronics, plastics, rubber, textiles, energy saving and so forth, the project size going up to Rs 25 lakh to Rs 50 lakh and offer employment to as many as 50 to 200 people each. The majority come from middle-class families. There are findings by a few authors that the start-up rate of EDP is quite low but on-the-job experience had contributed positively.

On constraints for women entrepreneurs, several studies including Gunnerud (1997), Singh (1992) and Manimekalai and Rajeswari (2000) underlined that it is more difficult for women to start and be in business due to (a) lack of previous opportunity to develop business skills, (b) expectations of financers/managers of entrepreneurship and women that influence the granting of business credit and (c) domestic responsibilities that make them face a conflict of roles.

It is thus concluded that female entrepreneurs want freedom to combine family responsibilities and a fair income, and they express the need for flexibility that had not been found among male entrepreneurs. In addition, a woman's entire socialization process makes her fearful of failure, doubtful of success and reluctant to take risks, and the social, economic and cultural constraints, including lack of encouragement from the family, support from institutions, and so forth, constrain women to become as successful as male entrepreneurs.

Definitions of Concepts

Woman Entrepreneur

In this study, a woman entrepreneur is defined as 'an adult woman who undertakes to organize, own and run an enterprise'.

Women Enterprises

Women enterprises, in this study, are defined as those enterprises which are primarily owned and controlled by women, either supported by other members or individually managed.

Microenterprises

A microenterprise is an enterprise where the size of investment is within Rs 1 lakh including the cost of the plant and the machinery. In these enterprises, the entrepreneur would be owner and labourer, mostly employing family members along with hired labourers. In some cases, the entrepreneur is self-employed.

Objectives

The studies undertaken in the field of women entrepreneurship from different countries and different perspectives revealed that women invariably choose entrepreneurship mainly due to distress factors. Only a few could start their enterprises primarily to use their leisure and to use the technology learnt, and so forth. Moreover, the women entrepreneurs' scale of operations and the nature of activities also exhibit that they choose to work in a business of microscale, part-time self-employment-oriented activities largely confining to service or trading activities rather than manufacturing or production-oriented. It is in this backlog that this study has been attempted to identify the nature of women entrepreneurial activities and their size and scale of operations. Studies have also proved that the scale and size of women-owned enterprises lagged behind men-owned enterprises mainly due to the dual responsibilities of the women. Accordingly the following objectives are framed:

1. To find out the socioeconomic characteristics of the sample women entrepreneurs and men entrepreneurs.
2. To identify the factors which influenced the sample entrepreneurs to assume an entrepreneurial role.
3. To analyze the comparative performance of women-owned and men-owned enterprises in relation to various socioeconomic characteristics, extent of income contribution of women to the household and the reach of the institutional support.
4. To identify through the SWOT analysis, the problems faced by them in running the enterprises and managing home and business.

Methodology

The database on women in microenterprises has been very weak, given the characteristics that they are mostly found in the informal sector and their contributions to the household and economy go largely unaccounted in the national income accounting. It was really an adventure in the conceptualization stage as to how to identify the women enterprises at the microscale of operation. Repeated visits to District Industries Centres, Inspector of Factories, District Small and Tiny Industries Association, Confederation of Indian Industry, Women Associations, Tamil Nadu Adi-Dravidar Housing and Development Corporation (THADCO), banks financing the women enterprises: Lead Bank, NGOs, and so forth, could not help in furnishing the necessary information. In fact, the lack of database on such enterprises as they have not registered and work as home-based activities, posed problems for the researcher in the beginning. Hence, it is was realized that a complete enumeration using census survey would be the best option to identify the microenterprises run by women and accordingly a preliminary survey, literally stepping into a door-to-door service to all shops and services was made and finally succeeded in identifying around 550 units. These units were classified as per their product line and only 432 units could be retained which had furnished full information in the baseline survey. Moreover, repeated visits to many units did not get results and so they had to be eliminated in the beginning itself. Of the 432 units retained, 30 per cent of the units from each category were chosen for an intensive study, which came to 130 units using the stratified systematic random sampling. The distribution of the units as per their line of production is furnished in the subsequent pages (see Table 12.1).

Table 12.1   Distribution of the Activities of the Sample Women Entrepreneurs

Code no.	Activities	Universe	Samples
1.	Tailoring Shops	150	45
2.	Beauty Clinics	60	18
3.	Readymade Garments Trade	17	5
4.	Tailoring Institutes	7	2
5.	Stationery Stores	24	7
6.	General Stores	34	10
7.	Vendors	6	2
8.	Confectionary Stores	30	9
9.	Xerox and Communication Services	22	7
10.	Typewriting Inst. and Computer Edu.	27	8
11.	Repairing and Services	6	2
12.	Catering Units	10	3
13.	Printing and Binding	7	2
14.	Others	32	10
	Total	**432**	**130**

For the purpose of comparison, 38 men-owned similar enterprises have also been chosen to analyze the differential performance and problems from gender perspective. Table 12.1 brings the distribution of the sample units as drawn from the universe of women entrepreneurs in the study area (Tiruchirappalli in Tamil Nadu). It could be noticed that the majority of the units belong to tailoring shops and beauty clinics which they prefer as they exclusively deals with women. It is true and reflected in the findings of other studies also that the women entrepreneurs in the small and micro scale tend to choose products which are mostly used by women rather than mainstreaming to production or manufacturing or servicing the activities which involve male customers also. This again is gender socialization, which reinforces that a woman is comfortable dealing with women-related products. Sensitization can be given in EDPs to diversify entrepreneurial activities to non-feminine products which may also widen their opportunities.

Table 12.2 explains the distribution of sample units owned by men and women sample entrepreneurs by the product line or service chosen. It attempts to identify similar units from the close vicinity of the women-owned sample enterprises. However, not a fully satisfactory distribution that matches exactly with the distribution of the women-owned enterprises could be identified. The characteristics exhibited by men-owned enterprises have been more or less similar to those run by women. The nature of activities, in general, indicates that the women have not chosen the processing or manufacturing of production-oriented units because in the sample district, the real entrepreneurship to assume risk and realize profit as not been found. Rather, the majority of them had chosen entrepreneurship under distress conditions to support and supplement the income of their families, which were mostly at the subsistence level.

Table 12.2 Distribution of the Sample Units by Their Nature of Activities

Sl. no.	Activities	No. of entrepreneurs			
		Female	Per cent	Male	Per cent
1.	Tailoring Shops	45	34.62	9	23.68
2.	Beauty Clinics	18	13.85	7	18.42
3.	Readymade Garments Trade	5	3.85	2	5.26
4.	Tailoring Institutes	2	1.54	–	–
5.	Stationery Stores	7	5.38	1	2.63
6.	General Stores	10	7.69	6	15.79
7.	Vending	2	1.54	–	–
8.	Confectionary Stores	9	6.92	1	2.63
9.	Xerox and Communications	7	5.38	3	7.9
10.	Typewriting Institutes	8	6.15	3	7.9
11.	Repairing and Services	2	1.54	1	2.63
12.	Catering Services	3	2.31	2	5.26
13.	Printing and Binding Services	2	1.54	1	2.63
14.	Others	10	7.69	2	5.26
	Total	**130**	**100**	**38**	**100**

Table 12.3 brings out the socioeconomic profile of the sample entrepreneurs. It could be seen from the table that relatively higher percentage of women entrepreneurs are married at the time of start-up and there is not much difference in the age-wise analysis. However, an interesting observation noticed about the nature of the families revealed that a majority of the women entrepreneurs tend to stay in nuclear families both at start-up and at present, whereas the men-owned enterprises exhibit a different trend, showing higher percentage choosing to stay in joint families. This is quite contradictory to the general expectation that the women, due to dual responsibilities, may prefer joint families to look after the children and household activities but it is true in this study.

Table 12.3   Socioeconomic Background of the Sample Entrepreneurs

Groups age	At start-up		At present	
	Female	*Male*	*Female*	*Male*
Average	29.68	30.03	36.7	39.08%
Marital Status				
Married	80.77%	47.37%	79.23%	76.32%
Nature of Family				
Joint	30%	68.40%	26.92%	36.80%
Nuclear	70%	31.60%	73.08%	63.20%
Size of the Family (Mean in No.)			4.3	4.7
Religion		Hindu	77.69%	68.42%
Community Backward Community			84.60%	71.05%
Previous Experience			10.75 years	14.24 years
Persons Supporting to		Self	24.62%	52.63%
Growth of Enterprises		Husband/Wife	61.54%	34%

In fact, among these sample enterprises, a majority of the entrepreneurs migrated from neighbourhood villages for job or marriage and accordingly chose a microeconomic activity which hardly adapts to joint family as their income earned does not suffice even to meet the nuclear family needs.

Other facts, such as the size of the family, religion and caste-wise distribution which tells us that majority had come from Hindu as well as the backward communities do not show much difference between genders. However, previous experience has been relatively more for men than women entrepreneurs. People supporting the enterprises revealed that relatively more women entrepreneurs are supported by family members, particularly husbands, as compared to men entrepreneurs who are mostly self-supported.

Factors

Entrepreneurship has not been taken as a factor which could be created. However, several attempts have been made to inculcate the spirit of entrepreneurship among the new communities and it could succeed partly in creating a new class of entrepreneurs.

Women entrepreneurs also fall in this category as a couple of decades ago, women entrepreneurship had not even been thought of. Table 12.4 explains the factors which determined the entry choice of the women and men in entrepreneurial activities.

Table 12.4 Factors Determining the Entry Choice to Entrepreneurship and the Activity

Rank	Factors determining the entry choice	
	Women Entrepreneurs	*Men Entrepreneurs*
I	Desire to be independent	Desire to be independent
II	To be able to give children a better life	To provide employment to others
III	To secure social prestige	To be able to give children a better life
	Reason for the Choice of the 'Present' Activity	
I	Easy marketing	Easy marketing
II	Training and education received	Previous experience
III	Can be done as a household activity	Family business

Closed-ended options could be found after a pilot study, enumerating various factors which have influenced the women and men to enter and run the enterprises, had been done in the first stage. The respondents were asked to rank the factors in the order of preference of at least three factors.

The entry choice to entrepreneurship explains that there is not much difference between male and female entrepreneurs for becoming entrepreneurs as more or less similar reasons were given.

As far as the factor determining the choice of the present activity as their entrepreneurial activity is concerned, it is revealed that one of the reasons is that it can be done as a household activity—a reason which is absent with men-owned enterprises. Hence, women prefer to balance the dual role of a homemaker and a business woman, and accordingly, choose to work on household-based activities.

Table 12.5 Details of Organization of the Sample Entrepreneurs

Sources	Women-owned units	Men-owned units
Ownership of the Premises		
Rented	79.23%	97.37%
Nature of Organization		
Sole Proprietorship	83.85%	92.11%
Area of the Marketing		
Within the District	80%	76.92%
Registration Status		
Registered	56.17%	65.79%

Details of the organization of the sample entrepreneurs revealed that the relatively larger percentage of women chose not to locate to rented premises and a slightly higher percentage of the men-owned enterprises was sole proprietorship. Although women work on a very tiny or micro scale, yet they depend on others for help, particularly in marketing. Hence, relatively lower percentage of them is on a sole proprietorship concern as compared to men-owned enterprises. On the marketing aspects, the women are found to produce and market only in their own localities and at the most within the district, unlike men-owned enterprises which market outside the district also. The women-run units are not registered—rather they are running as household enterprises and some have chosen to register with the Tamil Nadu General Sales Tax Act.

Performance Analysis

Sample units were started in different years and as such the data on performance indicators such as investment, turnover, profit, and so forth, need to be either deflated or inflated and mean growth is calculated. In this study, they were deflated to the base year to make the values uniform

Table 12.6 Mean Performance in Terms of Sales Turnover for Women-
owned Enterprises

Sales Turnover (Rs in '000)	Start-up	1997	1998	1999	2000	2001
Below 100	52042	55578	58673	57690	55486	54832
100–150	122915	126603	125074	122779	124362	123431
150–200	171589	173117	171219	164781	173548	172275
200–250	215377	228296	214980	211438	216388	216388
250 and above	456156	785421	831356	778586	799859	803302
Mean for Total	**135981**	**249570**	**259949**	**272939**	**291242**	**292847**

to compare the performance of all the sample units. Accordingly, the mean growth of sales turnover has been found to have more than doubled over the years. The sales turnover performance has been fluctuating in almost all the size groups, indicating that the business performance in such micro scale of operations also tends to show cyclical fluctuations.

Although by the mean performance it is shown that there is a doubling of performance in terms of mean growth, yet the annual percentage growth in terms of deflated index shows that the overall growth has moved from 8.4 per cent to 11.5 per cent, which is not an appreciable growth. Since the enterprises are micro in scale, they are not able to show a growth rate to an appreciable percentage. For men-owned enterprises, the data given was not complete enough to be compared.

Certain variables have been taken for both men-owned and women-owned enterprises and a comparison of the variables revealed that the mean size of the investment of men-owned enterprises is slightly higher than that of the women-owned ones. On the other hand, the working capital exhibits a significant variation as the women-owned enterprises have just one-fourth of what the men-owned enterprises have. Similarly, in other variables, such as employment and capacity utilization, women-owned enterprises lag behind the men-owned ones. A study of the capital that was owned and also borrowed by them at present also showed that men-owned enterprises could register a higher magnitude compared to those owned by women. Here again, it was attributed to the lack of time to fully concentrate on business, lack of mobility, and so forth, which made the women-owned enterprises lag behind men-owned enterprises in terms of certain indicators.

An analysis of the perceptions of the women entrepreneurs explained that the women after entering into running such microenterprises,

Table 12.7 Annual Average Growth Rate of Sales Turnover for Various Years

Sales Turnover (Rs in '000)	Start-up		1997		1998		1999		2000		2001	
	AAGR	CPI	AAGR	CPI	AAGR	CPI	AAGR	CPI	AAGR	CPI	AAGR	CPI
Below 100	–	100	0.68	107	1.27	113	1.09	111	0.66	107	0.54	105
100–150	–	100	0.25	103	0.16	102	–0.01	100	0.15	101	0.05	100
150–200	–	100	0.07	101	–0.62	100	–0.33	96	0.08	101	0.03	100
200–250	–	100	0.86	106	–0.03	100	–0.30	98	0.08	100	0.08	100
250 and above	–	100	7.22	172	8.23	182	7.07	171	8.37	175	7.61	176
Overall mean	–	**100**	**8.4**	**184**	**10.1**	**191**	**11.2**	**201**	**12.7**	**214**	**11.5**	**215**

Table 12.8 Comparative Analysis of the Variables of the Sample Men- and Women-owned Enterprises

Sources	Women-owned	Men-owned enterprises
Investment (in Rs)	122322	147342
Working Capital (in Rs)	35461	148584
Employment (in No.)	1.37	3
Capacity Utilization (in per cent)	49.93	62.68
Profit (in per cent)	33.5	–
Reinvestment (in per cent)	36.61	27.24
Current Average Own Capital	61519	90950
Current Average Borrowed Capital	9480	113888

Table 12.9 Gain and Loss after Entry into Business as Perceived by Women Entrepreneurs

Gain	Per cent	Loss	Per cent
Double Income	86.92	Time pressure and resultant health problems	80
Economic Freedom	79.23		
Contribution to the Public Society	77.69	Indirect abuse of customers, relatives and others	61.54
Decision-making in Family Matters	75.39		
Better Education	73.08	Lack of leisure time	58.46
Better Saving for Future	70		
Better Respect and Requirements in Society/ among Relatives	48.46	Unable to concentrate on children education	56.15
Able to Provide More Comforts to the Family	46.92	Taking care of the self	30

experienced gains in certain aspects, such as income, economic freedom, contribution to society, decision-making in family, education of the children, improved saving, mobility and improved recognition among the relatives. However, they also felt that they had lost on certain aspects including time pressure, as they had to look after home and business, customer's abuse, lack of time to devote to children and their education, self-care, and so forth. It is true that as far as women confine themselves only to household activities, their entire time is devoted to such work alone and when they move out and concentrate on business, a balancing is required to avoid conflicts between work and home.

Multiple Regressions

Multiple regressions have been made to find out the determinants of entrepreneurial performance in terms of growth in investment. It is estimated to explain the variations in investment size, identifying relevant variables explaining the growth of investment.

Table 12.10   Multiple Regression for Growth of Investment

Dependent Variable: Annual Average Growth Rate (AAGR) of Investment			
Independent Variables	'T' value	'T' significance	Sign Obtained
1. Previous Experience	1.149	0.2528	−
2. Caste of Entrepreneurs	0.672	0.5026	+
3. Region of Location	0.615	0.5395	+
4. Business Premises	0.662	0.5096	−
5. AAGR of Capacity Utilization	2.464	0.0152	+
6. AAGR of Fixed Own Capital	6.717	0.0000	+
7. AAGR of Fix. Borrowed Capital	5.096	0.0000	+
8. AAGR of Sales Turnover	0.346	0.7298	+
9. AAGR Growth of Profit	2.467	0.0151	+
10. AAGR of Reinvested	0.428	0.6693	−
11. AAGR of Own Working Capital	5.840	0.0000	+
12. AAGR of Borrowed Working Capital	1.826	0.0705	+
13. AAGR of Employment	1.475	0.1428	−
Constant	1.124	0.2632	

Notes: R^2 = 0.76191; Adjusted R^2 = 0.58050; F Value = 12.34784; Sig. F = 0.0000

The possible independent variables identified are able to explain the variations in growth of investment to the tune of 0.76, indicating that around 76 per cent of variations in the growth of investment could be caused by the identified variables but still there are other variables which need to be identified to fully explain the variations in the growth of investment.

Problems

The problems faced by the women-owned and men-owned enterprises are furnished in Table 12.11.

Table 12.11 **Important Problems of the Sample Entrepreneurs**

General problems	Percentage of entrepreneurs	
	Female	Male
Lack of Mobility	62.31	44.74
Lack of Marketing Facilities	58.46	–
Insufficient Individual Swareness	43.85	42.11
Lack of Financial Resources	36.92	–
Initial Lack of Confidence in Their Own Abilities	36.15	13.16
Banker's Reluctance to Take Risk of Helping a Woman Entrepreneur	33.85	26.32

A majority of the women entrepreneurs felt that a lack of mobility as restricted by family has been the major problem which causes problems of marketing the products or services outside their locality, and expanding the scale of operations. Moreover, it was expressed that a lack of awareness of various programmes and schemes of the government, procedures to be followed to avail bank credit, and so forth, have also been mentioned by a few of them as major problems. Male entrepreneurs also face these problems but it is less pronounced.

From the gender perspective, it is noticed that women have additional family-related problems compared to men. The percentage of women facing such problems are more than that of men. This is also true when it comes to business-related problems. Competition is a common problem faced by both women and men, but other issues are more pronounced in women-owned enterprises as compared to male-owned units.

In general, not much difference could be observed with respect to business-related problems but there has been a significant difference with respect to the family problems for women.

Hypotheses Testing

The women entrepreneurs' families depend on their income; without their income, their families would have faced survival difficulties.

It has been proved by Economic Dependency Ratio.

Economic Dependency Ratio was developed by Annemettee Sorensen and Sara McLanahan (1987). Dependency of women is defined as the

Table 12.12 Problems Related to Family and Business

Problems related to family	Percentage of entrepreneurs	
	Female	Male
Duel responsibility of family and business	61.54	2.63
Lack of support from parents/husband/wife	38.46	23.68
Lack of time to concentrate on business;		
Ultimately depending on others for decisions	25.38	2.63
Problems Related to Business		
Competition	91.54	92.11
Changing consumers' tastes and preferences	71.54	63.16
Lack of support from peer group	60	26.32
Lack of awareness about the existing scheme		
of assistance	59.23	47.37
Lack of knowledge about the latest technologies	51.54	36.84

Note: The percentage includes the number of women who face the problems mentioned in the table.

difference between the income contribution of the women towards the income bowl of the family and contribution made by the other earning members of the family. The level of dependency has been explained with the following formula:

$$ DEP. = \frac{INCF}{INCF + INCW} - \frac{INCW}{INCF + INCW} $$

where

DEP. = Dependency level

INCF = Income of the family

INCW = Income of the sample women entrepreneurs

This dependency model explains that if the household is completely a dependent unit of the women entrepreneurs' income, that is, INCF is greater than INCW, the level of dependency is −1.

INCF < INCW = −1 (HHs depend on women's income)

If the woman is completely a dependent person on the household income, say INCF is less than INCW, the level of dependency is +1.

INCF > INCW = + 1 (Women depend on HHs income)

When the dependency value is zero, it indicates that the family is an independent unit, which can survive without the earning of its women entrepreneurs.

INCF = INCW = 0 (Family is an independent unit)

By applying this dependency model, the dependency level of the respondents and respondent households are analyzed as follows: the variables taken into consideration are the size of income of the respondents and income of the household by activity.

Table 12.13   Economic Dependency of Women Entrepreneurs by Activity

Activity	Proportion of women's contribution	Level of dependency
Tailoring shops	52.30	−0.46
Beauty clinics	44.12	+0.12
Readymade garments trade	52.75	−0.06
Tailoring institutes	48.39	+0.03
Stationery stores	68.54	−0.37
General stores (grocery and fancy stores)	93.51	−0.87
Vending	100	−1
Confectionary stores	52.94	−0.06
Xerox and communications services	43.53	+0.13
Typewriting institutes and computer edu.	33.48	+0.33
Repairing and services	88.24	−0.77
Catering services	51.28	−0.03
Printing and binding services	100	−1
Others	37.63	+0.25
Total	**51.63**	**−0.03**

It may be inferred from Table 12.13 that the dependency level of the women is positive for beauty clinic, tailoring institute, xerox and telecom centres, typewriting and computer centre, and other activities, indicating that the women in these activities might have assumed entrepreneurial activities merely for economic need to support the subsistence of the family. The availability of time, skill acquired, education, and so forth, might have contributed to the women's taking up entrepreneurial activities. On the other hand, the negative dependency level in tailoring, readymade garments, stationery stores, general stores, and vending, confectionary stores, repairing services, catering services, printing and binding indicates that the family has been a unit dependent on women's income. Therefore, in the study area among the 14 women's activities, the families of those involved in tailoring, readymade garments, stationery stores, general stores, vending, confectionery stores, repairing services, catering services, and printing and binding activities depend mostly on the women's income than other activities. This may be attributed to the absence of adult male earner, low income of male members, unemployment of husband or unskilled wageworkers, aged father or no adult male in those families. On the basis of this evidence, is the hypothesis that sample women entrepreneurs' families are dependent on women's income (Hypothesis 1).

Table 12.14 Economic Dependency of Women Entrepreneurs by Marital Status

Marital Status	Proportion of Women's Contribution	Level of Dependency
Unmarried	48.77	+0.03
Married	50.29	−0.01
Widow	63.7	−0.27
Divorcee	38.46	+0.23
Total	**50.84**	**−0.02**

The dependency level of women entrepreneurs by marital status reveals that the unmarried and divorcees have positive dependency ratio, which means that women are completely dependent on the household income. On the other hand, unmarried and widowed women have negative dependency ratio wherein the household is completely dependent on women entrepreneurs' incomes. However, the overall dependency ratio has been found to be negative, indicating the dependence of families on women's income.

Hypothesis 2

Women entrepreneurs are less likely to have access to credit from formal financial institutions (see Table 12.15).

The schemes of assistance available for women entrepreneurs have not reached the women who have already initiated an enterprise on their own. Moreover, it was observed that the men-owned enterprises also face the difficulties in availing the existing support. This tends to conclude that the formal credit access and search are very poor for microenterprises in general, irrespective of whether they are owned by men or women.

Table 12.15 Percentage of Sample Entrepreneurs Who Availed Institutional Support

Schemes	Women-owned enterprises	Men-owned enterprises
No Loan	78.4	81.58
PMRY	8.4	7.89
SSI	0.8	10.53
Direct loan from bank	9.2	–
JRY	0.8	–
Refugee welfare loan	0.8	–
TAHDCO	0.8	–
Co-operative Bank	0.8	–

SWOT Analysis

Every initiative, be it economic, social or political, will necessarily have strengths and weaknesses influenced by the environment. Micro-enterprises rarely identify these influences before commencing their work. The simplest way to conduct environmental scanning is through SWOT analysis. The external environment consists of variables, opportunities and threats that are outside the business and not typically within the short run control of the entrepreneurs. The key environmental factors are depicted in Figure 12.1. The internal environment consists of variables relating to strengths and weaknesses that are within the organization control of the entrepreneur. Those variables form the context in which work is done. They include the unit's structure, culture and resources. Key strengths form the set of core competencies which the enterprise can use to gain competitive advantage.

In this study, the strengths identified among the sample women entrepreneurs are: their determination to stay in business, to be successful and expand the enterprises, to avail government assistance for expansion, support of the family members, friendly customers, no role conflict with family and business, and the courage to withstand ups and downs in business.

The weaknesses are that they are still unaware of various assistance available at the government levels, unable to be patient enough to fulfil the formalities of formal credit, complete dependency on informal credit, unable to face competition, not expanding the scale of operation, lack

Figure 12.1 SWOT Analysis

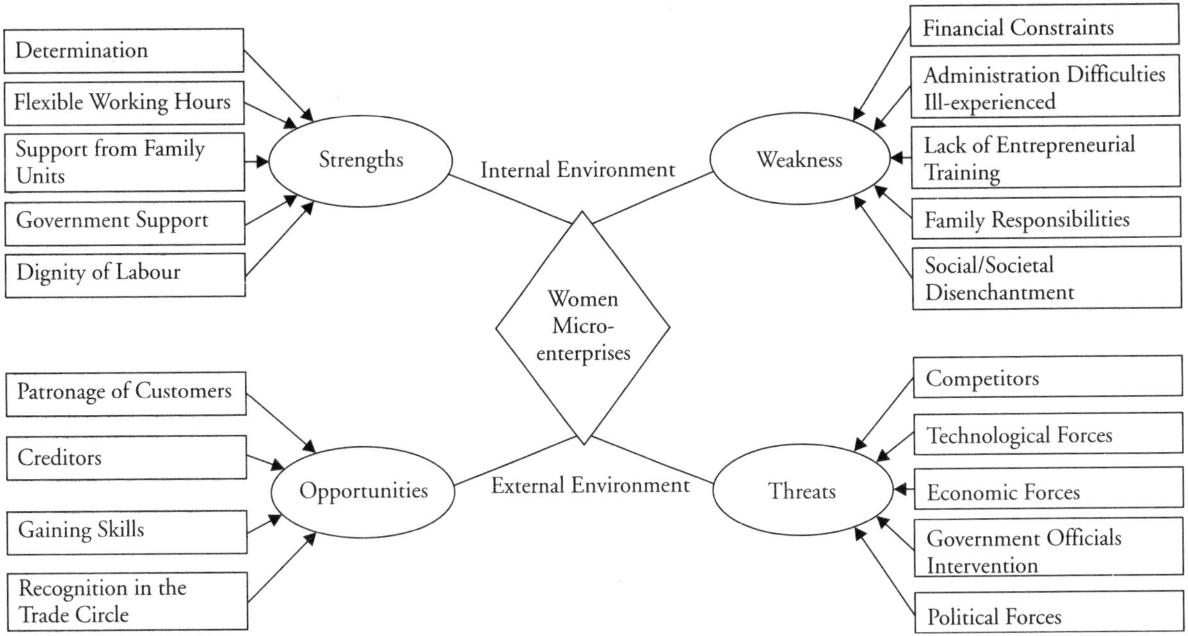

Source: Compiled from primary data.

of financial support from family and banks, absence of networking, inability to devote full time on business, feeling of guilty on non-attending the household responsibilities, and so forth.

The opportunities are that the microscale units are meeting their demands right from the lower income to the upper income group. Several schemes of assistance are available to them from the government and non-government agencies, financial institutions with special subsidies and incentives for women, male members' support, guidance from similar male-run enterprises, education, previous experience, and so forth.

The threats to the women entrepreneurs are competition from similar male and female enterprises, lack of education and experience on the innovative way of doing things, technological backwardness, confining to microscale of operations, service or trade and business rather than manufacturing, lack of risk-taking ability, lack of financial support, lack of encouragement and co-operation from family in a few cases, lack of reach of government schemes, lack of initiatives or networking to represent their problems collectively, and so forth.

However, the women were confident that if proper financial and marketing support is extended, they would convert the weaknesses into strengths and threats into opportunities.

Recommendations

From the findings that emerged from this study, the following recommendations are worth mentioning:

- The reach of formal credit must be made easier through the networking of the microenterprises, which is completely absent.
- A majority of the enterprises are service- and trade-oriented in the traditional entrepreneurial activities. In the modern activities, there is lack of technological upgradation. These issues need to be addressed by regularly updating knowledge on the latest developments taking place.
- Government programmes do not reach the deserving—this must be done away with if these women form an association and represent collectively.

- There is a lack of awareness about various schemes of assistance available with banks, government departments, and so forth, due to a lack of publicity. Hence, any programmes introduced must be publicized periodically through grass-root level functionaries.
- Women must understand the rules, regulations, procedures and laws to be followed to avail any type of support and assistance from the banks or government departments.
- Women must seek to undergo training on their own either through their association or collectively forming a group and representing the training institutions. This would help them in converting the threats into opportunities.
- Products of the women enterprises must be invited to trade fairs, exhibitions, etc., so that they would get advertised and also the associations can periodically arrange to exhibit their products.
- Having come to face both business and home, a balancing has to be done without any guilt as pursuing a business is also a service to the society and family. Hence a suitable alternative arrangement to look after the work of the entrepreneurs at home may be made so as to concentrate more on business and expand further.
- Banks are now coming forward to extend credit to women at the grassroot level of society. However, women without any association with non-government organizations (NGO) or self-help groups (SHGs) are not encouraged much. Such conditions may be relaxed for deserving women, taking their past performance into account.
- Women must also give up their docile nature to market their products everywhere, identifying suitable customers and expanding the market, thereby.
- Women should not be confined to traditional services. Activities suiting their requirements, namely education, experience, knowledge, must be taken up, may be, in processing and manufacturing which are more rewarding with relatively high risk. This has to be promoted with the support of the other members of the family.
- The predominance of the informal credit among the sample microenterprises may be eliminated by accommodating the 'existing entrepreneurs' also into the stream of assistance. This would serve twin purposes of (a) promoting the women entrepreneurial base in the study as these entrepreneurs already started off and (b) it relieving these women from the trap of informal lenders.

- The easy availability of informal credit and non-accessibility to formal credit is due to the asymmetry of information to bankers which the informal lenders are able to win by directly dealing with borrowers on a small scale which tend to eliminate the information gap. This can also be followed easily by the formal sector by extending support to group entrepreneurship.

Conclusion

This study has analyzed the entrepreneurial performance of men-owned and women-owned enterprises, taking various indicators, and found that there is no difference in the performance among the men-owned and women-owned enterprises except the fact that women face problems of lack of time to devote to family, undertake household chores, and so forth. The access to formal credit is very poor for microenterprises, irrespective of whether they are run by men or women. However, running enterprises had contributed to women empowerment, leading them to be independent, improving the education of their wards, postponing the age of marriage, sending girls outside for work and education, which were absent previously. However, the questioning of equal property, lack of asset base to avail bank credit, gender division of labour, feeling uncomfortable with activities with male customers, not encouraging the women workers to spend time on reading papers, interacting with men in neighbourhood, and so forth, are gender questions to be addressed. The fact that entrepreneurship among women does contribute to their empowerment cannot be denied and, therefore, entrepreneurial activities must be encouraged among women as instrument for empowerment.

References

Asath, Gulab Singh. 1987. 'Development of Entrepreneurship Among Rural Women—An Overview', *SEDME*, 15(2) (June).

Berg, Nina Gunnerud. 1997.'Gender, Race and Entrepreneurship', *Entrepreneurship and Regional Development*, 9: 209–268.

Berger, Margverite. 1985. 'An Initial Assessment of the Women's Role in Economic Development Program'. Report prepared for USAID/Bangladesh, Washington DC: International Centre for Research Women.

Bird, Barbara. 1989. *Entrepreneurial Behaviour*. Glenview, Illinois, London: Foresman and Co.

Buttner, E. Holly and B. Rosen. 1988. 'Bank Loan Officer's Perceptions of the Characteristics of Men, Women, and Successful Entrepreneurs', *Journal of Business Venturing*, 3(3): 249–258.

Buvinic, M. 1986. 'Projects for Women in Third World; Explaining Their Misbehaviour', *World Development*, 14(15): 653–664.

Carter, Nancy M., Mary Williams and Paul D. Reynolds. 1997. 'Discontinuance among New Firms in Retail; the Influence of Initial Resources, Strategy and Gender', *Journal of Business Venturing*, 12: 125–143.

Chandra, Shantha Kohil. 1997. *Development of Women Entrepreneurship*. New Delhi: Mittal Publications.

Everett, J. and M. Savara. 1984. 'Bank Loans to the Poor in Bombay, Do Women Benefit?', *SIGNS: Journal of Women in Culture and Society*, 10(Winter): 272–290.

Hisrich, Robert, D. and C. G. Brush. 1986. *The Women Entrepreneurs: Starting Financing and Managing a Successful New Business*. Washington, D.C: Health and Co.

Jean, Berns M. 1986. 'Communication Variables and Female Entrepreneurs Exploratory, Case Studies of Six Former Corporate Executive Women', Dissertation Abstract, International.

Kilby, Peter and D'Zmura David. 1985. 'Searching for Benefit', US Aid Evaluation Special Studies, 28.

Kirve, Harsha and Ajit Kanitkar. 1993. 'Entepreneurship at the Grass Roots: Developing the Income Generating Capabilities of Rural Women', *Journal of Entrepreneurship*, 2(2) (July–December): 177–197.

Le, Anh T. 2000. 'The Determinants of Immigrant Self-Employment in Australia', *International Migration Review*, 34(1) (Spring): 183–214.

Langowitz, Nan. 2004. GEM 2004 Report on Women and Entrepreneurship. Available online at www.gemconsortium.org.

Manimekalai, N. 1993. 'Studies on Entrepreneurship Development in Industrial Estates', *Small Enterprises Development, Management and Extension Journal (SEDME)*, 20(2) (June): 66–72.

————. 1999. 'Nature and Characteristics of Women Entrepreneurs in India', in M. Soundrapandian (ed.), *Women Entrepreneurship, Issues and Strategies*, pp. 33–40. New Delhi: Kanishka Publishers.

Manimekalai N. and G. Rajeswari. 2000. 'Nature of Women Entrepreneurs a Profile', *SEDME* (July).

Patel, V. G. 1988. 'Women Entrepreneurship Development', Keynote Address at the Fifth National Convention of Women Entrepreneurs', *National Association Young Entrepreneurs (NAYE)*, Feb 6–8, Ahemadabad.

Reichmann. 1992. 'Women Entrepreneurs—A Case Study, Women and Development', in Chetana Kalbagh (ed.), *Women in Enterprise and Profession*. New Delhi: Discovery Publishing House.

Poojaray, Chandra. 1996. 'Who Creates Entrepreneur? Some Observation from a Micro Study', *Journal of Entrepreneurship*, 5(2) (July–December): 253–260.

Shah, A. M. 1996. 'The Judicial and Sociological View of Other Backward Classes', in M. N. Srinivas (ed.), *Caste, Its Twentieth Century Avatar*. New Delhi: Viking.

Shah, Hina and D. D. Bhuptani. 1989. 'Fostering Women Entrepreneurship', *Nirnay*, 4(4): 96.
Shantha Kohil Chandra. 1997. *Development of Women Entrepreneurship*. New Delhi: Mittal Publications.
Singh, Kamala. 1992. *Women Entrepreneurs*. New Delhi: Ashish Publishing House.
Singh, N. P., P. Sehgal, Madam Tinani and Rita Sengupta. 1986. 'Successful Women Entrepreneurs; Their identity, Expectations and Problems: An Explanatory Research Study', *Research Report Serial Two*, National Institute for Entrepreneurship and Small Business Development, New Delhi.
Sorensen, Annemette and Sara McLanahan. 1987. 'Married Women's Economic Dependency, 1940–1980', *American Journal of Sociology*, 43(3): 659–687.
Surti, K. and D. Sarupriya. 1983. 'Psychological Factors Affecting Women Entrepreneurs: Some Findings', *Indian Journal of Social Work*, 44(3): 287–295.
Symons, Gladys L. 1987. 'Women's Occupational Careers in Business: Managers and Entrepreneurs in France and Canada', *International Studies of Management and Organization*, 16: 61–75.
Tendler, Judith. 1989. 'What Ever Happened to Poverty Alleviation', *World Development*, 17(7): 1033–1044
Vineze and Medha Dubashi. 1987. *Women Entrepreneurs in India: A Socio-economic Study of Delhi*. New Delhi: Mittal Publicationss.

Strategic Role of Engineering Institutions for Entrepreneurship Developments in India

13

DINESH KHANDUJA AND
RAJEEV KHANDUJA

Engineering education plays a significant role in entrepreneurship development. Since entrepreneurship is a dynamic process of vision, change and creation, education provides energy and passion towards creation and implementation of new ideas on a continual basis. In India, engineering institutions have mostly played a passive role, resulting in many myths and fears among students on entrepreneurship. Survey reports amply indicate the abundant existence of entrepreneurial aptitude among students but, ironically, entrepreneurial capability is lacking among them on account of poor inputs on entrepreneurship. This paper gives an account of trends in engineering graduates towards wage employment/self-employment as career options. The paper also analyzes the prevalent myths and fears on entrepreneurship. As a remedial measure, strategic counselling by engineering institutions is proposed, which will significantly improve the involvement of engineering faculty for the sustainable growth of entrepreneurship in India.

Introduction

The challenges and opportunities of economic liberalization and global market have shaken the economies of developing countries like India where industrial growth often gets retarded because of higher population growth, declining GDP, growing inflation, illiteracy and unemployment. In today's dynamically changing society, there is an urgent need to create an environment of entrepreneurship to effectively counter these socioeconomic ills (Sanghvi, 1996). Entrepreneurship is a dynamic process of vision, change and creation. Vision is to recognize the opportunity where others see chaos, contradiction and confusion (Kuratko and Hodgetts, 2004). Change and creation involve the application of energy and passion towards creating and implementing new ideas and creating solutions (Kent, 1990). An engineering education plays an important role in developing the technical manpower required for the industrial sector for its sustainable growth. In this context, many have observed that the engineering education today does not adequately prepare graduates for engineering practice (Brawner and Miller, 2003). Employers argue that graduates are academic experts but lack job skills, such as team work, leadership and operations management (Wani and Sharma, 2000). Sparks (1993) feels that engineering graduates need to be sensitive towards economic, social, political, cultural and ethical dimensions of their work. Entrepreneurship is perceived to bring benefits at both the macro level of economic development and the micro level of personnel development. In this scenario, small and medium-sized entrepreneurs play a vital role in the social and economic development of the country by improving the efficiency of resources 'use, reducing risks and hazards, minimizing wastage, and safe-guarding environmental qualities' (Wani and Sharma, 1999).

The changing needs of employers, away from specialization and towards flexibility and life-long learning, make a case for change in engineering education. Change needs to be built on a sound understanding of the factors that affect student learning. One approach, which inculcates in students the urge to take up the responsibilities for learning and thus ensures deep and active involvement, is problem-based learning (Ditcher, 2001).

Engineering Education in India

Education is the most important resource in any country. It has multiple effects in all facets of development in a society and among various educational resources. Engineering education holds the key to economic viability of a nation. India has formally recognized the importance of higher education in science and technology and committed herself to the development of manpower in the field of science and technology (Constitution of India, 1949; Government of India, 1958). Over the past 50 years, the country has provided full policy support (Government of India, 1968, 1986a, 1986b) and substantial public funds to create one of the world's largest network systems of higher education. This network includes:

1. Seven Indian Institutes of Technology (these institutes are globally acknowledged for quality education).
2. Some front-ranking universities/institutes for engineering and applied sciences education (for example, Anna University, Jadavpur University, Indian Institute of Science, Bangalore, B.H.U., Varanasi, and so forth.
3. Eighteen National Institutes of Technology (almost one institute for every state in India)
4. National Institutes for Technical Teachers Training and Research.
5. Well-established state engineering colleges in all states.
6. Around 500 engineering colleges managed by the private sector.
7. Around 1,100 polytechnics managed by both the government and the private sector.

This vast network of institutions should have brought unparalleled technological dominance for India. But this could not happen on account of certain faults, fallacies and failures of our educational planners. So, a re-engineering of the education system is needed to improve the quality of education. This will directly improve the entrepreneurial capability of the engineering graduates with more focus on project-based learning, practical skills and problem-solving.

Entrepreneurship in India: Some Aspects

Entrepreneurship is more than a mere creation of business. The characteristics of seeking opportunities, taking risks and possessing the tenacity to push an idea through to reality combine into a special perspective that permeates entrepreneurs (Hitt et al., 2001).

An 'entrepreneurial perspective' can be developed in individuals. This perspective can be exhibited inside or outside an organization, in profit or not-for-profit organizations and in business or non-business activities for the purpose of bringing forth creative ideas. Thus, entrepreneurship is an integrated concept that permeates an individual's business in an innovative manner. The USA has achieved its highest economic performance during the last 10 years by fostering and promoting entrepreneurial activity (Kuratko et al., 2001). In the USA, researchers are continuously striving to learn more about the entire entrepreneurial process to understand the driving forces within entrepreneurs better (Bygrave and Hofer, 1991; Bull and Willard, 1993; Gartner, 2001). The time has come for our country to wake up and re-plan the education system in order to create a better entrepreneurial environment. Entrepreneurial education has become one of the hottest topics in the US business and engineering schools, where the number of schools teaching entrepreneurial courses has grown from as few as two dozen 20 years ago to more than 1,600 at this time (Katz, 2003; Solomon et al., 2002). India must follow this US strategy as the entrepreneurial spirit is universal, judging by the enormous growth of interest in entrepreneurship around the world in the past few years (Peng, 2001; McDougall and Oviatt, 2003). In India, more than 50,000 engineering students are passing out every year and only 25 per cent of them get immediate employment in public/private sectors. The government must perceive this vast unemployment as an alarming waste of talent, knowledge, skills and 'youthful' passion. The development of entrepreneurship can be a viable solution to many economic evils in India. Entrepreneurship development in India is urgently needed for solving the following problems:

1. National production and low productivity levels
2. Uniform regional development
3. Unemployment
4. Dispersal of national wealth
5. Exploitation of national resources

Entrepreneurial Myths among Engineering Students: A Case Study

The entrepreneurs, in today's dynamic society, should be opportunistic, money-grabbing, aggressive and autocratic (Casson, 1997). They must imbibe skills of invention, innovation and incubation (Samiuddin and Rehman, 1989). Tandon (1975) finds the entrepreneurs as individuals who conceive an industrial enterprise for a purpose, display considerable initiatives, grit and determination in bringing the project to function and, during this process, perform different operations to jump start units from the conceptualization to the operational stage. Entrepreneurship Development Institute, Ahmedabad (1994), identifies essential qualities of an entrepreneur as desire to achieve, perseverance, moderate risk-taking aptitude, ability to find and explore opportunity, analytical ability, ability to face uncertainty, urge for independence, flexibility, planning skills, motivation, positive self-concept and future orientation. With these entrepreneurial concepts in mind and to access the entrepreneurial traits in engineering graduates, a survey was conducted among final-year students at the National Institute of Technology, Kurukshetra, for four consecutive years. The questionnaire was given to assess the entrepreneurial inclination among students, analyze the aptitude and capability of students wanting to be entrepreneurs, and analyze the myths and fears among students not wanting to be entrepreneurs. Table 13.1 and Table 13.2 present the main findings.

Table 13.1 Survey Break-up

Branch	Civil Engg.		Mechanical Engg.		Electrical Engg.		Electronics Engg.		Computer Engg.		Total	
Year	M	F	M	F	M	F	M	F	M	F	Males	Females
2001	07	03	28	02	18	12	08	07	09	06	70	30
2002	06	04	38	02	15	10	10	05	06	04	75	25
2003	06	04	49	01	30	15	15	10	15	05	115	35
2004	08	02	48	02	28	17	14	11	12	08	110	40

Table 13.2 Entrepreneurial Inclination

	Do you want to set up your own industry?							
	2001		2002		2003		2004	
	Yes	No	Yes	No	Yes	No	Yes	No
Males	74%	26%	72%	28%	70%	30%	75%	25%
Females	38%	62%	42%	58%	40%	60%	45%	55%
General	64%	36%	65%	35%	63%	37%	67%	33%

The findings help us infer the following conclusions (see Figures 13.1, 13.2 and 13.3):

Figure 13.1 First Career Option (2001–2004)

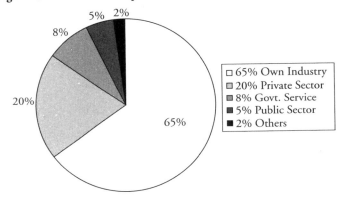

**Figure 13.2 Entrepreneurial Programmes Attended (2001–2004)
(For Engg. Students Wanting to be Entrepreneurs)**

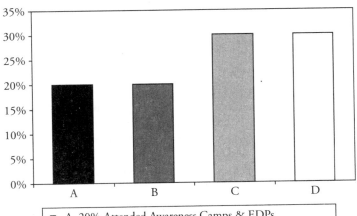

Figure 13.3   Myths and Fears on Entrepreneurship (2001–2004)
(For Engg. Students Not Wanting to be Entrepreneurs)

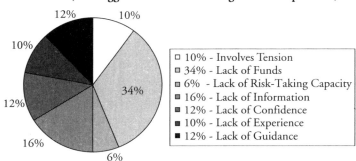

- ☐ 10% - Involves Tension
- ▥ 34% - Lack of Funds
- ▩ 6% - Lack of Risk-Taking Capacity
- ■ 16% - Lack of Information
- ■ 12% - Lack of Confidence
- ■ 10% - Lack of Experience
- ■ 12% - Lack of Guidance

Survey Observations

The following observations are made from the survey findings of over four years on almost 500 engineering graduates. These are:

1. There is an abundance of entrepreneurial aptitude among engineering graduates, as almost 65 per cent of them want to set up their own industries in different areas.
2. As compared to girls, boys have a much higher level of aptitude for entrepreneurship.
3. Among 35 per cent of the graduates who do not want to be entrepreneurs, private sector jobs are most popular (57 per cent), followed by government service (23 per cent), public sector jobs (14 per cent) and others like defence, research, and so forth (6 per cent).
4. Exposure to entrepreneurial programmes and teaching subjects has a significant impact on entrepreneurial aptitude of engineering students as 70 per cent of students opting for self-employment were exposed to some of these EDP programmes.
5. Most prevalent myths and fears on entrepreneurship among the students were lack of funds (34 per cent), lack of information (16 per cent), lack of confidence (12 per cent), lack of guidance (12 per cent), stressful work (10 per cent), lack of experience (10 per cent) and lack of risk-taking capacity (6 per cent).

Remedial Analysis

Despite the presence of entrepreneurial aptitude among students in a large measure, a meagre percentage of students are actually setting up their enterprises. Sickness among the small industries has assumed an alarming proportion as it results in locking up of resources, wastage of capital assets, loss of production and increase in unemployment. Here, engineering institutions have a crucial role to play as inputs by the faculty not only include knowledge enhancement, but these must also include skill enhancement and increasing entrepreneurial awareness. Some of the suggested remedial measures by the institutions for entrepreneurship development are:

1. Expose students to publications on entrepreneurship, which can be research-based as well as popular. Some of these are academic journals, text books and books on entrepreneurship, biographies and autobiographies of entrepreneurs, compendiums about entrepreneurs, news periodicals, venture periodicals, newsletters, proceedings of conferences, and so forth.
2. Make students directly observe the successful entrepreneurs. They should be asked to take their interviews, trace their history, and analyze their success factors.
3. Arrange speeches and presentations by practicing entrepreneurs on their mission, strategies and experiences.
4. Compulsory attendance at EDPs and related camps at regular intervals for all engineering students.
5. Continual counselling of students and regular career guidance by expert faculty and can be in different forms. The counselling model, as in Figure 13.4, can be adopted by the institutions in stages to monitor the progress made by student-teacher interaction on career plans.

Personal counselling helps in increasing entrepreneurial awareness and helps in identification of students with entrepreneurial aptitude. It helps in clearing individual doubts and removing related myths and fears on entrepreneurship. Educational counselling helps in enhancing the skills and capability of these students. Vocational counselling is a procedure of self-appraisal under experienced faculty members wherein the student

Figure 13.4 Strategic Counselling by Institutions

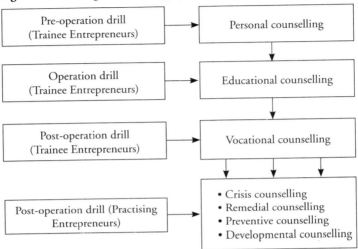

learns to prepare reports, identify products, plan production, purchase and arrange marketing of necessary documents, and so forth. Once their entire business is in operation, the entrepreneurs can even seek the help of parent institutions to ward off unforeseen crises or to prevent them. These steps shall be useful for the development of entrepreneurial culture among students, effecting industry-institute partnership, industrial exposure to faculty of engineering institutions, effective incubation of established industries and socioeconomic development of the country.

Conclusion

Engineering institutions have a moral duty in churning out successful engineering graduates who should be a national asset. These graduates can serve the nation well if only they adapt themselves to the prevailing socioeconomic scenario, which demands them to go in for self-employment. They should be job givers rather than being job seekers. Their entrepreneurship shall help in the equitable distribution of wealth, removal of unemployment and optimum utilization of resources. To remove many myths and fears about entrepreneurship among engineering graduates, all concerned institutions should formulate new strategies, change existing curriculum, and install new programmes to foster entrepreneurship. The faculty of these institutions need to be enriched and updated on the latest technological developments and economic conditions so that they can be effectively involved to boost engineering graduates towards entrepreneurship. The faculty must become a tool to bring about a revolution in entrepreneurship development. Besides, the existing industries must also be incubated on different levels for a sustainable growth under the watchful guidance of these faulty members. All these steps must be adopted and pursued with a missionary zeal to make our country economically stronger.

References

Brawner, C. E. and T. K. Miller. 2003. 'Engineering Design Using an Entrepreneurial Model'. Available online at *http://www4.ncsu.edu/-browner/enterprio.htm*, accessed: 5 February 2007

Bull, I. and G. E. Willard. 1993. 'Towards a Theory of Entrepreneurship', *Journal of Business Venturing*, 8(2): 183–196.

Bygrave, W. D. and C. W. Hofer. 1991. 'Theorizing about Entrepreneurship', *Entrepreneurship Theory and Practice*, 2(1)(Winter): 12–22.

Casson M. 1997. *The Entrepreneur—An Economic Theory*. London: Martin Roberston and Co. Ltd.

Constitution of India. 1949. Available online at *http://alfa.nic.in/const/a1.html*, accessed: 2 February 2007.

Ditcher, A. K. 2001. 'Effective Teaching and Learning in Higher Education with Particular Reference to the Under Graduate Education of Professional Engineers', *International Journal of Engineering Education*, 17(1): 24–29.

Entrepreneurship Development Institute. 1994. *A Hand book for New Entrepreneurs*. Ahemdabad: Entrepreneurship Development Institute.

Gartner, W. B. 2001. 'Is There an Elephant in Entrepreneurship? Blind Assumptions in Theory Development', *Entrepreneurship Theory and Practice*, 25(4): 27–39.

Government of India. 1958. *Scientific Policy Resolution*.

———. 1968. *National Education Policy*.

———. 1986a. *National Policy on Education* (Modified in 1992).

———. 1986b. *Technology Policy Statement*.

Hitt, M. A., R. D. Ireland, S. M. Camp and D. L. Sexton. 2001. 'Strategic Entrepreneurship: Entrepreneurial Strategies for Wealth Creation', *Strategic Management Journal*, (special issue), 22(6): 479–492.

Katz, J. A. 2003. 'The Chronology and Intellectual Trajectory of American Entrepreneurship Education', *Journal of Business Venturing*, 18(2): 283–300.

Kent, C. A. 1990. 'Entrepreneurship Education at the Collegiate Level: A Synopsis and Evaluation', in Kent, C. A. (ed.), *Entrepreneurship Education*, pp. 111–122. New York: Quorum Books.

Kuratko, D. F., R. D. Ireland and J. S. Hornsby. 2001. 'Improving Firm Performance Through Entrepreneurial Actions: Acordia's Corporate Entrepreneurship Strategy', *Academy of Management Executive*, 15(4): 60–71.

Kuratko, D. F. and R. M. Hodgetts. 2004. *Entrepreneurship: Theory, Process, Practice*. Mason, OH: South-Western Publishers.

McDougall, P. P. and B. M. Oviatt. 2003. 'Some Fundamental Issues in International Entrepreneurship', Coleman White Paper Series. Available online at *www.usasbe.org*, accessed: 5 February 2007.

Peng, M. W. 2001. 'How Entrepreneurs Create Wealth in Transition Economies', *Academy of Management Executive*, 15(1): 95–110.

Samiuddin and H. Rehman. 1989. 'Entrepreneurship Development—A Key to Economic Growth', in Samiuddin (ed.), *Entrepreneurship Development in India*, pp. 49–58. New Delhi: Mittal Publications.

Sanghvi, A. N. 1996. 'Promotion of Technical Entrepreneurship through Technical Education', *Journal of Engineering Education*, 19(2): 42–44.

Solomon, G. T., S. Duffy, and A. Tarabishy. 2002. 'The State of Entrepreneurship in the United States: A Nationwide Survey and Analysis', *International Journal of Entrepreneurship Education*, 1(1): 65–86.

Sparks, J. J. 1993. 'Engineering Education in a World of Rapidly Changing Technology': 1–6, 10–12, Association of Engineering Education in Southeast Asia and the Pacific. (AEESEAP)/Federation of Engineering Institutions of Southeast Asia and the Pacific. (FEISEAP)/International Association of Continuing Engineering Education. (IACEE). International Conference on Engineering Education, Singapore.

Strengthening the role of business and industry http://www.unep.org/Documentry/Default.asp?DocumentID=52&ArticleID=78

Tandon, B. C. 1975. *Environment and Entrepreneur*. Allahabad: Chugh Publications.

Wani, V. P. and S. K. Sharma. 1999. 'Technocrat as an Entrepreneur: Avenues': 38–40, National Seminar on Recent Trends in Manufacturing Systems, HMT Pinjore.

———. 2000. 'Technocrat as An Entrepreneur: A Necessity in Changing Indian Economic Scenario' III: 17–23, National Seminar on New Perspectives and Prospects for Technical Education, Thiruvnanthapuram, Kerala.

Building Entrepreneurial Society in India through Business Incubation

14

M.K. Sridhar and M.V. Ravikumar

Preamble

Wealth creation by pursuing an enterprise is not new in India. Kautilya, one of the earliest exponents of 'Artha Shastra' (Art of State Craft) emphasized the fact that the source of livelihood of men is wealth, and wealth alone enabled the creation of more wealth. The existence of enterprise, both public and private, very elaborate internal and external trade, taxation systems, certain amount of distrust on the activities and motivations of the traders are all detailed in Kautaliya's abovementioned pioneering work (Jha et al., 2000).

Economic growth and development constitute a dominant item on the agenda of most of the nations, as it increases employment opportunities, thus contributing to the social development. In economics and commerce, an entrepreneur is an economic leader who possesses the ability to recognize opportunities for the successful introduction of new products, techniques and new sources of supply. Whatever be the economic and political set-up of a nation, 'entrepreneurship' is thus essential for economic development (Ramana and Papaiah, 1998).

Evolution of Entrepreneurship in India

Entrepreneurship is all too often taken to mean the creation of new business. Another widely held view is that entrepreneurial behaviour is all about individual initiative. Entrepreneurship in India was originally limited to very few communities who were adept in certain skills like negotiation, public relations and so forth. Cawsji Nanabhoy Davar set up the first cotton mill in 1854 which was an instant success and spawned many others in its wake. By 1860, there were already 10 and the industry was firmly established by 1875 (Manimala et al., 2001).

Entrepreneurship During Pre-Independence

India had a long tradition of highly-skilled master craftsmen and skill-based small and tiny industries, which were known the world over for their quality products. The development of entrepreneurial attitude being a complex and long-term phenomenon is closely associated with the culture and the social norms prevailing in the country. India being a multicultural society, its cultural diversity presents pockets of high and low entrepreneurial activity. For example, India has a long tradition of trading and certain communities like the Marwari community of Rajastan, the Vysyas or Setty community of Andhra Pradesh, the Parsi community of Gujarat, the Chettiar community in Tamil Nadu have been involved in trading for centuries. Although Indian entrepreneurial expertise brought the English, Dutch, Portuguese and French traders to India, with the British establishing their governance in most parts of India, yet British India saw the decline of Indian entrepreneurship side-lined by the British-made goods. The end of World War II marked a boom period when a large number of skilled and semi-skilled workers started small production units using old machinery and borrowed capital from moneylenders, kin-groups, banks, and so forth (Sampath, 2001).

Post-Independence Initiatives

After gaining independence, the country embarked on a planned economic development with emphasis on rapid industrialization of the economy. During the first three decades after independence, a lot of small and tiny industries were cropping up in clusters around the various major public sectors, organized private sector industries and where natural resources/skills were available. The government pronounced several policies and programmes to develop, promote and support the small industry movement.

Entrepreneurship Promotion through Small Industry Development

The 1956 Industrial Policy Resolution mentioned four factors in favour of the small scale industries. They were employment, equality, latent resources and decentralization. The policy sought to create maximum job opportunities, ventures with small doses of investment, mobilization of local skill and capital, and the disbursal of the units into semi-urban and rural areas. It was planned that the small units have to be developed along with the large units. A number of institutional mechanisms have been set up to encourage entrepreneurship among the people. The Small Industry Development Organisation (SIDO), through the network of Small Industries Service Institutes (SISIs) has been a pioneer in conducting Entrepreneurship Development Programmes for various sectoral groups. In the late sixties, it was seen that this policy had not resolved the income and regional disparities and, therefore, the emphasis got shifted to industrial promotion in relatively backward states and districts. Fiscal and financial incentives alone were insufficient.

Developing Individuals as Entrepreneurs

To identify and train potential entrepreneurs, the Gujarat Industrial and Investment Corporation pioneered several programmes for Entrepreneurship Development. A programme for creating opportunities of self-employment for the educated unemployed came into operation in 1973. The Small Industries Extension Training (SIET) initiatives launched activities for stimulating entrepreneurship in Jammu and Kashmir (1972), Andhra Pradesh (1973), Assam (1974) and Karnataka (1975). Financial institutions like the State Bank of India too had been conducting Entrepreneurship Development Programmes. Several state governments like Karnataka, Tamil Nadu, Maharashtra, and so forth, established special organizations during 1970s like Technical Consultancy Service Organisation of Karnataka (TECSOK), Industrial and Technical Consultancy Organisation of Tamil Nadu (ITCOT), Maharashtra Centre for Entrepreneurship Development (MCED), respectively, mainly for promoting entrepreneurship. Among the several institutions set up during this period and later for developing research knowledge on entrepreneurship and guiding the training and development activities were the National Institute of Small Industry Extension Training (NISIET) at Hyderabad, National Institute for Entrepreneurship and Small Business Development

(NIESBUD), New Delhi, and Entrepreneurship Development Institute of India (EDII) at Ahmedabad (Ravikumar, 2004a).

Entrepreneurship in the Science and Technology Sector

Recognizing the role that technology can play in the development of society, a Technology Policy Statement (TPS) was formulated in 1983 with the basic objective of developing indigenous technology and ensuring efficient absorption of imported technology appropriate to national priorities and availability of resources. The TPS also aimed at using traditional skills and capabilities, making them commercially competitive (Menon et al., 2002).

To encourage the entrepreneurial spirit among the science and technology (S and T) individuals, the Government of India established the National Science and Technology Entrepreneurship Development Board (NSTEDB) in 1982 under the Department of Science and Technology (DST). NSTEDB in a period of two decades has been able to initiate entrepreneurial awareness among the S and T individuals on a large-scale spread all over India. For strengthening institute–industry interaction, NSTEDB set up Science and Technology Entrepreneurs' Park (STEPs) in collaboration with the financial institutions (IDBI, IFCI, and ICICI) in academic institutions of excellence and also established Entrepreneurship Development Cells (EDCs) in universities and engineering colleges (Singh et al., 2000). So far, NSTEDB has catalyzed 15 STEPs in different parts of India which have promoted 788 units generating an annual turnover of Rs 1,300 million and employment for over 5,000 persons. The STEPs promoted entrepreneurs have developed more than 100 new products and technologies (Gupta, 2000).

Institutional Support—Development Finance

The Small Industries Development Bank of India (SIDBI) was created in April 1990, exclusively to look after the developmental finance requirements of the small scale sector through the existing state finance corporations and banking institutions. SIDBI also supported Entrepreneurship Development Programmes, Market Development Programmes, Technology Upgradation Programmes, and similar growth programmes through recognised Industry Associations (Annual Report 1995, SIDBI). SIDBI actively supports various programmes envisaged in the policy through financial participation, managerial advice and performance review.

Promotion of Entrepreneurship in the Software Sector

The Software Technology Parks of India (STPI), an autonomous society promoted by Department of Electronics, Government of India, mainly to provide connectivity for software exporters, had only 13 IT companies registered with them when they started in 1990, whereas at present it has over 1,050 companies (Naidu, 2002). STPI also provides infrastructural facilities for software entrepreneurs on monthly instalments basis till the time they can establish themselves. Technology Business Inculators (TBI) have been initiated at N.S. Raghavan Centre for Entrepreneurial Learning (NSRCEL), Indian Institute of Management, Bangalore, Indian Institute of Technology, and Indian Institute of Science, and at a few more institutions during the last six years (Ravikumar, 2004a).

Even NSTEDB, DST under their development of entrepreneurship through the institutional mechanism programme, have supported the establishment of many TBIs with the main objective to catalyze development and growth of technology-led enterprises and creating value-added jobs and services, besides developing new tools of technology transfer for fostering the entrepreneurial spirit (www.nstedb.com).

With many such policy support and promotional programmes, there was a significant growth of the small scale industry. Although the contribution of small scale sector to GDP, employment and exports significantly grew over four decades, there was no measure of 'entrepreneurial activity' in the country. The first research study to measure entrepreneurial activity was undertaken by the Indian Institute of Management, Bangalore (IIM-B), in 2000.

Measure of Entrepreneurial Activity

Global Entrepreneurship Monitor (GEM) is an international research project designed for assessing the level of entrepreneurial activity along with the entrepreneurship framework conditions prevailing in the country. This project was launched in 1999 as a joint initiative of the London Business School, UK, and the Babson College, USA. IIM-B joined the project as a partner in 2000. The GEM conceptual model is based on three sets of variables and their interrelationships. The dependent variable is the economic growth of the country. The other two variables are the level of entrepreneurial activity and the conduciveness of entrepreneurial framework conditions. Of these, the entrepreneurial activity is an independent variable with reference to the national economic growth and dependent variable with reference to the entrepreneurial framework conditions. In other words, the hypothesized relationship among the three sets of variables is that the entrepreneurship conditions stimulate entrepreneurial activity which, in turn, stimulates the national economic growth. The generalized relationship among the three sets of variables can be stated as shown in Figure 14.1 (Manimala, 2002).

Figure 14.1 GEM Conceptual Model

The findings of the research are given in Table 14.1.

Table 14.1 Growth of Entrepreneurship Activity in India as Compared with GDP Growth

Sector	1999	2000	2001	2002
Entrepreneurial activity (in %)	–	8.97	11.55	17.88
Growth in GDP (in %)	6.71	5.36	4.08	–

Source: Global Entrepreneurship Monitor India Report (2002).

It can be seen from the findings of the GEM research that the level of entrepreneurial activity in India is consistently increasing. This is contrary to the overall finding of the GEM global project that entrepreneurial activity declines following the decline of the GDP in the previous year. The IIM-B research team has reasoned out that this may be due to the fact that the economic liberalization was being carried out with renewed vigour during this period, which may have thrown up opportunities of different kinds of businesses rather than market replication of existing businesses stimulated by increasing demand.

Indian Entrepreneurship at Crossroads

With this background of various policy and promotional support for entrepreneurship from the Union Government and the state governments, and growth in the overall entrepreneurship activity, which includes both 'survival' entrepreneurship as well as 'opportunity'-based entrepreneurship, it may be worth looking at the status of growth and contribution of the small scale sector in the pre-liberalization and post-liberalization decades. As, in developing countries like India, the small scale industry is the potent way by which maximum employment can be generated with comparatively low investment and is also helpful in the removal of regional imbalance in industrial development.

Table 14.2 Growth of Small Industry in Terms of No. of Units, Employment, Output and Exports

Period	Units*	Employment*	Output*	Exports*
1980s	18.40	5.84	18.66	19.38
1990s	5.62	4.00	15.31	20.62

Sources: SIDBI (1999).
Notes: *Figures represent Compounded Average Rate of Growth (CAGR) in %.

Table 14.3 Contribution of Small Industry to National Income (GDP), Exports and Employment (in %)

Year	National income	Exports	Employment
1980–1981	9.2	24.5	31.0
1990–1991	11.0	29.7	47.6
2000–2001	6.4	30.9	66.4

Sources: EPW Research Foundation (2002).

The share of the small industry in the national income increased in the protection period of the eighties, but declined considerably in the transitional period of the nineties. The share of the small industry in exports and its employment in relation to the organized employment has consistently increased both in the protection period and in the transition period. The increase in the relative share of small industry employment as well as in exports during the transitional nineties is a significant issue to be considered. This has happened in spite of reduction in the growth rate of the actual number of units (Balasubrahmanya, 2004).

The other pertinent issue is why liberalization and globalization should affect the Indian small industry to such an extent? A survey-based study which emanated from the Entrepreneurship Development Institute of India, Ahmedabad, indicated that the small industry in general is characterized by technological obsolescence and, therefore, its products are of inferior quality. Also, small industry suffers from low productivity (Awasthi, 1993).

In the current challenging business environment, entrepreneurship could be viewed as a function of few important parameters like:

1. Technology
2. Core competence in the chosen area
3. Business environment governed by national and entrepreneurship framework conditions
4. Effective strategy formulation
5. Speed and process of decision-making for a given business situation (Ravikumar and Sridhar, 2003).

For a long time, Indian entrepreneurship has been built around 'trading' and the individuals' skill set for survival rather than perceiving market opportunities, evaluating and managing 'risks'. In India, generally, businesses, including professional firms, are inherited, which also means that the market status and risk of continuing old businesses are not properly evaluated.

Considering the accelerated pace of change and demise of job security, it has become very important that a strong *entrepreneurial culture*-based on right fundamentals is built. This would call for a holistic training and mentoring programme in an appropriate environment to ensure that good business ideas based on market opportunities are well-supported.

Evolution of Entrepreneurial Society

The Concept

Economists have generally seen entrepreneurship as an effect of a constellation of particular economic conditions, rather than as a cause of their growth. The cultural, social and political context is the primary determinant of the way of economic life. More generally, the unique features of all facets of a nation's way of life arise out of this context. For instance, India is different from other nations in that it is agriculturally-oriented, has a huge unorganized business sector and a parallel economy of a significant size. Such contextual factors are very influential and are difficult to change quickly since they have deep roots in the nation's psyche. Entrepreneurial opportunities in the nation and entrepreneurial capacity of individuals are more influenced by the *entrepreneurial characteristics of the society.* These characteristics are determined by the *entrepreneurship framework conditions,* such as government policies, education levels, quality of infrastructure, and so forth.

Entrepreneurship Framework Conditions

As societies (and their economies) evolve, opportunities are thrown up for new firms to replace the older ones whose efficiency and ability to meet the society's needs have declined. When capable and motivated individuals perceive these opportunities, the outcome is entrepreneurial activity, that is, creation of new firms. Creation of new firms that replace the old ones is inevitable. Creative destruction or business churning can be observed in most economies. Depending on the entrepreneurial characteristics of the system, entrepreneurial process is smoothly facilitated. The GEM model examines the specific conditions prevailing in a country that have a direct bearing on the exploitation of entrepreneurial opportunities (Manimala, et al., 2001). This could be understood well from the schematic (see Figure 14.2).

There are 14 dimensions as listed in Figure 14.2, which measure the conduciveness of the entrepreneurial framework conditions, which in turn decide how entrepreneurial the society is. Higher this measure and more positive it correlates with the growth of the GDP of the nation and jobs created, would herald emergence of *entrepreneurial society.* Such society facilitates creation of more small and medium enterprises (SMEs).

Building Entrepreneurial Society

In order to flourish, small scale entrepreneurs are compelled to develop all sorts of technical and social skills. The social skills that they are forced to nurture are distinctly modern, rational-instrumental patterns of interaction at several levels. Chief among them are those relating commercial activities: interaction networks have to be constructed between

Figure 14.2 GEM Conceptual Model: Elaboration of Entrepreneurial Framework Conditions

**Entrepreneurial Framework
Conditions**

- Financial Support
- Govt. Policies
- Govt. Programmes
- Education & Training
- R & D Transfer
- Commercial Infrastructure
- Internal Market Openness
- Physical Infrastructure
- Cultural Norms
- Social Status & Esteem
- Opportunities for New
  Venture Creation
- Entrepreneurial Capacity
- Intellectual Property Rights
- Facilitation of Women
  Entrepreneurs

Social,
Cultural,
Political
Context

Entrepreneurial
Opportunities

Entrepreneurial
Capacity

Business
Churning

National
Economic
Growth

GDP

Jobs

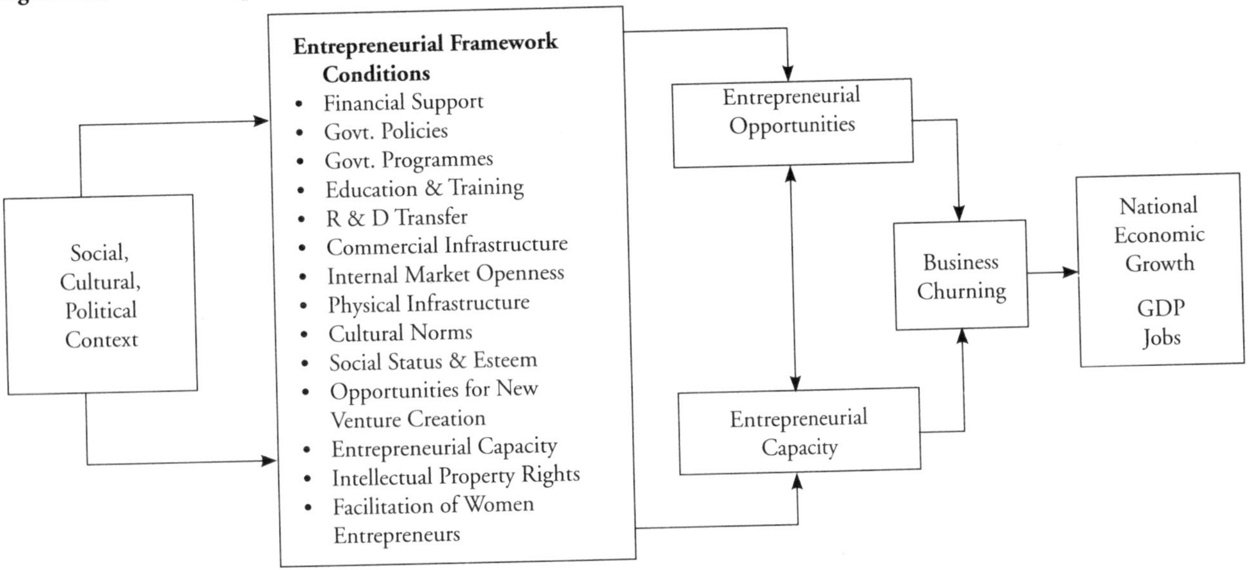

Source: GEM India Report (2002).

entrepreneurs and suppliers, between sellers and customers, between entrepreneurs and other actors on the local as well as on the more distant scene. Propelled by the need to adapt to the demands of a modern economy, which can no longer be understood in terms of local needs alone, the individual entrepreneur is eager for information on larger issues of technology, economy, markets and funding. The entrepreneurial mindset transcends the confines of family and tradition, opening up individuals to modern styles of consciousness and securing them a place in the modern industrial society (Berger, 1991).

When a nation embarks on establishing an entrepreneurial society, there has to be a stable and efficient handholding mechanism available at a low cost to start-ups as well as family-based entrepreneurs who would like to diversify into new sectors. This paper proposes that establishing *business incubators* suiting regional conditions and local resources based on the appropriate and effective framework on a public-private, private, in-company or co-operative basis could be the ideal method to build an *entrepreneurial society*.

Concept of Business Incubation

The concept of an *incubation* was first initiated in the early 20th century itself at the Stanford University, California, USA, when the University President David Starr Jordan urged his staff to make personal investments in a company founded in the early nineties by Cyril Elewell, an engineering school graduate who worked on the first round of 'wireless' technologies, ship-to-shore radio communications, where later many Stanford graduates began their career. The Stanford University staff knew that if they did not work hard and support to build industry infrastructure around Stanford, they would lose an advantage of making an early alliance with companies and thus not have a mechanism in place where they could send their graduates to cut their teeth (Richards, 2002).

It was not too long after that time when Stanford's then President Ray Lyman Wilber, in return for half of the royalties on any patents developed, agreed to provide lab space and US$ 100 in parts to two brothers Sigurd and Russel Varian, thus giving them a chance to develop what turned out to be the Klystron tube. Russel had a Ph.D. in physics and

Sigurd was a pilot for Pan Am, interested in building a landing system that would work in fog and bad weather. The technology that the two brothers developed led to the possibility of building Radar system that was critical to the Battle of Britain and winning World War II!

About the same time, Professor Fred Terman brought together Bill Hewlett and David Packard, the names behind Hewlett Packard, together. Prof. Terman was concerned that electronics engineering graduates of Stanford could not find employment on the west coast. As a solution, he encouraged his students and others to form companies in the San Francisco bay area and Stanford faculty to consult with them to help to create products. Prof. Terman made a personal investment of US$ 500 to the start-up efforts of Hewlett Packard (popularly known as HP) apart from lending his expertise. Recently, William and Flora Hewlett Foundation gave US$ 400 million to Stanford, the largest amount ever left to an educational institution. Stanford had no rights to anything created by HP (Richards, 2002). Thus, technology grew in 60 square miles around Stanford University rapidly through the establishment of a strong 'entrepreneurial culture'. Figure 14.3 depicts a simple schematic to understand how a Business Incubator (BI) was conceived (Ravikumar, 2004b).

Figure 14.3   Block Schematic Highlighting the Four Basic Elements that are Essential for Establishing BI

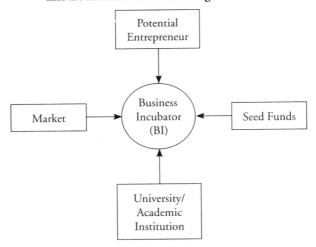

Evolution of Business Incubators

Definition

The term *incubator* literally means a climate-controlled environment that supports the early development, sometimes even saving the life of a 'new born'. In the economic development context, 'incubators' support the transformation of selected early stage businesses with high potential, into self-sufficient, growing and profitable enterprises. By reducing the risks during the early period of business formation, the incubator is intended to contribute to economic growth through sustaining new enterprises (Lalkaka and Bishop, 1996). An incubator can also be defined as 'a facility that provides affordable space, shared office services and business development assistance in an environment conducive to new venture creation, survival and early stage growth' (Allen and McCluskey, 1990).

Historic Development of Business Incubators (BIs)

In a rapidly changing global economy, small enterprises (SEs) are increasingly a force for national economic growth. Since 1980s, SEs—and the entrepreneurs who drive them—have received serious attention by planners, legislators and development practioners the world over. New structures and strategies are being explored that will help small businesses to start, survive and grow. In this quest, the business incubation centre has emerged as a recent innovation, harbouring great potential as a tool for economic development (Lalkaka and Bishop, 1996).

The new global economy is increasingly characterized by three processes: the overall lowering of trade barriers and concurrent emergence of regional trading blocs; the shift towards information and service-oriented activities, in order to create new competitive advantages in the world market; and the downsizing of large organizations, together with mergers and acquisitions, in the face of this restructuring. These factors are, in turn, shrinking opportunities for people to join labour force. Thus, those unemployed who are able, are increasingly turning to the creation of entrepreneurial small businesses (Lalkaka et al., 1996). Thus, there is a pressing need to build an *entrepreneurial society* which would facilitate smooth establishment and operation of enterprises.

Incubators originally derive from the various initiatives discussed in section on post-Independence initiatives of this paper. Early focus

Figure 14.4   Schematic Historical Development of Business Incubators

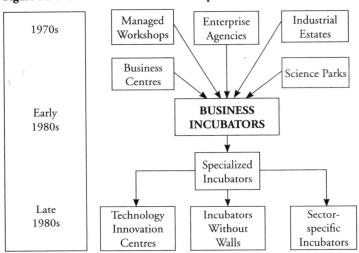

of many entrepreneurship development programmes was in creating awareness and training in the essentials of business operation, often for individual entrepreneurs. With the increasing need to understand technology, business strategies, forming the right management teams and management practices, emphasis is more on 'technical' and 'managerial' mentoring. Thus Business Incubators (BIs) emerged in the early eighties out of precursor to SE programmes developed over two decades earlier (Lalkaka and Bishop, 1996). Figure 14.4 explains the historic development of business incubators.

Establishing Business Incubator

Key Aspects

Business incubator (BI) focusses on nurturing the process of SE development. This kind of business development requires the provision of workspace and value-adding technical and managerial support. While establishing an incubator, the following aspects have to be considered:

a.   Mobilizing *government support* through funding, fully or partly, to initiate the concept, implement the operations plan and cover initial operations

  b. Promoting active *community participation* and private industry membership of the governing and advisory boards, and their involvement as mentors, suppliers and customers
  c. Organizing tenant support by a small but *experienced management* staff
  d. Implementing the *selection and graduation criteria*, because the essential feature of the incubator is the development of viable tenant businesses within a relatively short period of time
  e. Ensuring the *financial stability* of the incubator itself

The fiscal discipline by management is a must, to enable the incubator to survive changes in the climate of government support and to set a proper example for entrepreneurs in reaching sustainability themselves (Lalkaka and Bishop, 1996).

Facilities and Services

The physical *workspace* of incubators can be leased on a short term, initially below-market basis, to enable an entrepreneur without substantial resources to gain access to working space. The space is furnished with the basic requirements of business (desk, file cabinets, computer, telephone, work area) or fitted with specific equipments (as in the case of electronics or biotechnology sectors). The space will be generally vacated within a specified period of time (12 to 36 months) to allow tenancy by another client-entrepreneur.

The *facility-associated services* can include receptionist, secretary, conference facilities, a cafeteria, commonly shared items like fax machine, paper copying machine and broadband connectivity for the Internet, laser printer, and so forth. Thus, the incubator provides an entrepreneur the opportunity to begin work almost immediately, offering substantial savings in fixed and working capital and avoidance of the problems inherent in establishing an office (Lalkaka and Bishop, 1996). Normally, incubators take the help of a panel of attorneys, chartered accountants, tax consultants and patent lawyers drawn from the community, based on the needs of the client-entrepreneur.

Structure and Operations

Depending on the type of incubator, facilitating agency (government/ private), capital outlay and the regional conditions where the incubator is being established, the structure and operations will vary to an extent.

However, a minimum set of personnel like *incubator manger and secretary* are essential. *The manager, guided by a competent board of directors/governing council, is the key to the success of the incubator.*

Types of Incubators

Developing a theme for an incubator involves creating special programmes directed towards specific kinds of businesses. During the past couple of decades, a variety of themes have emerged to serve specific kinds of business needs:

1. *A targeted population incubator* enhances a conventional incubation programme with specific features to support empowerment of specific populations, for example, women, fresh graduates, minorities.
2. *An international incubator* encourages foreign investment, both financial and technological. Such an incubator often includes a range of services for international and expatriate professionals.
3. An *industrial subcontracting* orientation is built on linkages to large enterprises, supporting the development of new businesses as vendors. Key features include quality control and scheduling.
4. *Single business incubators* will have programmes specifically tailored to the needs of a particular class of industrial products/services, for example, IT services, biotechnology, handicrafts, and so forth.
5. *University incubators* specialize in supporting the development technology or new processes initiated by the faculty and staff of the university or based on some relationship to the university.
6. *Technology business incubators* focussing on an overall local or national economic development programme, providing the expectation of highly paid, environmentally friendly, employment opportunities. Although direct job creation may be modest, yet the ripple effect of their actions can extend the positive range of their impact.
7. A *hub incubator*, with a full management team, can support a number of satellite incubators with a minimal staff and greater outreach possibilities. Such an incubator can reduce operational costs and increase impact of the incubator.
8. *Virtual incubator* or the incubator without walls has recently emerged, focussing on the provision of counselling to client businesses.

9. *Regional or rural incubator* is focussed on stimulating businesses which utilize local materials and other resources, including local skill sets, primarily serving specified geographical areas (Lalkaka and Bishop, 1996).

Value Framework of Business Incubator

Figure 14.5 indicates how when a BI is established, taking into account the key aspects explained in the section on the Key Aspects of Establishing Business Incubator of this paper, it creates a value by ensuring balance between *business ecosystem* and *social ecosystem.*

Entrepreneurship Development

Entrepreneurship development is the key value process that any government is looking at in the absence of growth in jobs, as this process would have greater possibility of job creation in the society.

Mentoring Relationship

Mentoring relationship will play a key role in ensuring the success rate of the formation of enterprise. India has a large pool of experienced academia and professionals who have either retired voluntarily or after attaining the superannuating age. This resource could be used for handholding the entrepreneurs in the initial stages with suitable soft skills training as well as technical support.

Opportunities Assessment and Risk Evaluation

Opportunities assessment and risk evaluation is an area that normally an individual entrepreneur finds difficult to tackle. With the experience of screening committee members and business networking support, business incubators can add value for this activity.

Seed Funding

Seed funding assumes importance once the business model and feasible business plan are in place. If the initial funding is tied up quickly, early launching of enterprise is possible. This will reduce the time to market the new product or service of the start-up. This is an area which rural

Figure 14.5 Business Incubator Framework for Value Creation

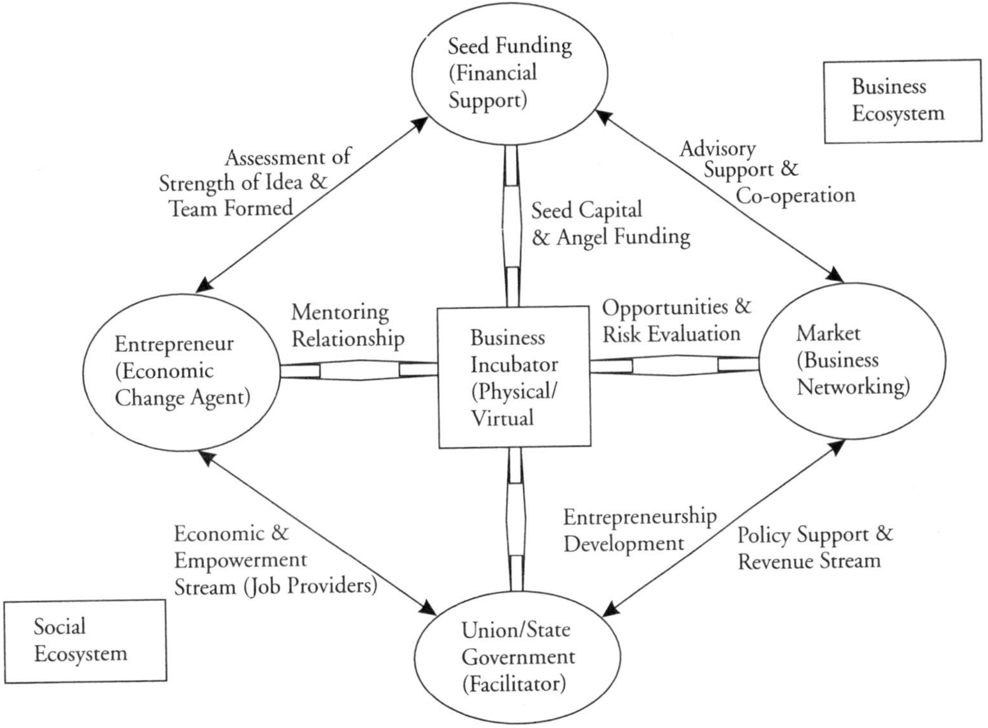

entrepreneurs especially would find difficult to handle and the BIs can play a significant role.

Business Networks

Business networks of the incubator should help the entrepreneurs in finding a market for their product or service to an extent. Sometimes the entrepreneurs can find a market even in the co-tenants of the incubator.

Thus, business incubators, through their 'value framework' bring about a fine balance between 'social eco-system' of creating jobs in the society, contributing to the economic growth and 'business eco system' of creating customers and suppliers for new products/services to meet the market needs by utilizing the funds that are available in the public/private organizations.

Performance of Business Incubators (BIs) in Industrially Developed Countries

The National Business Incubation Association (NBIA) reports that throughout the United States, small businesses generate approximately two out of every three new jobs. At almost any time, roughly seven million people are starting new businesses. All across the country, business incubators are providing entrepreneurs with tools that encourage technology transfer, enhance the local economy and create new jobs. NBIA has estimated recently that roughly 500 business incubators are operating in the United States alone (Frank, 1998).

The average single-site unit houses 19 tenant companies and incubates each one for around three years. In the UK, the survival rate of incubated businesses is around 80 per cent compared with around 50 per cent for those businesses based outside a unit. This is attributed to the level of support incubators offer (Whettingsteel, 2000).

Conclusion

In the current context of large unemployment and under-employment, estimates of which vary, it is time to think hard on how to improve employment. The success in the IT and telecommunication sector has helped the country in many ways, such as increasing export of services, facilitating entry of venture capitalists and catalyzing a change in thinking about the use of computers in schools, colleges, offices, and even in small enterprises and trading establishments. However, many of these aspects have happened in cities and created a great social divide between the English-speaking and those educated in regional languages, and between the rural and urban populations. The employment creation due to IT revolution seems to have made little difference to the total number of unemployed people.

Thus, it may be worthwhile to look at a well-designed *entrepreneurship policy* (EP) which could be broadly understood to stimulate and develop entrepreneurial activity based on integrated framework consisting of culture, choice of occupation, irrespective of social stratification, resource availability to entrepreneurs and the extent of opportunities available. This would call for a broad set of institutional participants including educators, government entities, media and civil society organizations in support role.

The EP should support the needs of the people as they move from the early stages of the process of entrepreneurship, say, from the very stage of intent to start a business, to pre-start-up and early post-start-up. This process would be generally long. The EP, therefore, requires mentoring and active promotion, foremost being access to information, advice about marketing, access to seed capital and technical support wherever needed. This should go hand in hand with the training of new entrants to business to learn the process of entrepreneurship and skills. Finally, the new entrants have to be facilitated with interfacing with small, medium or large enterprises about integration and networking (Vasudevan, 2005).

As explained in this paper, *business incubator* can perform all the above-mentioned functions successfully, provided a proactive policy support, knowledgeable governing council and effective incubator management are in place. The schematic diagram shown in Figure 14.6 explains how the business incubator helps in developing entrepreneurial society by interacting with the various stakeholders on a continuous basis. Success of any entity/organization lies in the value created not only by the entity, but also by the interaction between each of the entities/organizations/ institutions involved in the process.

However, designing such an overarching strategy is not going to be easy because, it depends on the willing cooperation and resources of a number of stakeholders in society—administrators, educators, financiers,

Figure 14.6 Business Incubator Linking All the Stakeholders of Entrepreneurial Society

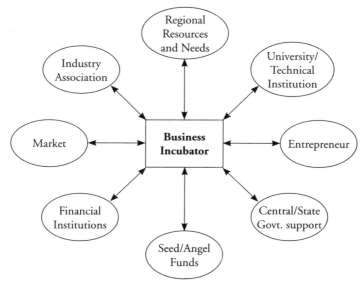

social organizations, technologists, social scientists and entrepreneurs themselves. The authorities and stakeholders would have to widely disseminate the content and workability of such a strategy because the need of the hour is to improve, not merely the size but also the quality of economic growth. This would go a long way in building *entrepreneurial society* which, in turn, would reduce joblessness and improve efficiency in the use of resources.

References

Allen, D. N. and R. McCluskey. 1990. 'Structure, Policy, Service, and Performance in the Business Incubator Industry', *Journal of Entrepreneurship—Theory and Practice* (Winter).

Annual Report. 1995. Small Industries Development Bank of India (SIDBI).

Awasthi, Dinesh. 1993. 'Impact of New Economic Polices on Small, Tiny industries sector', a Research report, Entrepreneurship Development Institute of India (EDII).

Balasubrahmanya, M. H. 2004. 'Small Industry in India in the Era of Globalization: Implications, Performance and Prospects', *Economic and Political Weekly*, (May).

Berger, Brigitte (ed.). 1991. *The Culture of Entrepreneurship: 31*, New Delhi: Tata McGraw-Hill Publishing Co. Ltd.

Frank, Bruno. 1998. 'The Fort Collins Virtual Business Incubator', *Business Source Premier*, Circle Drive: Athens USA. (March).

Gupta, Anita. 2000. 'Indian Experience on Promoting Business and Technology Incubation for Improved Competitiveness of Small and Medium-sized Industries through Technological Developments'. A country paper presented at the national workshop on 'Promotion of Business and Technology Incubation for Improved Competition of SMEs through Applications of Modern and Efficient Technologies at Phnom Penh, October.

Jha, Mithileshwar, D. R. V. Seshadri and Malathi V. Gopal. 2000. *Global Entrepreneurship Monitor India Report 2000*, NSRCEL, IIM-B.

Lalkaka, Rustam and Jack Bishop. 1996. *Business Incubators in Economic Development: An Initial Assessment in Industrializing Countries. 20*, New York.

Manimala, Mathew J., Srinivas Parakya, Malathi V. Gopal and Joseph Shields. 2001. *Global Entrepreneurship Monitor India Report 2001: 16*, NSRCEL, IIM-B.

Manimala, Mathew J. 2002. *Global Entrepreneurship Monitor India Report 2002*: 47, NSRCEL, IIM-B.

Menon, P. K. B., Anita Gupta, M. N. Shivaram, R. M. P. Jawahar and A. Raghavendra. 2002. 'Promoting business and technology Incubation for Improved Competitiveness of Small- and Medium-Sized Industries through Application of Modern and Efficient Technologies in India'. Country paper presented at the national workshops on promoting business and technology incubation for improved competitiveness of small- and medium-sized industries through the application of modern and efficient technologies at Hanoi, Vietnam and Dhaka, Bangladesh.

Naidu, B. V. Director. 2002. 'Software Technology Parks of India (STPI),' Bangalore: *The Economic Times*, (May 3, 2002).

Ramana, A. V. and R. Papaiah. 1998. 'Nuances of Entrepreneurship Development', *Indian Management*, (Feb.): 48.

Ravikumar M. V. and Dr M. K. Sridhar. 2003. 'Entrepreneurial Innovativeness in Team Formation—A Conceptual Model'. Paper presented at the Third International Entrepreneurship Forum (IEF) conference held at IIM-B, March 6–8.

Ravikumar M. V. 2004a. 'Entrepreneurship and India's Economic development', *Golden Jubilee Commemorative Issue of Bangalore Management Association*, (August): 31–34.

———. 2004b. 'Business Incubation for Industrial Growth'. Monthly newsletter of Indian Institute of Productivity Engineers, (December).

Richards, Sally. 2002. *Inside Business Incubators and Corporations: 28–29*, New York: John Wiley and Sons Inc.

Sampath, D. 2001. *Inheriting the Mantle: 31–32*, New Delhi: Response Books (A division of Sage Publications).

Singh, Nagendra (ed.) and B. K. Jain, B. P. Sinha and Nithya Nanda. 2000. *Changing Frontiers of Techno Entrepreneurship: 8*. New Delhi: ASEED.

Vasudevan, A. 2005. 'Time for An Entrepreneurship Policy', *Business Line*, (Sept.).

Whettingsteel, Heidi. 2000. 'Going to Work on An Egg', *Business Source Premier*, (March). Available online at www.nstedb.com.

About the Editor and Contributors

Editor

Shivganesh Bhargava is Professor at the Shailesh J. Mehta School of Management, IIT, Bombay, in the area of Organizational Behavior, Human Resource Management and Entrepreneurship. His past teaching and research associations include IIM, Lucknow and Ahmedabad. Dr Bhargava has various accolades to his credit, including being the first recipient of the V.K.R.V. Rao Award in Management. He has also been awarded the ICSA Young Scientist (1986) and the MPCOST Young Scientist (1988) awards. He has contributed to numerous national and international journals and authored the book, *Transformation Leadership: Value-based Management for Indian Organization* and edited the volume: *Developmental Aspects of Entrepreneurship*.

Contributors

A. Mohammed Abdullah is Faculty Member at the Bharathidasan University, Tiruchirapalli.

R. Ganesan is Assistant Professor at the School of Management, SNS College of Technology, Sathy Main Road, Vazhiyampalayam, Coimbatore.

Sanjay S. Gaur is Associate Professor at the Shailesh J. Mehta School of Management, IIT, Bombay.

Francis Jose is Faculty at the Department of Commerce, Loyola College, Chennai.

T.J. Kamalanabhan is Professor at the Department of Management Studies, IIT, Madras.

Dinesh Khanduja is Assistant Professor (Mechanical) at the National Institute of Technology, Kurukshetra.

Rajeev Khanduja is Assistant Professor (Mechanical) at the S.J.P.M.L. Institute of Technology, Radaur (Yamuna Nagar).

R.C. Maheshwari is Professor at the Centre for Rural Development and Appropriate Technology, IIT, Delhi.

N. Manimekalai is the Director of the Centre for Women's Studies, Bharathidasan University, Tiruchirapalli.

N. Nagesha is a Doctoral Student at the Department of Management Studies, Indian Institute of Science, Bangalore.

R.P. Pradhan is Faculty Member and the Public Relations Officer at the Humanistic & Management Group, Birla Institute of Technology & Science (BITS), Pilani, GOA Campus.

R. Raghunathan is Lecturer at the Management Group, Birla Institute of Technology & Science, Pilani.

M.V. Ravikumar is Doctoral Student at the Canara Bank School of Management Studies, Bangalore University, Bangalore.

Deeksha A. Singh is Doctoral Student at the Department of Business Policy, National University of Singapore, Singapore.

Shailendra Singh is Professor at the H.R.M. Group, Indian Institute of Management, Lucknow.

M.K. Sridhar is Reader at the Canara Bank School of Management Studies, Bangalore University, Bangalore.

Kailash B.L. Srivastava is Professor at the Department of Humanities and Social Sciences, IIT Kharagpur.

Hari Vasudevan is Assistant Professor at the Dwarkadas J. Sanghvi College of Engineering, Mumbai.

V. Vijaya is Faculty Member at the Manipal Institute of Management, Bangalore.

V.P. Wani is Workshop Superintendent at the National Institute of Technology, Kurukshetra.

Index